Test Bank

to Accompany

Social Psychology

Charles G. Lord

prepared by

Charles F. Bond, Jr.
Texas Christian University

Harcourt Brace College Publishers

*Fort Worth Philadelphia San Diego New York Orlando Austin San Antonio
Toronto Montreal London Sydney Tokyo*

Address for editorial correspondence:
Harcourt Brace College Publishers, 301 Commerce Street, Suite 3700, Fort Worth, Texas 76102

Address for orders:
Harcourt Brace & Company, 6277 Sea Harbor Drive, Orlando, Florida 32887-6777, 1-800-782-4479 or 1-800-435-001 (in Florida)

Printed in the United States of America

ISBN 0-03-019104-1

6789012345   023   987654321

TABLE OF CONTENTS

PREFACE

This test bank is designed for use in conjunction with the textbook Social Psychology By Charles G. Lord. The test bank includes 1125 questions: 70 multiple choice and 5 essay questions for each of the 15 chapters in the accompanying Social Psychology text. Questions have been designed to assess students' ability to recall factual information and to test their analytic ability to apply concepts introduced in the text.

Using the Question Codes

Each question in this test bank is followed by three attributes which may be helpful to you in selecting and using test question. These codes are as follows:

ANS:		Correct answer to question
Type:	M	Multiple-choice question
	E	Essay question
KEY 1:	F	Question that tests recall of factual information
	A	Question that tests analytic ability to apply concepts
PAGE:		Textbook page on which the correct answer can be found

I would like to thank Nancy Crochiere and Charles Lord for editorial comments on earlier versions of the test bank.

Charles F. Bond, Jr.

Chapter 1

Introduction to Social Psychology

MULTIPLE CHOICE

1. While flying to Pittsburgh, Albert (who's scared to death of flying) is seated beside Alice, an attractive female. Albert considers asking Alice for a date. Research indicates that Albert's fear

   a) increases the likelihood that he will ask for the date
   b) decreases the likelihood that he will ask for the date
   c) has no effect on the likelihood that he will ask for the date
   d) increases the likelihood that he will ask for the date if Alice seems hard to get, and decreases the likelihood otherwise

   Answer: a   Type: M   Page(s): 1   Key 1: A

2. In a well-known study, male subjects were asked questions by either a male or female experimenter after crossing either a scary or a safe bridge. As the results showed, the subjects

   a) showed off when crossing the scary bridge in front of the female experimenter
   b) showed off when crossing the scary bridge in front of the male experimenter
   c) were more attracted to the female experimenter after crossing the scary bridge than the safe bridge
   d) were more attracted to the female experimenter after crossing the safe bridge than the scary bridge

   Answer: c   Type: M   Page(s): 2   Key 1: F

3. Which of the following statements about social psychological research is true?

   a) One experiment can prove beyond a doubt that an idea is correct or that an idea is incorrect.
   b) Although one experiment can prove beyond a doubt that an idea is correct, it cannot prove beyond a doubt that an idea is incorrect.
   c) Although one experiment cannot prove beyond a doubt that an idea is correct, it can prove beyond a doubt that an idea is incorrect.
   d) No one experiment can prove beyond a doubt that an idea is correct or that an idea is incorrect.

   Answer: d   Type: M   Page(s): 2   Key 1: F

1

4. Social psychology is the scientific study of the way in which

   a) people's thoughts, feelings, and behaviors are influenced by social institutions and societal trends
   b) people's thoughts, feelings, and behaviors are influenced by the real or imagined presence of other people
   c) social institutions influence, and are influenced by, the people who occupy key roles in those institutions
   d) social institutions evolve over time in response to the demands of competing constituencies

   Answer: b   Type: M   Page(s): 3   Key 1: F

5. Unlike philosophers, social psychologists answer questions

   a) about physical reality
   b) about ethical issues
   c) with scientific methods
   d) with logic

   Answer: c   Type: M   Page(s): 3   Key 1: F

6. Bertha has become fascinated with the question of why people fall in love. If Bertha is a social psychologist, she will try to determine the answer to this question by

   a) pure intuition
   b) collecting physical evidence
   c) using inductive logic
   d) using deductive logic

   Answer: b   Type: M   Page(s): 3   Key 1: A

7. Which of the following questions would be of most interest to a social psychologist?

   a) Why are certain people chronically depressed?
   b) Why do certain social institutions succeed, while others fail?
   c) How do we determine other people's attitudes?
   d) How can we tell if a person is about to have a heart attack?

   Answer: c   Type: M   Page(s): 4   Key 1: A

8. Which of the following questions would be of LEAST interest to a social psychologist?

   a) Which species of animals are the most and the least sociable?
   b) Does pornography cause violent crimes?
   c) What causes prejudice against women?
   d) What sorts of relationships do people have with one another?

   Answer: a   Type: M   Page(s): 4   Key 1: A

2

9. Carl, a young social psychologist, is trying to determine whether students' first impressions of a teacher are more important than the students' later impressions. Carl is studying

    a) attribution
    b) social inference
    c) interpersonal transference
    d) person perception

    Answer: d   Type: M   Page(s): 5   Key 1: A

10. Which of the following is the most basic field of study?

    a) person perception
    b) attribution
    c) social cognition
    d) the self

    Answer: c   Type: M   Page(s): 5   Key 1: F

11. The study of _____ primarily concerns people's thoughts.

    a) attitudes
    b) aggression
    c) attribution
    d) prejudice

    Answer: c   Type: M   Page(s): 5   Key 1: F

12. Darlene, a social psychologist, has found that distorted body images lead to eating disorders. Darlene's work focuses on

    a) person perception
    b) the self
    c) social cognition
    d) attribution

    Answer: b   Type: M   Page(s): 5   Key 1: A

13. Earl has devoted his life to studying attitudes. Which of the following would be of greatest interest to him?

    a) why Fred, who favors gun control, votes for candidates who oppose gun control
    b) why Gail and Gary stayed married while Hal and Henrietta got divorced
    c) why people blame Irving, an AIDS victim, for his disease
    d) the thought processes that go into a verdict handed down by June, a local judge

    Answer: a   Type: M   Page(s): 5   Key 1: A

14. The study of _____ primarily concerns feelings.

    a) interpersonal power
    b) social influence
    c) attribution
    d) attitude change

    Answer: d   Type: M   Page(s): 5   Key 1: F

15. Kate, a social psychologist, is trying to determine why ordinary people will sometimes commit murder when told to do so by a charismatic leader. Kate will study

    a) altruism
    b) aggression
    c) prejudice
    d) interpersonal power

    Answer: d   Type: M   Page(s): 6   Key 1: A

16. Larry, an office worker, has found that he just can't do his job when other people are around, even if the other people aren't doing anything. To social psychologists, this is an issue in

    a) close relationships
    b) attribution
    c) social influence
    d) interpersonal power

    Answer: c   Type: M   Page(s): 1   Key 1: A

17. Most of the time, people

    a) adjust their initial impressions by taking into account additional information
    b) feel guilty about entertaining negative stereotypes
    c) go with their spontaneous reactions
    d) check on the validity of arguments they are hearing

    Answer: c   Type: M   Page(s): 7   Key 1: F

18. As research shows, subjects rate strawberry jams closest to the way experts rate those jams if

    a) they're paid a lot for making the ratings
    b) they're making the ratings just for fun
    c) they think carefully before making the ratings
    d) they make the ratings based on their first impressions

    Answer: d   Type: M   Page(s): 8   Key 1: F

19. Research shows that spontaneous reactions are

    a) inferior to deliberate reactions
    b) superior to deliberate reactions
    c) sometimes inferior to deliberate reactions, sometimes superior to deliberate reactions
    d) inferior to deliberate reactions, but only when the issue is important

    Answer: c   Type: M   Page(s): 8   Key 1: F

20. Who's most likely to rely on their spontaneous reactions?

    a) Mary, who's in a foul mood
    b) Nancy, who's in a great mood
    c) Otto, who isn't doing much
    d) Paul, who's highly motivated to be correct

    Answer: b   Type: M   Page(s): 9   Key 1: A

21. Quincy and Robin are engaged. They view their relationship as a partnership, in which they share equally in costs and benefits. Their view of the relationship emphasizes

    a) spontaneous reactions
    b) deliberate reactions
    c) personal identity
    d) social identity

    Answer: c   Type: M   Page(s): 12   Key 1: A

22. Which of the following implies a social identity?

    a) Sam's helping Sharon because he empathizes with her.
    b) Ted's view of his relationship with Teresa as an equal partnership.
    c) Ursula's accepting responsibility for her softball team's losing.
    d) All of these imply a social identity.

    Answer: a   Type: M   Page(s): 12   Key 1: A

23. People in collectivistic cultures are most concerned with

    a) being right
    b) being likable
    c) personal identity
    d) social identity

    Answer: d   Type: M   Page(s): 12   Key 1: F

24. Relative to people in collectivistic cultures (like China), those in individualistic cultures (like New Zealand)

    a) are less likely to swear at authority figures
    b) are less likely to swear at their peers
    c) make new friends easier
    d) have longer-lasting friendships

    Answer: c   Type: M   Page(s): 13   Key 1: F

25. One of the basic themes of social psychology concerns the distinction between wanting to be right and

    a) needing to hear the truth
    b) dealing with being wrong
    c) wanting others to be wrong
    d) wanting to be likable

    Answer: d   Type: M   Page(s): 13   Key 1: F

26. Vanna, who suffers from very low self-esteem, asks Val if she is pretty. Vanna is most likely to want Val to tell her

    a) the truth
    b) that she's pretty no matter what
    c) that she's so intelligent that her appearance doesn't matter
    d) that she's so popular that her appearance doesn't matter

    Answer: a   Type: M   Page(s): 14   Key 1: A

27. Walter, who is chronically depressed, just met Wanda at a singles bar. Considering his depression, Walter is likely to

    a) initiate a long-term relationship with Wanda
    b) avoid a long-term relationship with Wanda
    c) form an accurate impression of Wanda
    d) form a positive impression of Wanda

    Answer: c   Type: M   Page(s): 14   Key 1: A

28. Sometimes people who are oppressed praise the system that oppresses them. What's the best explanation for this?

    a) These are people who have low self-esteem.
    b) These are people who want to believe the world is just.
    c) This is a spontaneous reaction.
    d) This is a deliberate reaction.

    Answer: b   Type: M   Page(s): 14   Key 1: F

29. Social psychologists use three major research methods. Which of the following is NOT one of them?

    a) field studies
    b) laboratory experiments
    c) correlational studies
    d) deductive reasoning

    Answer: d   Type: M   Page(s): 16   Key 1: F

30. An experiment is a procedure used to determine whether one event (which is _____) causes a second event (which is measured).

    a) observed
    b) measured
    c) manipulated
    d) held constant

    Answer: c   Type: M   Page(s): 17   Key 1: F

31. In an experiment, the investigator tries to hold constant

    a) the aspect of the participant's experience that the investigator wishes to measure
    b) the factor the investigator wishes to manipulate
    c) both of these
    d) neither of these

    Answer: d   Type: M   Page(s): 17   Key 1: F

32. The aspect of the participant's experience that an experimenter wishes to manipulate is called a(n)

    a) intrinsic variable
    b) extraneous variable
    c) independent variable
    d) dependent variable

    Answer: c   Type: M   Page(s): 17   Key 1: F

33. A test of whether the independent variable worked is called a

    a) manipulation check
    b) measurement validation
    c) test for independence
    d) factor indemnification

    Answer: a   Type: M   Page(s): 18   Key 1: F

34. Social psychologists hold extraneous variables constant when they conduct

    a) field studies
    b) computer simulations
    c) experiments
    d) correlational studies

    Answer: c   Type: M   Page(s): 18   Key 1: F

35. Xerxes, a social psychologist, did an experiment to see whether experts are more effective than non-experts in getting people to recycle. In Xerxes' experiment, the independent variable is

    a) the gender of the research participants
    b) the ethnicity of the research participants
    c) the degree to which research participants recycle
    d) expertise (or non-expertise)

    Answer: d   Type: M   Page(s): 18   Key 1: A

36. Yolanda, a social psychologist, conducted an experiment to determine whether humor influenced people's attitudes about women. In this experiment, the dependent variable is

    a) humor
    b) people's attitudes about women
    c) the women about whom people had attitudes
    d) the gender of the experimenter

    Answer: b   Type: M   Page(s): 18   Key 1: A

37. The goal of social psychology is to see

    a) what people say they would do when they are aware that they are being studied
    b) what people say they would do when they are not aware that they are being studied
    c) what people do when they are aware that they are being studied
    d) what people do when they are not aware that they are being studied

    Answer: d   Type: M   Page(s): 18   Key 1: F

38. In a well-known experiment, female subjects were told by a "Dr. Zilstein" that they were about to receive painful electric shocks. As a consequence, the subjects

    a) wanted to wait for the experiment alone
    b) wanted to wait for the experiment with others
    c) were attracted to "Dr. Zilstein"
    d) were repulsed by "Dr. Zilstein"

    Answer: b   Type: M   Page(s): 19   Key 1: F

39. In an experiment, subjects are randomly assigned to

    a) an experimenter
    b) receive or not receive a manipulation check
    c) different levels of the dependent variable
    d) different conditions

    Answer: d   Type: M   Page(s): 20   Key 1: F

40. What's the biggest disadvantage of a laboratory experiment?

    a) Subjects must be randomly assigned to conditions.
    b) Subjects must be systematically assigned to conditions.
    c) Subjects may perceive the situation as artificial.
    d) Subjects may become overinvolved in the situation.

    Answer: c   Type: M   Page(s): 20   Key 1: F

41. _____ concerns the extent to which subjects react in a laboratory as they would to some important, involving event outside the laboratory.

    a) Experimental realism
    b) Extra-experimental realism
    c) Mundane realism
    d) Psychological realism

    Answer: a   Type: M   Page(s): 20   Key 1: F

42. In one investigation, male subjects were asked questions by a male or a female experimenter after crossing either a scary or a safe bridge. This investigation was a

    a) role-playing simulation
    b) correlational study
    c) field study
    d) laboratory experiment

    Answer: c   Type: M   Page(s): 20   Key 1: F

43. In one investigation, male subjects were asked questions by a male or a female experimenter after crossing either a scary or a safe bridge. Prior to the experiment, the investigators performed a manipulation check to determine whether

    a) romantic attraction leads to fear
    b) fear leads to romantic attraction
    c) romantic attraction could be measured successfully
    d) the "scary" bridge aroused anxiety

    Answer: d   Type: M   Page(s): 21   Key 1: F

9

44. In a typical field study,

    a) subjects are randomly assigned to conditions
    b) subjects are not randomly assigned to conditions
    c) the experimenter is male
    d) the experimenter is female

    Answer: b   Type: M   Page(s): 22   Key 1: F

45. The best way to study a social psychological question is with

    a) a laboratory experiment
    b) a field study
    c) a correlational study
    d) all of these methods

    Answer: d   Type: M   Page(s): 22   Key 1: F

46. Zelda, a social psychologist, did an investigation at a local hospital to see whether patients who were awaiting life-threatening surgery would be more interested in having a roommate than patients who were awaiting minor surgery. So she went to patients' hospital rooms and asked them whether or not they would like to have a roommate. The subject's answer constituted Zelda's dependent variable. Zelda's investigation is a

    a) laboratory experiment
    b) field study
    c) panel survey
    d) correlational study

    Answer: b   Type: M   Page(s): 22   Key 1: A

47. A correlation is

    a) an independent variable
    b) a dependent variable
    c) the degree of association between two variables
    d) the degree of association between two constants

    Answer: c   Type: M   Page(s): 23   Key 1: F

48. The more introverted a person is, the smaller the number of friends they have. From this we can conclude that the correlation between introversion and number of friends is

    a) positive
    b) negative
    c) non-existent
    d) nothing can be concluded from the information given

    Answer: b   Type: M   Page(s): 23   Key 1: A

49. People who have an avoidant attachment style

    a) avoid being alone whenever possible
    b) avoid overattachment to material possessions
    c) find it difficult to trust others completely
    d) like to depend on other people

    Answer: c   Type: M   Page(s): 23   Key 1: F

50. Alice, who has a secure attachment style, has been frightened by a prank phone call. Research indicates that Alice is likely to

    a) seek out her boyfriend Albert
    b) avoid her boyfriend Albert
    c) seek out and confront the person who placed the call
    d) avoid the person who placed the call

    Answer: a   Type: M   Page(s): 24   Key 1: A

51. In an archival study, researchers found that the number of lynchings in fourteen states of the southern U.S. was negatively associated with

    a) the number of inter-racial marriages
    b) the price of cotton
    c) the rise of the civil rights movement
    d) the number of lynchings in sixteen states of the northern U.S.

    Answer: b   Type: M   Page(s): 24   Key 1: F

52. In an archival study,

    a) subjects read materials that are chosen by the investigator
    b) subjects read materials of their own choosing
    c) researchers keep records of their results
    d) correlations are applied to old records

    Answer: d   Type: M   Page(s): 24   Key 1: F

53. What's the biggest disadvantage of correlational studies?

    a) They're unethical.
    b) They're artificial.
    c) They can't determine what caused what.
    d) They can't be applied to old records.

    Answer: c   Type: M   Page(s): 25   Key 1: F

54. What is the "third variable" problem?

    a) Relationships involving three variables are too complex to be systematically studied.
    b) Two variables may be associated because they are both caused by some third variable.
    c) There are three methods for studying social psychology, and often they give variable results.
    d) In addition to an independent variable and a dependent variable, every experiment has a third variable: the subjects.

    Answer: b   Type: M   Page(s): 26   Key 1: F

55. There is a positive correlation between the number of bars in a town and the number of churches in a town because (relative to small towns) large towns have lots of bars and lots of churches. This illustrates the

    a) ecological fallacy
    b) correlational fallacy
    c) third variable problem
    d) problem of mundane realism

    Answer: c   Type: M   Page(s): 26   Key 1: A

56. Social psychology

    a) is highly mathematical
    b) involves no mathematics whatsoever
    c) is one of the most difficult of research topics
    d) is a relatively easy research topic

    Answer: c   Type: M   Page(s): 27   Key 1: F

57. In one study, researchers had shoppers evaluate some items of clothing, then asked them why they preferred one item of clothing over another. Results showed that subjects

    a) liked all of the items equally well
    b) liked best the items that cost the least
    c) knew why they preferred the items that they did
    d) did not know why they preferred the items that they did

    Answer: d   Type: M   Page(s): 28   Key 1: F

58. Why don't social psychologists simply ask people how they would react in various social situations?

    a) People are motivated to make a favorable impression.
    b) Few people would agree to answer the questions.
    c) It would be unethical to ask them.
    d) Most social psychologists haven't been trained in face-to-face interview techniques.

    Answer: a   Type: M   Page(s): 28   Key 1: F

59. Research shows that people

    a) think that they have been affected by factors that haven't affected them
    b) give plausible explanations for their actions
    c) don't know that they have been affected by factors that have affected them
    d) all of these are true

    Answer: d   Type: M   Page(s): 30   Key 1: F

60. Bob, who just participated in a social psychology experiment, has been asked by Bertha, the experimenter, why he behaved the way that he did. If Bob is a typical research subject, he will

    a) refuse to answer Bertha's questions
    b) give plausible reasons for his behavior
    c) correctly identify the immediate causes of his behavior
    d) correctly identify the ultimate causes of his behavior

    Answer: b   Type: M   Page(s): 30   Key 1: A

61. Cathy has just designed an experiment that virtually forces subjects to behave in the way that she's predicted they'll behave. Cathy's study suffers from the problem of

    a) predictive confirmation
    b) predictive instantiation
    c) experimental demand
    d) forced compliance

    Answer: c   Type: M   Page(s): 31   Key 1: A

62. Experimental demand occurs when

    a) subjects are forced to participate in an experiment
    b) the subjects participating in an experiment are forced to do something that they wouldn't usually do
    c) the design of an experiment virtually forces subjects to act in the predicted way
    d) the demand for experimental research is so great that there aren't enough social psychologists available to conduct the needed research

    Answer: c   Type: M   Page(s): 31   Key 1: F

63. Clever Hans was a horse who developed the ability to add, subtract, multiply, and divide. Professors discovered that Clever Hans was

    a) exceptionally bright at mathematics
    b) exceptionally good at "reading" body language
    c) exceptionally good at distracting questioners from the answers Hans was giving
    d) a complete fraud

    Answer: b   Type: M   Page(s): 32   Key 1: F

64. Mr. van Osten of Germany taught his horse to add, subtract, multiply, and divide. Further studies indicated that the horse was simply reading van Osten's body language. The horse was named

    a) Clever Hans
    b) Intelligent Albert
    c) Mathematica
    d) Claus

    Answer: a   Type: M   Page(s): 32   Key 1: F

65. In a well-known study, students had rats learn a maze. Some of the students had been told that their rats were bright; the others had been told that their rats were dull. The study concluded that

    a) there are genetic influences on learning
    b) there are no genetic influences on learning
    c) experimenters' expectations can influence their results
    d) experimenters' expectations do not influence their results

    Answer: c   Type: M   Page(s): 33   Key 1: F

66. David was recruited by his social psychology professor to run an experiment. David wasn't, however, told the professor's hypothesis in advance. Why?

    a) David would be in a better position to appreciate the hypothesis after he'd run the study.
    b) The professor thought that David would learn more if he had to discover the hypothesis on his own.
    c) The professor was probably too busy to explain the hypothesis to David.
    d) The professor didn't want David's expectations to influence the results of the experiment.

    Answer: d   Type: M   Page(s): 34   Key 1: A

67. Research participants must be told in advance as much as possible of what will happen to them. This is the principle of

    a) prior notice
    b) prebriefing
    c) debriefing
    d) informed consent

    Answer: d   Type: M   Page(s): 35   Key 1: F

68. After subjects have finished participating in an experiment, the experimenter is obligated to

    a) pay them
    b) ask them not to reveal the purpose of the experiment to others
    c) fully inform them about the experiment
    d) inform them only to the extent that the experimenter wishes

    Answer: c   Type: M   Page(s): 35   Key 1: F

69. Social psychologists believe that deception

    a) is always unethical
    b) can always be morally justified
    c) is ethical until proven otherwise
    d) is unethical unless the benefits from deception outweigh the costs

    Answer: d   Type: M   Page(s): 35   Key 1: F

70. Just after participating in a social psychology experiment, Erving was told all about the purpose of the experiment. He learned that during the experiment he had been misled. Erving was receiving

    a) a debriefing
    b) an independent variable
    c) a dependent variable
    d) informed consent

    Answer: a   Type: M   Page(s): 35   Key 1: A

ESSAY

71. Sometimes people's reactions are spontaneous; at other times, their reactions are deliberate. Summarize some of the conclusions that social psychologists have reached about spontaneous and deliberate reactions. Is one kind of reaction better than the other? Be specific.

    Answer:
    Students could answer this question by summarizing the material on pages 7-9 of the text. They should note that spontaneous reactions are more common than deliberate reactions, and that the latter take time and energy. People rely on spontaneous reactions unless they have the motivation and ability to do otherwise. Students should note that spontaneous reactions are sometimes better than deliberate reactions, and sometimes worse.

    Type: E   Page(s): 7   Key 1: F

72. Sometimes, people want to be right; sometimes, they want to be likable. Summarize some of the conclusions that social psychologists have reached about these two goals that people have. When are people most concerned about being right? When are they most concerned about being likable? Is one of these goals better than the other? Be specific.

Answer:
Students could answer this question by summarizing the material on pages 13-15 of the text. They should note that people who are depressed and people who have low self-esteem are very concerned about being right. People who have high self-esteem are more concerned with being likable. Neither of these goals is inherently superior to the other.

Type: E   Page(s): 14   Key 1: F

73. Suppose that you wanted to test the idea that people become uncomfortable when they are praised. Describe an experiment that you could design to test this idea. In describing your experiment, be sure to use the terminology used in your text. Be specific in describing the experiment you would design.

Answer:
In an experimental test of this idea, subjects would be randomly assigned either to be praised or not to be praised. Then the experimenter would somehow measure their level of discomfort. The best answer to this question would elaborate on this design, and identify an independent variable and a dependent variable in the proposed experiment.

Type: E   Page(s): 16   Key 1: A

74. Social psychologists use three major research methods. Identify the three methods, and discuss their relative advantages and disadvantages. Is one method best? Is one worst? Be specific.

Answer:
Social psychologists use three major research methods: laboratory experiments, field studies, and correlational studies. The best answer to this question would summarize the advantages and disadvantages of each of these methods, as listed on page 26 of the text.

Type: E   Page(s): 26   Key 1: F

75. A critic was recently heard saying, "Social psychology is totally unethical! I cannot believe that social psychologists are permitted to do what they do!"
In a paragraph, react to the critic's concern. In doing so, review the ethics of social psychological research, and ethical safeguards that social psychologists follow.

Answer:
Students could answer this question by summarizing the material on pages 34-37 of the text. In discussing the ethics of research, students should review the issues of informed consent, experimental deception, and debriefing.

Type: E   Page(s): 35   Key 1: A

Chapter 2

Social Cognition

MULTIPLE CHOICE

1. Research shows that rapists receive the most severe sentences if their victims offer

    a) no resistance
    b) a low degree of resistance
    c) a medium degree of resistance
    d) a high degree of resistance

    Answer: c   Type: M   Page(s): 42   Key 1: F

2. Zelda realized that she was about to be raped by Zed. If Zelda's goal is to maximize the punishment Zed will receive from a jury, Zelda should

    a) scream obscenities at Zed and kick him
    b) kick Zed, but not scream obscenities at him
    c) calmly inform Zed that she doesn't want to have sex
    d) calmly inform Zed that he's committing rape

    Answer: b   Type: M   Page(s): 42   Key 1: A

3. Your textbook defines social cognition as the process by which

    a) others' motivations and emotions are understood
    b) others' attitudes and personalities are understood
    c) society instills values in individuals
    d) people acquire and use knowledge about each other

    Answer: d   Type: M   Page(s): 42   Key 1: F

4. A research study showed that rapists receive the most severe punishments if their victims offer a moderate degree of resistance, neither too little nor too much. How did the researchers explain this result?

    a) Jurors imagine that victims who offer too little or too much resistance might not have been raped if they offered moderate resistance.
    b) Jurors don't like to think about crimes in which victims offer too little or too much resistance.
    c) Jurors believe that if they (the jurors) had been the victim, they would never have put themselves in a position to be raped.
    d) Female jurors believe that victims who don't resist enough are "asking for it"; male jurors believe that victims who resist a lot are "turning the rapist on".

    Answer: a   Type: M   Page(s): 43   Key 1: F

17

5. The spontaneous stage of social thinking involves greater _____ than the deliberative stage.

   a) accuracy
   b) inaccuracy
   c) personal investment
   d) automaticity

   Answer: d   Type: M   Page(s): 43   Key 1: F

6. Models of social thinking are called

   a) absolute inference algorithms
   b) relative inference algorithms
   c) information-processing models
   d) neural network models

   Answer: c   Type: M   Page(s): 44   Key 1: F

7. Which of the following occurs during the spontaneous stage of social cognition?

   a) application of general world knowledge
   b) application of person knowledge
   c) organization and categorization of people and events
   d) use of current goals

   Answer: c   Type: M   Page(s): 44   Key 1: F

8. Which of the following occurs during the deliberative stage of social cognition?

   a) application of goal knowledge
   b) generation of new thoughts which are mixed with incoming information
   c) categorization of people and events
   d) initial comprehension

   Answer: a   Type: M   Page(s): 44   Key 1: F

9. The deliberative stage of social thinking occurs

   a) a long time prior to the spontaneous stage
   b) just prior to the spontaneous stage
   c) at the same time as the spontaneous stage
   d) just after the spontaneous stage

   Answer: d   Type: M   Page(s): 45   Key 1: F

10. Yolanda was serving as a juror on a case in which a man was charged with murder. Which of the following would require Yolanda to use a deliberative stage of social thinking?

   a) to comprehend the defense attorney's opening statement
   b) to disregard inadmissible evidence the prosecutor presented
   c) to recognize that the defendant was a white male
   d) to recognize that the defendant was elderly

   Answer: b   Type: M   Page(s): 46   Key 1: A

11. In a research study, subjects who were considering two crimes saw false statements on a computer screen about the two defendants. The results showed that subjects who were distracted

   a) were unusually lenient toward both defendants
   b) were unusually harsh toward both defendants
   c) were influenced by the false statements to treat one defendant more harshly than the other
   d) "bent over backwards" so as not to be influenced by the false statements

   Answer: c   Type: M   Page(s): 46   Key 1: F

12. To be completely automatic, thinking must be all of the following EXCEPT

   a) intentional
   b) highly efficient
   c) difficult to control
   d) outside of awareness

   Answer: a   Type: M   Page(s): 47   Key 1: F

13. Research shows that automatic thinking processes, like negative stereotyping, are

   a) easy to control
   b) difficult, but not impossible, to control
   c) impossible to control
   d) unlikely to be used by a person who is distracted

   Answer: b   Type: M   Page(s): 47   Key 1: F

14. Psychologists agree that

   a) most cognitive processes are completely automatic
   b) most cognitive processes are completely deliberative
   c) about half of cognitive processes are completely automatic; the other half are completely deliberative
   d) it is difficult to separate automatic processes from deliberative processes

   Answer: d   Type: M   Page(s): 48   Key 1: F

15. In the middle of a movie, Wanda was exposed to a photograph so quickly that she was not consciously aware of having seen the photograph. Research indicates that this rapid exposure of the photograph should

    a) have no effect on Wanda
    b) affect Wanda's motivational processes, but not her thinking processes
    c) influence Wanda's automatic thinking processes, but not her deliberative processes
    d) influence Wanda's deliberative thinking processes, but not her automatic processes

    Answer: c   Type: M   Page(s): 48   Key 1: A

16. Social thinking is governed by three operating principles. Which of the following is NOT one of them?

    a) introspection
    b) recency
    c) the cognitive miser principle
    d) self-generation

    Answer: a   Type: M   Page(s): 48   Key 1: F

17. Of the following, who is the biggest "cognitive miser"?

    a) Val, who never spends a dime
    b) Ursula, who reacts spontaneously to everything
    c) Teresa, who is always planning ahead
    d) Sarah, who is always lost in thought

    Answer: b   Type: M   Page(s): 49   Key 1: A

18. According to the cognitive miser principle,

    a) some people enjoy thinking for its own sake
    b) some people would prefer to do others' thinking for them
    c) most people prefer to daydream, rather than study
    d) most people do only as much thinking as they have to

    Answer: d   Type: M   Page(s): 49   Key 1: F

19. One important principle in social information-processing states that people use

    a) algorithms whenever they can
    b) more thought than is necessary
    c) the most complex categories they can comprehend
    d) the most recent information they have received

    Answer: d   Type: M   Page(s): 50   Key 1: F

20. According to the principle of self-generation,

    a) people generate their own thoughts
    b) people generate their own sense of self
    c) generic information is more self-relevant than personal information
    d) personal information is more self-relevant than generic information

    Answer: a   Type: M   Page(s): 48   Key 1: F

21. A heuristic is a

    a) type of category
    b) rule of thumb
    c) stage in deliberative thinking
    d) set of steps that guarantees that a problem will be solved

    Answer: b   Type: M   Page(s): 51   Key 1: F

22. Roger was asked whether there were more than 1 million people in the world; Randy was asked whether there were less than 1 trillion. Then Roger and Randy independently estimated how many people there were in the world. According to the anchoring and adjustment heuristic,

    a) Roger and Randy should give the same estimate.
    b) Both Roger and Randy's estimates should be too high.
    c) Roger's estimate should be higher than Randy's.
    d) Roger's estimate should be lower than Randy's.

    Answer: d   Type: M   Page(s): 52   Key 1: A

23. By virtue of the anchoring and adjustment heuristic,

    a) people underadjust from an anchor point
    b) people overadjust from an anchor point
    c) people adjust their anchor point to fit their preconceptions
    d) people adjust their anchor point to give a socially desirable answer

    Answer: a   Type: M   Page(s): 52   Key 1: F

24. The recency principle in information processing is most helpful in explaining

    a) the anchoring and adjustment heuristic
    b) the availability heuristic
    c) the simulation heuristic
    d) the representativeness heuristic

    Answer: b   Type: M   Page(s): 53   Key 1: F

21

25. Pauline thought that more people died in fires than died from cancer because it was easier for her to think of a person dying from fires. Pauline is using the

    a) simulation heuristic
    b) representativeness heuristic
    c) availability heuristic
    d) anchoring and adjustment heuristic

    Answer: c   Type: M   Page(s): 53   Key 1: A

26. The representativeness heuristic states that people make judgments by

    a) conforming to the imagined judgments of representative others
    b) making an adjustment away from judgments made by representative others
    c) how similar a case is to their idea of a typical case
    d) the ease with which a representative example comes to mind

    Answer: c   Type: M   Page(s): 53   Key 1: F

27. Oscar, who was accused of kidnapping, got a light sentence because he had committed an atypical kidnapping. The jurors who sentenced Oscar were most likely using the

    a) representativeness heuristic
    b) anchoring and adjustment heuristic
    c) indivisibility heuristic
    d) simulation heuristic

    Answer: a   Type: M   Page(s): 54   Key 1: A

28. According to the simulation heuristic, people

    a) are strongly influenced by the results of computer simulations
    b) are strongly influenced by live re-enactments of events
    c) judge events by trying to imagine what else might have happened
    d) judge whether or not an event is real by the ease with which it could be faked

    Answer: c   Type: M   Page(s): 54   Key 1: F

29. Jurors are most likely to believe a lawyer if the lawyer tells a good "story." This reflects the jurors' use of the

    a) anchoring and adjustment heuristic
    b) availability heuristic
    c) overinformation heuristic
    d) simulation heuristic

    Answer: d   Type: M   Page(s): 55   Key 1: F

30. People use a number of heuristics in their social thinking. Which of the following is NOT one of them?

    a) the simulation heuristic
    b) the intensification heuristic
    c) the availability heuristic
    d) the representativeness heuristic

    Answer: b   Type: M   Page(s): 56   Key 1: F

31. A mental model is

    a) a set of steps that guarantees that a problem will be solved
    b) a rule of thumb
    c) what people imagine to be a "typical" person or event
    d) how people imagine their minds to work

    Answer: c   Type: M   Page(s): 56   Key 1: F

32. Mental maps or blueprints for how familiar people, objects, and events work are what social psychologists call

    a) abstractions
    b) instantiations
    c) schemas
    d) prototypes

    Answer: c   Type: M   Page(s): 56   Key 1: F

33. A _____ is a stereotyped sequence of actions that defines a well-known situation.

    a) prototype
    b) role
    c) script
    d) teleograph

    Answer: c   Type: M   Page(s): 55   Key 1: F

34. When Nancy and Ned went out on their first date, they both knew exactly what to do -- where they would go, what they would say, when they kiss. This occurred because Nancy and Ned had the same first-date

    a) script
    b) stereotype
    c) prototype
    d) heuristic

    Answer: a   Type: M   Page(s): 57   Key 1: A

35. Social psychologists define a prototype as

    a) the very first (or original) member of a category
    b) the best-fitting member of a category
    c) an event schema
    d) a role schema

    Answer: b Type: M Page(s): 58 Key 1: F

36. Your textbook discusses three types of mental models used in social thinking. Which of the following is NOT one of them?

    a) schema
    b) prototype
    c) script
    d) simulation

    Answer: d Type: M Page(s): 59 Key 1: F

37. How accurate is social thinking?

    a) It is always very accurate.
    b) It is usually very accurate.
    c) It is usually very inaccurate.
    d) It is always very inaccurate.

    Answer: b Type: M Page(s): 61 Key 1: F

38. While participating in a psychology experiment, Mary had to memorize a set of words like "reckless", "conceited", and "stubborn". Later, she read about a man who climbed mountains, and went white-water canoeing. Mary is participating in a study of

    a) mental simulations
    b) the anchoring and adjustment heuristic
    c) construct accessibility
    d) thought suppression

    Answer: c Type: M Page(s): 62 Key 1: A

39. What's the difference between the availability of information and the accessibility of information?

    a) There is no difference.
    b) A piece of information can be available without being accessible; but the opposite cannot happen.
    c) A piece of information can be accessible without being available; but the opposite cannot happen.
    d) A piece of information can be available without being accessible; or it can be accessible without being available.

    Answer: b Type: M Page(s): 62   Key 1: F

40. While participating in a social psychology experiment, Lonnie was asked to think of 6 incidents in which she was assertive; Mary was asked to think of 12 such incidents. Lonnie will think of herself

    a) as more assertive than Mary thinks of herself
    b) as less assertive than Mary thinks of herself
    c) as having a better memory than Mary
    d) as having a worse memory than Mary

    Answer: a Type: M   Page(s): 63   Key 1: A

41. To the social psychologist, a prime is a

    a) heuristic
    b) mental model
    c) piece of information that calls attention to itself
    d) piece of information that calls a construct to mind

    Answer: d Type: M   Page(s): 63   Key 1: F

42. As part of an experiment Katrina, a devout Roman Catholic, was required to read about a sexual dream. Afterwards, Katrina was presented with a picture of the Pope so fast that Katrina was unaware that any picture had been shown. Research indicates that this brief exposure to a picture of the Pope should

    a) have no effect on Katrina
    b) make Katrina feel secure
    c) make Katrina feel proud of being a Roman Catholic
    d) make Katrina feel guilty

    Answer: d Type: M   Page(s): 64   Key 1: A

43. Assimilation occurs when

    a) thoughts become more similar to earlier thoughts
    b) thoughts become more different from earlier thoughts
    c) the process of thinking is deliberative
    d) primes have no effect

    Answer: a   Type: M   Page(s): 64   Key 1: F

44. The set-reset hypothesis has been developed to explain

    a) why thinking is so often automatic
    b) why certain mental models are used more often than others
    c) assimilation and contrast effects in judgment
    d) the impact of counterfactual thinking on judgment

    Answer: c   Type: M   Page(s): 65   Key 1: F

45. John heard from some friends about two people that he'd never met: Ida and Ellen. John heard that Ida was introverted and that Ellen was extroverted. Later, John met these two women at a party; where both were acting like extroverts. Based on research, we could expect John to remember

    a) Ida better than Ellen
    b) Ellen better than Ida
    c) the woman he liked more better than the woman he liked less
    d) the woman about whom he felt less strongly better than the woman about whom he felt more strongly

    Answer: a   Type: M   Page(s): 66   Key 1: A

46. Research shows that you're most likely to remember information about a person if the information is

    a) consistent with your initial impression of that person
    b) inconsistent with your initial impression of that person
    c) irrelevant to your initial impression of that person
    d) identical to your initial impression of that person

    Answer: b   Type: M   Page(s): 66   Key 1: F

47. Social psychologists use the phrase positive-negative asymmetry to refer to the fact that

    a) people are more often in positive moods than negative moods
    b) people are more often in negative moods than positive moods
    c) negative information affects certain judgments more than positive information
    d) being in a positive mood has a bigger effect on a person's thought processes than being in a negative mood

    Answer: c   Type: M   Page(s): 66   Key 1: F

48. People weight negative information more heavily than positive information when making judgments about

    a) a person's competence
    b) a person's morality
    c) the past
    d) the future

    Answer: b   Type: M   Page(s): 67   Key 1: F

49. Helen heard that Hal had flunked one exam but gotten an A on a second exam. Research on positive-negative asymmetry suggests that Helen will rate Hal as

    a) more intelligent than the average person
    b) precisely as intelligent as the average person
    c) less intelligent than the average person
    d) either intelligent or unintelligent, depending on what Helen thinks about Hal's sense of morality

    Answer: a   Type: M   Page(s): 67   Key 1: A

50. To explain how we remember people, social psychologists have proposed a

    a) hindsight bias hypothesis
    b) process-content hypothesis
    c) set-reset hypothesis
    d) recapitulation hypothesis

    Answer: d   Type: M   Page(s): 67   Key 1: F

51. According to the recapitulation hypothesis, it would be easiest to remember

    a) an extrovert
    b) an introvert
    c) a person you had come to hate
    d) a doctor

    Answer: d   Type: M   Page(s): 67   Key 1: A

52. Research shows that subjects remember the most information about people if they

    a) are instructed to memorize the information
    b) are trying to form impressions of the people
    c) know they'll never have to interact with the people
    d) don't personally know any of the people

    Answer: b   Type: M   Page(s): 68   Key 1: F

53. On the first day at his new job, Gary wanted to remember everything that he possibly could about all of his new coworkers. In order to maximize his memory for these people, Gary should

    a) try to memorize everything about his coworkers that he can
    b) try not to memorize anything about them
    c) form impressions of his coworkers
    d) avoid forming impressions of them

    Answer: c   Type: M   Page(s): 68   Key 1: A

54. Research shows that if you try to form an impression of a person, later on you'll remember a lot about that person. Social psychologists explain this effect by saying that in forming an impression, you

    a) focus on the person's positive characteristics
    b) focus on the person's negative characteristics
    c) think about the characteristics about which you care most strongly
    d) think about the relationships among the person's characteristics

    Answer: d   Type: M   Page(s): 68   Key 1: F

55. According to the hindsight bias, people

    a) remember the past as being more positive than it was
    b) prefer the past to the future because the past is known
    c) believe that they knew all along what would happen
    d) believe that their own past is harder to understand than others' pasts

    Answer: c   Type: M   Page(s): 69   Key 1: F

56. After hearing that Fred's plane had left 2 minutes before Fred arrived at the airport, Frannie told Fred "I knew all along that you'd be late for that plane!" Frannie's remark reflects

    a) counterfactual thinking
    b) the availability heuristic
    c) the foresight bias
    d) the hindsight bias

    Answer: d   Type: M   Page(s): 70   Key 1: A

57. Why does the hindsight bias occur?

    a) People selectively remember information that is congruent with the known outcome.
    b) People selectively remember information that is incongruent with the known outcome.
    c) It's easier to think about negative information than positive information.
    d) It's easier to think about positive information than negative information.

    Answer: a   Type: M   Page(s): 70   Key 1: F

58. Research shows that people who imagine future events

    a) are more outgoing than people who reminisce over past events
    b) are less outgoing than people who reminisce over past events
    c) overestimate the likelihood that the events will occur
    d) underestimate the likelihood that the events will occur

    Answer: c   Type: M   Page(s): 71   Key 1: F

59. As part of a psychology experiment, Edgar was asked to imagine that he had been run over by a drunk driver. Research indicates that Edgar will now

    a) believe that he's likely to be run over by a drunk driver
    b) believe that he'll never be run over by a drunk driver
    c) have difficulty thinking about anything other than drunk drivers
    d) have difficulty ever again thinking about drunk drivers

    Answer: a   Type: M   Page(s): 71   Key 1: A

60. After imagining an event, people overestimate the likelihood that the event will occur. Why?

    a) They can't stop thinking about the event.
    b) They don't realize that circumstances might change.
    c) They will assume that others have imagined the event too.
    d) The event will seem more representative than it should.

    Answer: b   Type: M   Page(s): 72   Key 1: F

61. Counterfactual thinking involves

    a) reviewing past events as they occurred
    b) imagining future events as one expects them to occur
    c) imagining future possibilities which one expects never to happen
    d) imagining past events that "might have been"

    Answer: d   Type: M   Page(s): 72   Key 1: F

62. People are most likely to think about how a negative outcome might have been avoided if the outcome

    a) is extremely negative, not just annoying
    b) resulted from something they failed to do, rather than something they did
    c) resulted from something they didn't normally do, rather than something they normally did
    d) resulted from something they were forced to do, rather than something they chose to do

    Answer: c   Type: M   Page(s): 73   Key 1: F

63. There are two kinds of counterfactual thinking: taking back actions and

    a) putting forward actions
    b) simulating past events
    c) simulating future events
    d) undoing outcomes

    Answer: d   Type: M   Page(s): 74   Key 1: F

64. Why do people use downward counterfactual thinking?

    a) to make themselves feel better
    b) to make themselves feel worse
    c) to prepare for the future
    d) to understand the past

    Answer: a   Type: M   Page(s): 74   Key 1: F

65. To win $100 million in the state lottery drawing, a contestant had to have selected (in writing) seven numbers in the order in which they were drawn out of an urn. On Monday May 29, the numbers drawn out of the urn were 3-2-7-9-3-6-1 (in that order).
    According to research on counterfactual thinking, which of the following contestants should feel the worst about losing?

    a) Danielle, who had selected the numbers 3-2-7-9-3-6-0.
    b) David, who had selected the numbers 3-2-7-9-3-6-8.
    c) Charlie, who had selected the numbers 3-2-8-9-3-6-1.
    d) Carla, who had selected the numbers 3-2-0-9-3-6-1.

    Answer: a   Type: M   Page(s): 75   Key 1: A

66. Sometimes, trying NOT to think about your weight makes you think about it more. According to research on thought suppression, why?

    a) You have to be on the lookout for thoughts about your weight.
    b) You're motivated to do what you're told not to do.
    c) You try not to think about anything.
    d) Thoughts about your weight are completely automatic.

    Answer: a   Type: M   Page(s): 77   Key 1: F

30

67. Alice, Albert, Bob, and Betty were participating in a social psychology experiment. As part of the experiment, these subjects were told either to think about purple ink-blots or not to think about purple ink-blots. Which of the four would have been thinking the most about purple ink-blots at the end of the experiment?

    a) Alice, who had always been trying not to think about them
    b) Albert, who had always been trying to think about them
    c) Bob, who had earlier tried to think about purple ink-blots, but was now trying not to
    d) Betty, who had earlier tried not to think about purple ink-blots, but was now trying to think about them

    Answer: d   Type: M   Page(s): 78   Key 1: A

68. In an experiment, chronically depressed subjects were instructed not to think about a sad story. Results indicated that these subjects

    a) made no attempt to follow instructions
    b) successfully followed the instructions
    c) tried to distract themselves with positive thoughts
    d) tried to distract themselves with negative thoughts

    Answer: d   Type: M   Page(s): 78   Key 1: F

69. Social psychologists did a study of people who had experienced the unexpected death of their spouse. Results showed that the people who had discussed this traumatic experience with others _____ than people who had not.

    a) reported more health problems
    b) reported fewer health problems
    c) were more likely to brood about "what might have happened"
    d) were less likely to brood about "what might have happened"   .

    Answer: b   Type: M   Page(s): 81   Key 1: F

70. Experiments show that talking about a traumatic experience

    a) encourages a person to dwell on the experience
    b) is more beneficial than writing about it
    c) increases the likelihood of subsequent illness
    d) reduces the likelihood of subsequent illness

    Answer: d   Type: M   Page(s): 55   Key 1: F

ESSAY

71. There are two stages in social thinking: a spontaneous stage and a deliberative stage. Describe these two stages, being sure to note the ways in which they differ from one another. Then use this two-stage model to explain a recent instance in which you acquired and used knowledge about other people. In explaining this example of your own social thinking, draw on as many research-based concepts and ideas as you can.

Answer:
To answer this question, students would begin by summarizing the spontaneous and deliberative stages of social thinking, as outlined on page 44 of the text. They would then need to relate this model to an example of social thinking from their own life. In explaining the example, they would need to correctly distinguish spontaneous from deliberative aspects of their thinking process; and would ideally discuss some operating principles (p. 51), heuristics (p. 56), and mental models (p. 59) underlying their thinking.

Type: E   Page(s): 44   Key 1: A

72. People use a number of heuristics in social thinking. Discuss four such heuristics, explain how each of these heuristics is applied, and summarize research on their use.

Answer:
In social thinking, people use the anchoring and adjustment heuristic, the availability heuristic, the representativeness heuristic, and the simulation heuristic. In answering this question, students should explain each of these heuristics (by, for example, summarizing the information on page 56) and would ideally document their points by citing specifics from the research studies described on pages 51-55.

Type: E   Page(s): 56   Key 1: F

73. As the defense attorney for a person accused of serial murder, you've learned that several members of the jury spent the evening before their final deliberations watching the movie "The Silence of the Lambs" -- which concerns serial murders similar to those of which your client has been accused. Do you believe that this movie will prejudice the jurors' judgment of your client? Will it make them more likely to find him guilty or less likely? In arriving at your answer to these questions, review research on priming, construct accessibility, and assimilation and contrast effects. Be sure to explain the relevance of these concepts to your case.

Answer:
In answering this open-ended question, students should draw on material from pages 60-65. Presumably, the movie would prime jurors to think about your client as a murderer. They might assimilate their judgment to this prime, or contrast their judgment away from it. Your client would be disadvantaged by an assimilation effect; and benefited by a contrast effect.

Type: E   Page(s): 61   Key 1: A

74. When are people most likely to think about what "might have been"? When are they least likely to engage in this kind of thinking? Answer this question by reviewing research on counterfactual thinking.

Answer:
Students could answer this question by reviewing the material on pages 72-75. Counterfactual thinking is most likely if an emotionally arousing outcome resulted from an abnormal action that the actor freely chose just prior to the occurrence of the outcome.

Type: E   Page(s): 72   Key 1: F

75. Having just flunked an examination in social psychology, you try not to think about it. Is this an effective strategy for dealing with your emotions? Based on social psychological research, what else might you do?

Answer:
It's not an effective strategy because often we're especially likely to think about things if we're trying not to think about, as is shown by Wegner's research on thoughts about a white bear. Even if we could temporarily avoid thinking about an academic failure, we might later suffer from a "rebound effect" (p. 78) and think about it more. It won't do us much good, either, to try to think about other things. Research suggests that in the long run, we'll be better off (in terms of psychological and physical health) if we talk about our failure with someone, as is shown by research on the health consequences of disclosing traumatic experiences (p. 81).

Type: E   Page(s): 77   Key 1: A

Chapter 3

Person Perception

MULTIPLE CHOICE

1. Research shows that sexually active college students

   a) almost invariably use condoms
   b) almost never use condoms
   c) use condoms until their partner has been tested and shown to be HIV-negative
   d) use condoms until they infer that their partner is HIV-negative

   Answer: d   Type: M   Page(s): 86   Key 1: F

2. Person perception concerns

   a) the visual and auditory hallucinations that are specific to perceiving social stimuli
   b) the process by which raw sensations are converted to percepts
   c) how we form impressions of others
   d) how we try to make the best possible impression on others

   Answer: c   Type: M   Page(s): 86   Key 1: F

3. The two stages of impression formation are analogous to the

   a) opening and closing heuristic
   b) anchoring and adjustment heuristic
   c) representativeness heuristic
   d) simulation heuristic

   Answer: b   Type: M   Page(s): 87   Key 1: F

4. Person perception involves four steps. Which of the following is NOT one of them?

   a) retrieval of prior information
   b) recategorization
   c) inferences
   d) categorization

   Answer: a   Type: M   Page(s): 87   Key 1: F

5. Person perception involves four steps. In order, the four steps are:

   a) inferences, categorization, gathering more information, recategorization
   b) inferences, gathering more information, categorization, recategorization
   c) categorization, gathering more information, recategorization, inferences
   d) categorization, inferences, gathering more information, recategorization

   Answer: d   Type: M   Page(s): 87   Key 1: F

34

6. Person perception involves two different stages:

    a) a spontaneous stage and a deliberative stage
    b) a nomographic stage and an ideographic stage
    c) a sensory stage and a cognitive stage
    d) an affective stage and a cognitive stage

    Answer: a Type: M Page(s): 86   Key 1: A

7. At a town meeting, Art heard a number of citizens make statements about a crime bill. Later, Art tried to remember which citizen made which statement. Research suggests that when Art makes mistakes in remembering "who-said-what", they will be based on

    a) the speaker's race, but not the speaker's sex
    b) the speaker's sex, but not the speaker's race
    c) both the speaker's race and the speaker's sex
    d) Art's impressions of the speakers' personalities

    Answer: c Type: M Page(s): 89   Key 1: A

8. If you know nothing about a person, many perceivers believe that the most useful piece of information you can get is the person's

    a) age
    b) educational level
    c) race
    d) sex

    Answer: d Type: M Page(s): 89   Key 1: F

9. In a large lecture hall, Betty has just glanced across the room at Bob. It's the first time she's seen him. Research on memory confusions suggests that the first thing Betty will notice about Bob is

    a) that he's an athlete
    b) that he's male
    c) that he's wearing blue jeans
    d) that he's highly intelligent

    Answer: b Type: M Page(s): 89   Key 1: A

10. Categorization of people by their sex and race is

    a) spontaneous for everyone
    b) spontaneous for sexists and racists, but deliberate for others
    c) deliberate for everyone
    d) deliberate for sexists and racists, but spontaneous for others

    Answer: a Type: M Page(s): 89   Key 1: F

11. Dayna had heard that Charlie and Charlene were lovers. The first time she met Charlie and Charlene, the two displayed a number of behaviors. Which of the following is Dayna most likely to remember?

    a) Charlie and Charlene talking at the same time
    b) Charlie listening while Charlene spoke
    c) Charlie and Charlene holding hands
    d) Charlie and Charlene yelling at each other

    Answer: c   Type: M   Page(s): 89   Key 1: A

12. Edgar had met Ellen at a wild drinking party, so he pegged her as an alcoholic. Later, Edgar interviewed Ellen for a job. Research suggests that in interviewing Ellen, Edgar will probe for information which

    a) verifies that Ellen's an alcoholic
    b) shows that Ellen's not an alcoholic
    c) fairly tests to determine whether Ellen is an alcoholic
    d) has nothing to do with Ellen's possible alcoholism

    Answer: a   Type: M   Page(s): 89   Key 1: A

13. Having heard that Fran (your new coworker) suffered from clinical depression, you had imagined that she would be gloomy. Now your boss has given you a long personality report which states that Fran is light-hearted and happy-go-lucky. Research on category-based versus individuating information indicates that you'll study this report most thoroughly if you

    a) have a Ph.D. in psychology
    b) don't have a Ph.D. in psychology
    c) have to rely on Fran to complete your own work
    d) don't have to rely on Fran to complete your own work

    Answer: c   Type: M   Page(s): 90   Key 1: A

14. Relative to normal people, the chronically depressed are

    a) more likely to make spontaneous trait inferences
    b) less likely to make spontaneous trait inferences
    c) more likely to rely on category-based impressions
    d) less likely to rely on category-based impressions

    Answer: d   Type: M   Page(s): 91   Key 1: F

15. In one study, college students saw a photograph of a person and a sentence below the photograph that said "I hate animals. I kick puppies just for fun." Results showed that the subjects inferred that the person was cruel

    a) spontaneously
    b) unless they were distracted by having to do another task
    c) unless they told not to draw inferences
    d) only if they were highly motivated to draw inferences

    Answer: a   Type: M   Page(s): 91   Key 1: F

16. Gary, Helen, Ira, and Jane heard Jack say "I never go to work, and I sleep 18 hours a day." Which of the four is LEAST likely to spontaneously infer that Jack is lazy?

    a) Gary, who is in the fourth grade
    b) Helen, who is a college student
    c) Ira, who suffers from panic disorders
    d) Jane, who prides herself on being an individualist

    Answer: a   Type: M   Page(s): 92   Key 1: A

17. "Face-ism" refers to

    a) the tendency to draw invalid inferences from a person's face
    b) the tendency to discriminate against males who have moustaches that resemble Hitler's
    c) a difference in photographic depictions of whites and non-whites
    d) a difference in memory for attractive faces versus unattractive faces

    Answer: c   Type: M   Page(s): 93   Key 1: F

18. In a study, American male college students rated the attractiveness of women from photographs. Results showed that the women they found most attractive had

    a) mature features
    b) baby features
    c) expressive features
    d) all of these features

    Answer: d   Type: M   Page(s): 93   Key 1: F

19. Research shows that

    a) perceivers can agree on the attractiveness of a person's voice
    b) perceivers cannot agree on the attractiveness of a person's voice
    c) although perceivers draw personality inferences from a person's face, they draw no such inferences from the person's voice
    d) you can't actually tell anything about an individual's personality from the sound of their voice

    Answer: a   Type: M   Page(s): 94   Key 1: F

20. One research team studied the voices of people who appeared on television. Results showed that

    a) men use more dominant voices when addressing women than when addressing men
    b) women use more submissive voices when addressing men than when addressing women
    c) all speakers use more dominant voices when addressing men than when addressing women
    d) all speakers use more dominant voices when addressing women than when addressing men

    Answer: c Type: M Page(s): 95   Key 1: F

21. In one study, college students watched a videotape of people walking. The videotape had been made under unusual circumstances so that the students didn't see the walkers themselves, only moving points of light. From this tape, students could accurately judge

    a) the personalities of the people who were walking
    b) the ages of the people who were walking
    c) that certain of the people were talking as they walked
    d) that certain of the people were lying as they walked

    Answer: b Type: M Page(s): 95   Key 1: F

22. In one study, college students watched a videotape of points of light that depicted people walking. Results showed that relative to young adult walkers, older walkers were seen as

    a) less intelligent
    b) less sexy
    c) happier
    d) more self-confident

    Answer: b Type: M Page(s): 95   Key 1: F

23. Karen and Larry have been married for 10 years. Research suggests that

    a) Karen is more likely to touch Larry than vice versa
    b) Larry is more likely to touch Karen than vice versa
    c) Karen is more likely to touch herself than Larry is
    d) Larry is more likely to touch himself than Karen is

    Answer: a Type: M Page(s): 96   Key 1: A

24. Accuracy in person perception has been measured in three ways. Which of the following is NOT one of them?

    a) agreeing with others
    b) agreeing with self-reports
    c) predicting future behavior
    d) describing past behavior

    Answer: d   Type: M   Page(s): 98   Key 1: F

25. Mel and Mona have just started dating. Which sort of accuracy in person perception would be most important to their getting along and forming a permanent relationship?

    a) Mel's ability to predict Mona's future behavior
    b) Mona's ability to predict Mel's future behavior
    c) Mel's agreeing with Mona's self-report of her sincerity
    d) Mel's agreeing with Mona's perception of Mary, Mona's friend

    Answer: c   Type: M   Page(s): 98   Key 1: A

26. Research shows that as two people become more acquainted with one another, their perceptions of one another

    a) become more accurate
    b) do not become more accurate
    c) are more influenced by nonverbal cues
    d) are less influenced by nonverbal cues

    Answer: b   Type: M   Page(s): 99   Key 1: F

27. Nan just met Ned. Nel has known Ned for nine years. Research suggests that

    a) Nel's perception of Ned is more negative than Nan's
    b) Nel's perception of Ned is not more negative than Nan's
    c) Nel's perception of Ned is more accurate than Nan's
    d) Nel's perception of Ned is not more accurate than Nan's

    Answer: d   Type: M   Page(s): 99   Key 1: F

28. In one study, subjects who had never met rated one another's personalities, had one-on-one interactions, then rated one another's personalities a second time. Results showed that

    a) the second ratings were more positive than the first ratings
    b) the second ratings were more negative than the first ratings
    c) the second ratings were more accurate than the first ratings
    d) the second ratings were less accurate than the first ratings

    Answer: d   Type: M   Page(s): 100   Key 1: F

29. Research shows that people are most accurate in judging others'

    a) intelligence
    b) extroversion
    c) honesty
    d) anxiousness

    Answer: b   Type: M   Page(s): 100   Key 1: F

30. Otto has had 40 sexual partners in the last year, and 38 of them were one-night stands. Social psychologists would classify Otto as high in

    a) introversion
    b) codependence
    c) sociosexuality
    d) all of these traits

    Answer: c   Type: M   Page(s): 101   Key 1: A

31. Research suggests that we are most accurate in perceiving traits that

    a) have been important to survival in evolutionary history
    b) have been unimportant to survival in evolutionary history
    c) are more important to us than to other people
    d) are less important to us than to other people

    Answer: a   Type: M   Page(s): 101   Key 1: F

32. A primacy effect occurs when a perceiver

    a) replaces a category-based impression with an individuated impression
    b) replaces an individuated impression with a category-based impression
    c) places greater weight on initial information than later information
    d) places greater weight on later information than initial information

    Answer: c   Type: M   Page(s): 101   Key 1: F

33. Pauline first heard that Roger was cruel. Then she heard that he was temperamental. Finally, she heard that he was brilliant. Pauline's strongest impression will be that Roger is

    a) cruel
    b) temperamental
    c) brilliant
    d) none of these

    Answer: a   Type: M   Page(s): 101   Key 1: A

34. A change-of-meaning explanation has been offered to explain

    a) face-ism
    b) primacy effects in person perception
    c) why acquaintance does not increase the accuracy of person perception
    d) why it is hard to detect lies

    Answer: b   Type: M   Page(s): 102   Key 1: F

35. Sam heard that Sally was intelligent, and later heard that she was foolish. Research suggests that Sam will

    a) have great difficulty resolving this apparent inconsistency
    b) have little difficulty resolving this apparent inconsistency
    c) weight the second piece of information more heavily than the first
    d) discount the first piece of information altogether

    Answer: b   Type: M   Page(s): 103   Key 1: A

36. According to _____, some traits are more central than other traits.

    a) primacy effects in person perception
    b) the elaboration likelihood model
    c) the traits versus situations debate
    d) implicit personality theory

    Answer: d   Type: M   Page(s): 104   Key 1: F

37. Teresa believed that people who are friendly also tend to be flexible. This is Teresa's

    a) category-based impression
    b) individuated impression
    c) implicit personality theory
    d) egocentric bias

    Answer: c   Type: M   Page(s): 104   Key 1: A

38. In implicit personality theory, warmth is a more central trait than politeness because warmth

    a) is harder to see than politeness
    b) is easier to see than politeness
    c) has more implications than politeness
    d) has fewer implications than politeness

    Answer: c   Type: M   Page(s): 104   Key 1: F

39. Ursula was frowning when she told Ted that she was happy. Ted will probably infer that Ursula is

    a) happy
    b) sad
    c) introverted
    d) extroverted

    Answer: b   Type: M   Page(s): 105   Key 1: A

40. Microexpressions are brief expressions conveyed by

    a) the sound of a person's voice
    b) a speaker's words
    c) the face
    d) the body

    Answer: c   Type: M   Page(s): 106   Key 1: F

41. Research shows that from hearing the sound of a person's voice,

    a) it's possible to detect microexpressions
    b) it's easy to determine whether or not the person is lying
    c) it's easier to recognize positive than negative emotions
    d) it's easier to recognize negative than positive emotions

    Answer: d   Type: M   Page(s): 106   Key 1: F

42. Hal was happy, but Sam was sad. Vanna saw Hal and Sam walking side-by-side. From their facial expressions, Vanna would

    a) not be able to recognize either Hal or Sam's emotions
    b) recognize Hal's emotion and Sam's emotion with equal ease
    c) recognize Hal's emotion more easily than Sam's emotion
    d) recognize Sam's emotion more easily than Hal's emotion

    Answer: c   Type: M   Page(s): 106   Key 1: A

43. Local display rules govern

    a) the expression of emotion
    b) the presentation of one's public self
    c) whether or not babies can be breast-fed in public
    d) whether or not pornography can be openly displayed

    Answer: a   Type: M   Page(s): 107   Key 1: F

44. The face-in-the-crowd effect refers to the fact that

    a) angry faces are easier to spot than happy faces
    b) angry faces are harder to spot than happy faces
    c) people who have distinctive faces tend to be popular
    d) people who have distinctive faces tend to be unpopular

    Answer: a   Type: M   Page(s): 107   Key 1: F

45. Secret Service agents immediately spotted the angry man who was waiting among the multitudes assembled for the President's speech. This illustrates the

    a) micro-expression effect
    b) face-in-the-crowd effect
    c) motivational improvement effect
    d) unbiased assimilation effect

    Answer: b   Type: M   Page(s): 107   Key 1: A

46. What is the one emotion that children communicate better than adults?

    a) fear
    b) anger
    c) joy
    d) surprise

    Answer: a   Type: M   Page(s): 108   Key 1: F

47. The oppression hypothesis states that people who have low power

    a) learn to display their own moods and intentions
    b) learn to read others' moods and intentions
    c) have unusually strong emotions
    d) have unusually weak emotions

    Answer: b   Type: M   Page(s): 108   Key 1: F

48. Wanda is a typical woman. Marvin is a typical man. Wanda is better than Marvin at

    a) communicating emotion but not interpreting it
    b) interpreting emotion but not communicating it
    c) communicating and interpreting emotion
    d) neither communicating nor interpreting emotion

    Answer: c   Type: M   Page(s): 108   Key 1: A

49. Xerxes has a baby-face. When adults see Xerxes, they would initially assume that he is

    a) dishonest
    b) strong and sophisticated
    c) weak and innocent
    d) they would make no assumptions from his baby-face

    Answer: c   Type: M   Page(s): 110   Key 1: A

50. A baby face has all of the following features EXCEPT

    a) a square jaw
    b) big eyes
    c) a small nose
    d) a round face

    Answer: a   Type: M   Page(s): 110   Key 1: F

51. Research shows that having a baby face

    a) makes a person more attractive to members of the opposite sex
    b) generally makes a person more attractive
    c) generally makes a person less attractive
    d) is independent of attractiveness

    Answer: d   Type: M   Page(s): 111   Key 1: F

52. Pyeong Su, a Korean college student, is perceived by his peers to have a baby face. Research suggests that Americans would

    a) also perceive Pyeong Su to have a baby face
    b) perceive Pyeong Su to have a mature face
    c) perceive that Pyeong Su was neither baby faced nor mature faced
    d) reach no agreement in judging Pyeong Su's face

    Answer: a   Type: M   Page(s): 111   Key 1: A

53. Research shows that people who have baby faces in childhood

    a) retain them their entire lives
    b) retain them into their fifties
    c) retain them through high school
    d) are no more likely than other people to have baby faces a few years later

    Answer: c   Type: M   Page(s): 111   Key 1: F

54. Teachers are more like to use baby talk when speaking to

    a) a man, rather than a woman
    b) a woman, rather than a man
    c) someone who has a baby face, rather than someone who does not
    d) someone who looks senile, rather than someone who does not

    Answer: c   Type: M   Page(s): 112   Key 1: F

55. In a study, adults tried to teach a complicated task to a preschooler over the phone. Results showed that adults who thought that the preschooler had a baby face

    a) were especially effective in teaching the task
    b) were especially ineffective in teaching the task
    c) were not especially effective nor ineffective in teaching the task
    d) avoided using baby talk

    Answer: c   Type: M   Page(s): 112   Key 1: F

56. Zelda, a baby-faced actress, is angling for a spot on a TV commercial. Research suggests that Zelda will be cast in a commercial which emphasizes

    a) sex appeal
    b) emotional well-being
    c) expertise
    d) trust

    Answer: d   Type: M   Page(s): 113   Key 1: A

57. Research shows that having a baby face

    a) has no impact on one's chances of being hired for any position
    b) reduces one's chances of being hired for low-status positions
    c) reduces one's chances of being hired for high-status positions
    d) increases one's chances of being hired for high-status positions

    Answer: c   Type: M   Page(s): 113   Key 1: F

58. Sometimes, baby faced defendants are especially likely to be convicted of a crime; sometimes they're especially likely not to be convicted of a crime. This depends on

    a) whether the defendant is a man or a woman
    b) whether the defendant is attractive or unattractive
    c) whether it is a crime of negligence of a crime of intention
    d) whether it is a property crime or a violent crime

    Answer: c   Type: M   Page(s): 113   Key 1: F

59. Elvira, a baby-faced defendant, is on trial for intentionally vandalizing her ex-husband's house. Elvira's baby face

   a) will make jurors believe that she is intelligent
   b) will make jurors believe that she is sophisticated
   c) makes it more likely that she will be convicted
   d) makes it less likely that she will be convicted

   Answer: d   Type: M   Page(s): 114   Key 1: A

60. Why do people lie?

   a) because it is advantageous to do so
   b) the culture tells them to lie
   c) it's a basic human instinct
   d) it reflects pathological tendencies

   Answer: a   Type: M   Page(s): 114   Key 1: F

61. Deceptive communication

   a) is unique to human beings
   b) is unique to human beings and gorillas
   c) is unique to human beings, chimpanzees, and gorillas
   d) occurs in a wide variety of species

   Answer: d   Type: M   Page(s): 115   Key 1: F

62. Perceivers tend to believe that

   a) people are lying
   b) people are telling the truth
   c) men are lying and women are telling the truth
   d) men are telling the truth and women are lying

   Answer: b   Type: M   Page(s): 115   Key 1: F

63. Lying

   a) usually fails
   b) usually succeeds
   c) is of no benefit to the liar
   d) is actually quite rare

   Answer: b   Type: M   Page(s): 115   Key 1: F

64. When asked where she had been on Friday night, Sally told Ted a lie. If Sally is like most people,

   a) she will later take back her lie
   b) she will later have to fabricate more lies to cover up this one
   c) her lie will probably succeed
   d) her lie will probably fail

   Answer: c   Type: M   Page(s): 115   Key 1: A

65. When Jack accused Jill of lying, Jill got so upset that she looked like she was lying, even though she wasn't. Jack took this as evidence that she was definitely lying. Jack has committed

   a) the Othello error
   b) the false confession error
   c) the visual primacy error
   d) the self-augmentation error

   Answer: a   Type: M   Page(s): 117   Key 1: A

66. Albert asked Bill how he had done on the exam. Bill responded nonverbally by putting his thumb and index finger in a circle to indicate that he'd done "OK". Social psychologists would call Bill's behavior a(n)

   a) emblem
   b) illustrator
   c) other-manipulation
   d) self-manipulation

   Answer: a   Type: M   Page(s): 118   Key 1: A

67. Connie, an unfaithful wife, was confronted by her husband; and had to lie to him about where she had been the previous night. Connie was highly motivated to be successful in her deception. Research shows that Connie's motivation would

   a) make it easier to detect her lie either verbally or nonverbally
   b) make it harder to detect her lie either verbally or nonverbally
   c) make it easier to detect her lie verbally, but harder to detect her lie nonverbally
   d) make it harder to detect her lie verbally, but easier to detect her lie nonverbally

   Answer: d   Type: M   Page(s): 120   Key 1: A

68. Research shows that people look dishonest if they

    a) look you right in the eye
    b) display unexpected behaviors
    c) don't have any special motivation to lie to you
    d) are attractive

    Answer: b   Type: M   Page(s): 121   Key 1: F

69. Which of the following groups is best at detecting lies?

    a) college students
    b) law enforcement officers
    c) customs officials
    d) These groups perform equally at lie detection.

    Answer: d   Type: M   Page(s): 122   Key 1: F

70. Research shows that

    a) Americans can tell when Jordanians are lying
    b) Jordanians can tell when Americans are lying
    c) Both of these statements are true.
    d) Neither of these statements are true.

    Answer: d   Type: M   Page(s): 124   Key 1: F

ESSAY

71. How do we perceive people? Answer this question by reviewing the four-step model of person perception presented in your textbook.

    Answer:
    Students could answer this question by reviewing the model presented on page 88 of the textbook. As noted there, person perception involves: 1) spontaneously categorizing the person, 2) spontaneously inferring that the person has certain stereotypical characteristics, 3) gathering more information, preferably information that confirms the initial impression, and if necessary 4) recategorizing the person into either a subcategory or a different category altogether.

    Type: E   Page(s): 88   Key 1: F

72. What sorts of information can people glean from nonverbal sources? Answer this question by reviewing research on the information available in facial cues, vocal cues, and movement cues. Be specific.

    Answer:
    Students could answer this question by reviewing the material on pages 92-97 of the text. In doing so, they might cover the work on face-ism in portraits of blacks and whites (p. 93), facial attractiveness (p. 93), vocal attractiveness (p. 94), gait (p. 95), and touching (p. 96).

    Type: E   Page(s): 92   Key 1: F

73. When are people's perceptions of others most likely to be accurate and when are they least likely to be accurate? Review research on factors that influence the accuracy of person perception.

Answer:
Students could answer this question by reviewing the material on pages 97-101 of the text. They might note, for example, that the accuracy of one's perceptions of a person is not enhanced by being acquainted with the person; and that accuracy is especially high for certain traits that are important to discern -- like extroversion and sociosexuality. Students might also note here that lie detection tends to be inaccurate.

Type: E   Page(s): 97   Key 1: F

74. Julie, a 20-year-old college student, has a baby face. Discuss the experiences Julie is likely to have by virtue of her face. Which aspects of her life will be affected by her baby face, which will not? Be specific, and cite relevant research studies.

Answer:
Students could answer this question by reviewing the material on pages 110-114 of the text. Julie would be perceived as warm, honest, naive, and dependent. She might be addressed with "baby talk". She might have an advantage in getting a job in which warmth and docility was valued, but have a disadvantage in getting a job in which strength and leadership was expected. If accused of an intentional crime, she might be acquitted; if accused of a negligent crime, she might be convicted.

Type: E   Page(s): 110   Key 1: A

75. You suspect that your best friend has been lying to you. Based on psychological research, how should you try to determine whether or not your best friend's statements have been lies? To what should you pay attention? What pitfalls should you try to avoid? How likely is it that you will succeed in determining whether or not your best friend has been lying?

Answer:
Students could answer this question by drawing on material from pages 114-125 of the text. It would be difficult to determine whether or not one's friend was lying; and one would be predisposed to a truthfulness bias. One would need to ignore the invalid cues to deception noted on page 117, and focus on the valid cues listed there. One might not want to accuse the friend of lying, so as to avoid the "Othello error" (p. 117); and one might want to factor in the friend's likely level of motivation (p. 120).

Type: E   Page(s): 114   Key 1: A

Chapter 4

Attribution

MULTIPLE CHOICE

1. Females believe that patients who are responsible for their own illness

   a) deserve lower quality medical care than other patients
   b) deserve the same quality medical care as other patients
   c) are just as likely as other patients to follow doctors' orders
   d) are no more likely than other patients to have the illness again

   Answer: b   Type: M   Page(s): 128   Key 1: F

2. Attributions offer answers to the question

   a) where
   b) what
   c) when
   d) why

   Answer: d   Type: M   Page(s): 128   Key 1: A

3. When people wonder why an event occurred and reach a conclusion about its cause, they are

   a) making an attribution
   b) forming an impression
   c) using an algorithm
   d) committing an error

   Answer: a   Type: M   Page(s): 129   Key 1: F

4. Causal attribution follows the

   a) simulation heuristic
   b) representativeness heuristic
   c) anchoring and adjustment heuristic
   d) seek and discover heuristic

   Answer: c   Type: M   Page(s): 129   Key 1: F

50

5. Three elements are spontaneously identified in the first stage of causal attribution. Which of the following is NOT one of them?

   a) person
   b) behavior
   c) situation
   d) object

   Answer: d   Type: M   Page(s): 130   Key 1: F

6. When all else is equal, the most important factor in causal attributions is

   a) behavior
   b) situation
   c) object
   d) person

   Answer: a   Type: M   Page(s): 131   Key 1: F

7. The identification stage of causal attribution is important because

   a) it is the final stage
   b) identifications can be ambiguous
   c) identifications require a lot of thought
   d) identifications are almost invariably erroneous

   Answer: b   Type: M   Page(s): 131   Key 1: F

8. Jack tripped over a chair. Which of the following would be a dispositional attribution for this event?

   a) The chair was in his way.
   b) It was dark, and no one could have seen the chair.
   c) Jack is clumsy.
   d) Lucia had placed the chair there temporarily, so she could stand on it and fix a light bulb.

   Answer: c   Type: M   Page(s): 131   Key 1: A

9. Jill saw Sally smile at the Christmas parade. Jill inferred that Sally was a cheerful person. Jill has just made

   a) a discounting error
   b) an augmentation error
   c) a situational attribution
   d) a dispositional attribution

   Answer: d   Type: M   Page(s): 131   Key 1: A

10. When making deliberative adjustments to their initial attributions, people use all of the following types of additional information EXCEPT

    a) constraints on the behavior
    b) effects of the behavior
    c) variance of the behavior
    d) identification of the behavior

    Answer: d   Type: M   Page(s): 132   Key 1: F

11. John plays golf every single day. From this fact, we can conclude that John's behavior is high in

    a) consensus
    b) consistency
    c) distinctiveness
    d) intensity

    Answer: b Type: M   Page(s): 132   Key 1: A

12. Albert was using cocaine that night, but so was everyone else. We can conclude that Albert's cocaine use was

    a) high in distinctiveness
    b) low in distinctiveness
    c) low in consensus
    d) high in consensus

    Answer: d Type: M   Page(s): 133   Key 1: A

13. In models of causal attribution, a behavior is said to be highly distinctive if

    a) no one else does the behavior
    b) everyone else does the behavior
    c) the behavior occurs only in this situation, and not other similar situations
    d) the behavior occurs in this situation, and other similar situations too

    Answer: c Type: M   Page(s): 133   Key 1: F

14. High consensus implies

    a) a dispositional attribution
    b) a situational attribution
    c) high distinctiveness
    d) high consistency

    Answer: b Type: M   Page(s): 133   Key 1: F

15. Models of causal attribution describe several ways in which behavior might vary. Which of the following is NOT one of them?

    a) distinctiveness
    b) consensus
    c) intensity
    d) consistency

    Answer: c   Type: M   Page(s): 134   Key 1: F

16. Cindy went home right after work. By doing so, she could avoid her ex-husband David and also watch her favorite TV show. If we wanted to explain why Cindy went home, the multiple effects of her behavior should

    a) detract from a confident dispositional attribution
    b) augment a confident dispositional attribution
    c) detract from a confident situational attribution
    d) have no effect on our attribution whatsoever

    Answer: a   Type: M   Page(s): 135   Key 1: A

17. Edgar ran a red light in his new car, but since he'd been drinking earlier in the night, you were reluctant to draw any inferences about his driving ability. You have engaged in

    a) the correspondence bias
    b) the actor-observer bias
    c) discounting
    d) augmentation

    Answer: c   Type: M   Page(s): 135   Key 1: A

18. Augmentation occurs when

    a) there was only one possible cause for a behavior
    b) there are several possible causes for a behavior
    c) a behavior occurred despite situational constraints
    d) a cause produced several behavioral effects

    Answer: c   Type: M   Page(s): 135   Key 1: F

19. While interviewing for a job, Fran told the interviewer that she hated his tie. You figured that she must really hate his tie to risk losing a job over it. You have engaged in

    a) discounting
    b) augmentation
    c) intensification
    d) counterfactual thinking

    Answer: b   Type: M   Page(s): 136   Key 1: A

Attribution

20. Behavior that carries a large emotional impact elicits

    a) strong situational attributions
    b) weak situational attributions
    c) strong dispositional attributions
    d) weak dispositional attributions

    Answer: c   Type: M   Page(s): 137   Key 1: F

21. The process that most people use for making causal attributions is

    a) inefficient
    b) ineffective
    c) efficient, but ineffective
    d) efficient and effective

    Answer: d   Type: M   Page(s): 139   Key 1: F

22. The correspondence bias is the tendency to assume that a person's words and deeds correspond with

    a) the situation that the person is in
    b) the person's dispositions
    c) the words and deeds of the person's friends
    d) the words and deeds of the person's family

    Answer: b   Type: M   Page(s): 139   Key 1: F

23. George had been assigned by his debate coach to argue for the death penalty. After hearing George's argument, people in the audience thought that George himself favored the death penalty, even though they knew he had been assigned to argue in favor of it. The members of this audience have

    a) engaged in discounting
    b) engaged in augmentation
    c) made a correspondence bias
    d) made a situational attribution

    Answer: c   Type: M   Page(s): 139   Key 1: A

24. The correspondence bias

    a) happens in the laboratory but not in real life
    b) happens in real life but not in the laboratory
    c) occurs among subjects who say they are aware of situational constraints
    d) is a very robust phenomenon

    Answer: d   Type: M   Page(s): 140   Key 1: F

25. Sally saw Judy struggling to finish her organic chemistry final exam. Which of the following attributions that Sally could make would reflect a correspondence bias?

    a) Sally infers that Judy is unintelligent, even though she knows that organic chemistry is a difficult subject.
    b) Sally infers that Judy is intelligent, but (like a lot of other people) has trouble with organic chemistry.
    c) Sally infers that Judy didn't really prepare for this exam, and that's why she's having trouble.
    d) Sally infers that since she (Sally) has no trouble with organic chemistry, Judy must be extremely unintelligent not to do well in the subject too.

    Answer: a   Type: M   Page(s): 140   Key 1: A

26. There are four causes of the correspondence bias. Which of the following is NOT one of them?

    a) insufficient augmentation
    b) failing to adjust accurately
    c) overlooking situational constraints
    d) unrealistic expectations

    Answer: a   Type: M   Page(s): 141   Key 1: F

27. The fundamental attribution error is to

    a) explain away failure
    b) take credit for success
    c) underestimate the power of the situation
    d) underestimate the power of dispositions

    Answer: c   Type: M   Page(s): 142   Key 1: F

28. To underestimate the power of situational constraints is

    a) to make the fundamental attribution error
    b) to make the derivative attribution error
    c) a tendency of actors, but not observers
    d) a rare occurrence

    Answer: a   Type: M   Page(s): 143   Key 1: F

Attribution

29. In a psychology experiment, Jane was assigned to ask Julie questions that Julie wouldn't be able to answer. Afterwards, Julie thought that Jane was incredibly knowledgeable. Julie has

    a) succumbed to a self-fulfilling prophecy
    b) shown a self-serving bias
    c) made an egocentric attribution
    d) made the fundamental attribution error

    Answer: d   Type: M   Page(s): 142   Key 1: A

30. LaVonne's boss told LaVonne to read aloud a series of statements opposing gun control. Research on the fundamental attribution error suggests that from hearing LaVonne read these statements aloud, LaVonne's boss will infer

    a) nothing about LaVonne
    b) that LaVonne opposes gun control
    c) that LaVonne favors gun control
    d) that he himself must favor gun control

    Answer: b   Type: M   Page(s): 143   Key 1: A

31. The correspondence bias occurs because attributers mistakenly assume that

    a) people won't argue against their own attitudes
    b) people will argue against their own attitudes
    c) they can set aside their own self-interest
    d) they cannot set aside their own self-interest

    Answer: a   Type: M   Page(s): 144   Key 1: F

32. As part of an experiment, Mary Jane, who favored the legalization of marijuana, was assigned to write an essay opposing the legalization of marijuana. After writing the essay, Mary Jane was told that someone else would read the essay and try to figure out Mary Jane's true attitude about marijuana. If Mary Jane is like most people, she will think that readers will infer

    a) that she opposes the legalization of marijuana
    b) that she has no attitude toward the legalization of marijuana
    c) that she was writing an essay opposite to her views
    d) none of these

    Answer: c   Type: M   Page(s): 144   Key 1: A

33. The correspondence bias results from emphasizing the

    a) behavior-situation link
    b) behavior-person link
    c) situation-person link
    d) links among behavior, situation, and person

    Answer: b   Type: M   Page(s): 145   Key 1: F

34. In the attribution process, there is an overemphasis on the behavior-person link

    a) only when the attributions concern morality
    b) only when the attributions concern ability
    c) from the very outset of the process
    d) only during deliberative adjustments

    Answer: c   Type: M   Page(s): 145   Key 1: F

35. Distraction influences attributions by preventing

    a) accurate identifications
    b) accurate categorizations
    c) deliberative adjustments
    d) the fundamental attribution error

    Answer: c   Type: M   Page(s): 146   Key 1: F

36. Dave is clinically depressed. Nick is not. In making causal attributions, Dave is

    a) more likely than Nick to adjust for situational constraints
    b) less likely than Nick to adjust for situational constraints
    c) more likely than Nick to identify behaviors correctly
    d) less likely than Nick to identify behaviors correctly

    Answer: a   Type: M   Page(s): 147   Key 1: F

37. The actor-observer difference holds that

    a) actors form more accurate impressions than do observers
    b) actors form less accurate impressions than do observers
    c) the correspondence bias is larger for actors than for observers
    d) the correspondence bias is larger for observers than for actors

    Answer: d   Type: M   Page(s): 148   Key 1: F

38. Ellen is taking a course in chemistry. According to research on the actor-observer difference, how should Ellen and Ellen's roommate explain why Ellen is taking this course?

   a) Ellen should say that she likes chemistry; her roommate should say that Ellen is fulfilling a requirement.
   b) Ellen should say that she is fulfilling a requirement; her roommate should say that Ellen likes chemistry.
   c) Ellen should say that she just couldn't find any other courses to fit her schedule; her roommate should say that it was just luck.
   d) Ellen should say that it was just luck; her roommate should say that Ellen couldn't find any other courses to fit her schedule.

   Answer: b   Type: M   Page(s): 148   Key 1: A

39. False consensus has been used to explain

   a) the accuracy of interpersonal impressions
   b) why certain traits are perceived more accurately than others
   c) why acquaintance does not improve the accuracy of impressions
   d) actor-observer differences in attribution

   Answer: d   Type: M   Page(s): 148   Key 1: F

40. One reason for actor-observer differences is that actors can see

   a) their own behavior better than observers
   b) situational constraints better than observers
   c) observers as well as observers can see actors
   d) what they are trying to do

   Answer: b   Type: M   Page(s): 148   Key 1: F

41. Waiting for an important job interview, Fred felt nervous. As part of the interview, Fred was shown a videotape of himself sitting in the waiting room. Research on visual salience in attributions suggests that seeing the tape should make Fred

   a) irate at the knowledge that he had been videotaped
   b) infer that the situation would have made anyone nervous
   c) infer that he is a nervous person
   d) infer that he is a relaxed person

   Answer: c   Type: M   Page(s): 149   Key 1: A

42. _____ is the tendency to view our own actions and choices as more common than they are.

   a) False consensus
   b) False consistency
   c) The egocentric bias
   d) Biased assimilation

   Answer: a   Type: M   Page(s): 150   Key 1: F

43. Which of the following is an example of false consensus?

   a) Mel believes himself to be completely unique.
   b) Nickie believes that everyone else is just like her.
   c) Otto believes that Oscar is just like Oscar's father
   d) Otto believes that Oscar is totally different from Oscar's father

   Answer: b   Type: M   Page(s): 150   Key 1: A

44. Research on false consensus indicates that we're most likely to make dispositional inferences about

   a) ourselves
   b) others who agree with us
   c) others who disagree with us
   d) others when we know nothing about them

   Answer: c   Type: M   Page(s): 150   Key 1: F

45. Who is most likely to display false consensus?

   a) Paul, who hangs out with people who are just like him
   b) Roger, who hangs out with people who are very different from him
   c) Samantha, who is chronically anxious
   d) Teresa, who is clinically depressed

   Answer: a   Type: M   Page(s): 151   Key 1: A

46. When people make attributions for success and failure, they use three dimensions: internal-external, stable-unstable, and

   a) distinctive-common
   b) consensual-idiosyncratic
   c) good-bad
   d) controllable-uncontrollable

   Answer: d   Type: M   Page(s): 152   Key 1: F

Attribution

47. Ursula has just lost an important tennis match. According to the self-serving bias, Ursula should attribute her failure to

    a) an external stable cause
    b) an external unstable cause
    c) an internal stable cause
    d) an internal unstable cause

    Answer: b   Type: M   Page(s): 153   Key 1: A

48. As a cause for Van's passing his bar exam, luck is an

    a) external, stable, controllable cause
    b) external, stable, uncontrollable cause
    c) external, unstable, controllable cause
    d) external, unstable, uncontrollable cause

    Answer: d   Type: M   Page(s): 153   Key 1: A

49. Walter just got fired from his job. In explaining why he got fired, Walter is likely to make a self-enhancing attribution

    a) only to his former boss
    b) only to prospective future bosses
    c) only to his wife
    d) even to himself

    Answer: d   Type: M   Page(s): 154   Key 1: A

50. Yolanda and Zed have been married for five years. If they're like most couples,

    a) Yolanda and Zed will agree that Yolanda does most of the housework
    b) Yolanda and Zed will agree that Zed does most of the housework
    c) Yolanda will believe that she does most of housework; Zed will believe that he does most of it
    d) Yolanda will believe that Zed does most of the housework; Zed will believe that Yolanda does most of it

    Answer: c   Type: M   Page(s): 155   Key 1: A

51. A majority of car drivers believe that they are

    a) average drivers
    b) above average drivers
    c) below average drivers
    d) more likely than average to be hit by a drunk driver

    Answer: b   Type: M   Page(s): 156   Key 1: F

52. In evaluating their life chances, most people show

    a) unrealistic optimism
    b) undue pessimism
    c) unrealistic optimism some days, undue pessimism other days-- depending on their recent experiences
    d) surprising accuracy

    Answer: a   Type: M   Page(s): 156   Key 1: F

53. Self-esteem depends on whether success is attributed to a(n)

    a) controllable cause or an uncontrollable cause
    b) common cause or a rare cause
    c) internal cause or an external cause
    d) stable cause or an unstable cause

    Answer: c   Type: M   Page(s): 158   Key 1: F

54. Albert, who just failed a psychology exam, blamed his failure on an external cause. This should

    a) make him believe that he can succeed in the future
    b) make him believe that he will fail in the future
    c) protect his self-esteem
    d) lower his self-esteem

    Answer: c   Type: M   Page(s): 158   Key 1: A

55. The attributed stability of a cause affects

    a) emotional reactions
    b) expectations for the future
    c) self-esteem
    d) self-consciousness

    Answer: b   Type: M   Page(s): 158   Key 1: F

56. Betty, who just got jilted by Carl, blamed the break-up on a stable cause. This is likely to make Betty

    a) try to reunite with Carl
    b) seek a new romantic partner
    c) decide she can be happy being alone
    d) become depressed

    Answer: d   Type: M   Page(s): 159   Key 1: A

Attribution

57. Attributional retraining programs are designed to encourage participants to attribute

    a) success to stable factors and failure to unstable factors
    b) success to unstable factors and failure to stable factors
    c) success to distinctive factors and failure to non-distinctive factors
    d) success to non-distinctive factors and failure to distinctive factors

    Answer: a   Type: M   Page(s): 159   Key 1: F

58. The attributed controllability of a cause affects

    a) self-esteem
    b) self-serving biases
    c) emotional reactions
    d) expectations for the future

    Answer: c   Type: M   Page(s): 160   Key 1: F

59. David and Ed are third-grade classmates. David is hyperactive; Ed is physically handicapped. Research indicates that other third graders will like Ed more than David because they will perceive

    a) David's hyperactivity as less stable than Ed's handicap
    b) David's hyperactivity as more stable than Ed's handicap
    c) David's hyperactivity as less controllable than Ed's handicap
    d) David's hyperactivity as more controllable than Ed's handicap

    Answer: d   Type: M   Page(s): 160   Key 1: A

60. Fred bumped into Glenn. Glenn is most likely to react aggressively if he believes that Fred's behavior was

    a) controllable
    b) uncontrollable
    c) internally caused
    d) externally caused

    Answer: a   Type: M   Page(s): 160   Key 1: A

61. Sometimes, flood victims are blamed for their own misfortune. This illustrates

    a) false consensus
    b) false uniqueness
    c) the egocentric bias
    d) the correspondence bias

    Answer: d   Type: M   Page(s): 161   Key 1: F

62. The just world hypothesis states that

    a) the world is, in fact, largely just
    b) perceivers want to believe that people get what they deserve
    c) perceptions of justice depend on considerations of equity
    d) perceptions of justice depend on procedural fairness

    Answer: b Type: M Page(s): 161 Key 1: F

63. Harry, a homosexual, just learned that he has AIDS. Ida said, "It serves you right! You got just what you deserved!" Ida's comment reflects

    a) unrealistic optimism
    b) false consensus
    c) the just world hypothesis
    d) an egocentric bias

    Answer: c Type: M Page(s): 161 Key 1: A

64. Conservatives are more likely than liberals to attribute poverty to

    a) dispositional causes
    b) situational causes
    c) unstable causes
    d) uncontrollable causes

    Answer: a Type: M Page(s): 163 Key 1: F

65. Julie believed that people are poor because of causes that are external, unstable, and uncontrollable. Julie is most likely a

    a) depressed person
    b) anxious person
    c) conservative
    d) liberal

    Answer: d Type: M Page(s): 163 Key 1: A

66. Larry is on trial for raping Mary. To get Larry off, Larry's lawyer should try to

    a) portray rape as an act of violence
    b) establish that Mary had been a virgin
    c) focus attention on Larry
    d) focus attention on Mary

    Answer: d Type: M Page(s): 164 Key 1: A

67. In judging the guilt of an alleged rapist, mock jurors are

    a) unwilling to believe that rape is an erotic act
    b) unwilling to believe that rape is a violent act
    c) not much affected by the victim's actions
    d) definitely affected by the victim's actions

    Answer: d   Type: M   Page(s): 164   Key 1: F

68. In a study of judgments about rape, male and female students read about a heterosexual couple who had earlier had intercourse with one another ten times. But on the current night, one member of the couple was forced into having sex. As the results of this study showed, students thought that

    a) the woman (but not the man) was now "obligated" to have sex
    b) the man (but not the woman) was now "obligated" to have sex
    c) both the man and the woman were now "obligated" to have sex
    d) neither the man nor the woman was now "obligated" to have sex

    Answer: c   Type: M   Page(s): 165   Key 1: F

69. In explaining murders,

    a) Americans emphasize situational causes; Chinese people emphasize dispositional causes
    b) Americans emphasize dispositional causes; Chinese people emphasize situational attributions
    c) both Americans and Chinese people emphasize dispositional causes
    d) both Americans and Chinese people emphasize situational causes

    Answer: b   Type: M   Page(s): 166   Key 1: F

70. People in collectivist cultures are more likely than people in individualistic cultures to attribute behavior to

    a) stable factors
    b) unstable factors
    c) controllable factors
    d) situational factors

    Answer: d   Type: M   Page(s): 166   Key 1: F

ESSAY

71. Compare and contrast impression formation and attribution. How are these two processes similar? How do they differ?

Answer:
Students could use this open-ended question as a vehicle for summarizing much of the material in chapters 3 and 4 of the text. Like impression formation, attributions involve two steps: a spontaneous step followed by a deliberative step. In both processes, the deliberative step involves an adjustment to the output of the first step. Like impressions, attributions are typically accurate, yet both impressions and attributions can in certain circumstances be inaccurate. Impressions are not, however, identical to causal attributions. Although one's impressions of a person may incorporate attributions for that person's behavior, impressions can be based on other information, too: like the person's face, voice, and gait. If attributions reflect the perceiver's attempt to understand behavior, impressions reflect the perceiver's attempt to understand people.

Type: E   Page(s): 85-167   Key 1: F

72. You've just seen a teenage boy driving a Corvette down main street at 120 miles per hour. Using the two-stage model of causal attribution presented in the textbook, explain this event. Apply each of the substages of this model of causal attribution to explaining the teenage boy's fast driving.

Answer:
To answer this question, students would need to apply the two-stage model of causal attribution presented on page 130. They would need to note how they would identify and categorize the behavior, situation, and person. This would constitute the spontaneous stage of causal attribution. They would then need to note how they might deliberatively adjust their spontaneous attribution, taking into account the variance of the behavior, the effects of the behavior, constraints on the behavior, and the emotional impact of the behavior. The ideal answer to this question would present a creative application of the concepts on pages 129-138 of the text.

Type: E   Page(s): 130   Key 1: A

73. Identify three important biases in attribution. Give an example of each bias, and explain the cause(s) of each. Which bias (in your opinion) distorts attributions the most seriously? Which is most harmless?

Answer:
Students could answer this question by defining and giving examples of the correspondence bias (p. 139), actor-observer differences (p. 148), and self-serving biases (p. 152). They would need to review the material in the text on the causes of each bias.

Type: E   Page(s): 139   Key 1: F

Attribution

74. What is the most "rational" way to make attributions for one's successes and failures? How do people actually make such attributions? Answer this question by reviewing social psychological concepts and research. Be sure to mention the three dimensions for making attributions for success and failure.

    Answer:
    In answering this question, students would need to note that attributions for success and failure vary from internal to external, from stable to unstable, and from controllable to uncontrollable. They would need to note that most people attribute their successes to internal, stable factors; and their failures to external, unstable factors. Although this may or may not be "rational", it keeps people from being depressed.

    Type: E   Page(s): 152   Key 1: F

75. John Q. Jones has been accused of raping 15 women. You are the prosecuting attorney. Using the principles of causal attribution, explain how you will convince a jury to convict John Jones of rape. Be sure to draw on social psychological concepts and research.

    Answer:
    Students could answer this question by reviewing the material on pages 164-165 of the text. They might also wish to develop legal strategies based on the correspondence bias, actor-observer differences, and perceivers' tendencies to use information about the variance of behavior over time, persons, and situations (p. 133).

    Type: E   Page(s): 164   Key 1: A

Chapter 5

The Self

MULTIPLE CHOICE

1. Research shows that college women eat less when talking to

   a) an attractive woman, rather than an unattractive woman
   b) an unattractive woman, rather than an attractive woman
   c) an attractive man, rather than an unattractive man
   d) an unattractive man, rather than an attractive man

   Answer: c   Type: M   Page(s): 170   Key 1: F

2. Zelda, a typical female college student, plans to eat lunch with classmates on four consecutive days this week. On Monday, she'll dine with Melvin, a highly desirable dating partner. On Tuesday, she'll dine with Ted, a complete loser. On Wednesday, she'll dine with Wanda, who is shockingly attractive. On Thursday, she'll dine with Thelma, who is downright homely. Based on research, we can predict that Zelda will eat more when dining with

   a) Melvin, rather than Ted
   b) Ted, rather than Melvin
   c) Wanda, rather than Thelma
   d) Thelma, rather than Wanda

   Answer: b   Type: M   Page(s): 170   Key 1: A

3. Historical scholarship suggests that

   a) it has become steadily easier to know oneself over the ages
   b) it has become steadily harder to know oneself over the ages
   c) it was hardest to know oneself in the 18th century
   d) it was hardest to know oneself in the 19th century

   Answer: b   Type: M   Page(s): 171   Key 1: F

4. As historical scholarship shows, the notion of "self-actualization" became dominant

   a) prior to the 18th century
   b) in the 18th century
   c) in the 19th century
   d) in the 20th century

   Answer: d   Type: M   Page(s): 171   Key 1: F

67

The Self

5. Personal identity has been emphasized over social identity

 a) in all cultures throughout history
 b) in all cultures, but only in modern times
 c) throughout history, but only in Western cultures
 d) only in Western cultures and only in modern times

 Answer: d   Type: M   Page(s): 172   Key 1: F

6. Who would have the easiest time achieving self-knowledge?

 a) Theus, a late medieval knight
 b) Alexander, an 18th century Puritan
 c) Jedadiah, an early 20th century American factory worker
 d) Bob, a late 20th century American college student

 Answer: a   Type: M   Page(s): 172   Key 1: A

7. Cindy thinks of herself as highly extroverted. Darlene doesn't really think of herself as either extroverted or introverted. Relative to Cindy, Darlene is

 a) schematic
 b) aschematic
 c) self-complex
 d) self-simple

 Answer: b   Type: M   Page(s): 174   Key 1: A

8. Self-schemas are

 a) techniques that people use to get along with others
 b) tactics that people use to exploit others
 c) beliefs that help people understand themselves
 d) beliefs that people have about their beliefs

 Answer: c   Type: M   Page(s): 174   Key 1: F

9. People use their self-schemas

 a) only in thinking about themselves
 b) in thinking about others, as well as themselves
 c) only when they are thinking about the past
 d) when they are thinking about the past and future, but not the present

 Answer: b   Type: M   Page(s): 174   Key 1: F

10. Jack is schematic, in thinking of himself as fiercely independent. If asked, "Are you the kind of person who is dependent on others?", Jack would

    a) remember that he was independent
    b) review all of the times he had been dependent on others
    c) review all of the times he had been independent of others
    d) do all of these

    Answer: a   Type: M   Page(s): 175   Key 1: A

11. Psychologists believe that

    a) everyone is schematic for every personality trait
    b) some people are schematic for every personality trait; others are aschematic for every personality trait
    c) there are certain traits for which everyone has a schema, and other traits for which no one has a schema
    d) although everyone is schematic for at least one trait, different people are schematic for different traits

    Answer: d   Type: M   Page(s): 175   Key 1: F

12. Jill thinks of herself as obese. Jane thinks of herself as obese, socially awkward, and intellectually gifted. Relative to Jill, Jane is high in

    a) self-schematicity
    b) self-aschematicity
    c) self-complexity
    d) self-simplicity

    Answer: c   Type: M   Page(s): 176   Key 1: A

13. Research suggests that a complex self-schema

    a) exaggerates the emotional impact of failure
    b) minimizes the emotional impact of failure
    c) results from a complex schema about one's mother
    d) results from a complex schema about one's same-sex parent

    Answer: b   Type: M   Page(s): 176   Key 1: F

14. Possible selves are

    a) a psychologist's projections of future possibilities for an individual
    b) an individual's projections of future possibilities for him- or herself
    c) selves that no one expects to materialize
    d) selves that one can be certain will materialize

    Answer: b   Type: M   Page(s): 177   Key 1: F

15. Surveys reveal that

    a) all college students expect to be sad in the future
    b) only college students who are currently sad expect to be sad in the future
    c) all college students expect to be happy in the future
    d) only college students who are currently happy expect to be happy in the future

    Answer: c   Type: M   Page(s): 177   Key 1: F

16. Jackie's possible selves are balanced. This means that

    a) Jackie has realistic views about the future
    b) Jackie has a realistic interpretation of the past
    c) Jackie's fears are offset by her hopes
    d) Jackie's thoughts are consistent with her emotions

    Answer: c   Type: M   Page(s): 178   Key 1: A

17. Jason, a 16-year-old, is in a training school for severe juvenile delinquents. Research suggests that Jason's possible selves will be

    a) realistic
    b) unrealistic
    c) balanced
    d) imbalanced

    Answer: d   Type: M   Page(s): 178   Key 1: A

18. Future selves

    a) have no impact on the present
    b) can affect current emotions, but not current behavior
    c) are at least as important as present self-schemas
    d) none of these

    Answer: c   Type: M   Page(s): 179   Key 1: F

19. Research shows that

    a) everyone has an equally complex future self
    b) future selves are more complex than present selves
    c) a given individual's future self is exactly as complex as that individual's present self
    d) a given individual can have a simple present self and a complex future self or vice versa

    Answer: d   Type: M   Page(s): 180   Key 1: F

20. Present selves can be divided into three types. Which of the following is NOT one of them?

    a) overlooked self
    b) actual self
    c) ought self
    d) ideal self

    Answer: a   Type: M   Page(s): 180   Key 1: F

21. The actual self, ideal self, and ought self can be seen from two perspectives:

    a) physical perspective and psychological perspective
    b) children's perspective and adults' perspective
    c) own perspective and other's perspective
    d) past perspective and present perspective

    Answer: c   Type: M   Page(s): 180   Key 1: F

22. John is a 40-year-old homeless alcoholic. John wishes that he were a rich stockbroker. This is John's

    a) actual self
    b) ought self
    c) impossible self
    d) ideal self

    Answer: d   Type: M   Page(s): 180   Key 1: A

23. Although Karen is overweight and unattractive, Karen believes that she is stunningly beautiful. This belief is Karen's

    a) ought self
    b) ideal self
    c) actual own self
    d) actual other self

    Answer: c   Type: M   Page(s): 180   Key 1: A

24. Self-discrepancies are discrepancies between

    a) the actual self and either the ideal or the ought self
    b) the ideal self and the ought self
    c) the past self and the present self
    d) the past self and the future self

    Answer: a   Type: M   Page(s): 181   Key 1: F

25. Luther perceives himself to be callous, but thinks that others feel that he ought to be sensitive. Research suggests that this discrepancy will make Luther feel

    a) contented
    b) angry
    c) sad
    d) anxious

    Answer: d   Type: M   Page(s): 181   Key 1: A

26. Research indicates that people feel dejected when there's a discrepancy between

    a) their actual self and their ideal self
    b) their actual self and their ought self
    c) their hopes and their fears
    d) their thoughts and their emotions

    Answer: a   Type: M   Page(s): 182   Key 1: F

27. Research shows that

    a) self-discrepancies have no impact on physical or mental health
    b) self-discrepancies can influence physical health, but not mental health
    c) all types of self-discrepancies lead to the same health problems
    d) different types of self-discrepancies lead to different types of health problems

    Answer: d   Type: M   Page(s): 182   Key 1: F

28. People use the social context to determine who they are by employing two processes: social comparison and

    a) self-comparison
    b) self-distinctiveness
    c) self-complexity
    d) self-simplicity

    Answer: b   Type: M   Page(s): 183   Key 1: F

29. Social comparison occurs when people

    a) use others as a standard for evaluating themselves
    b) use themselves as a standard for evaluating others
    c) compare people they like to people they hate
    d) compare people they know to famous people they have never met

    Answer: a   Type: M   Page(s): 183   Key 1: F

30. Alicia, a moderately good-looking teenager, is always comparing herself to the gorgeous women on the cover of fashion magazines. Alicia is engaged in

    a) spurious comparison
    b) realistic comparison
    c) upward comparison
    d) downward comparison

    Answer: c   Type: M   Page(s): 184   Key 1: A

31. Downward social comparison

    a) raises people's self-esteem
    b) lowers people's self-esteem
    c) can either raise or lower people's self-esteem
    d) has no effect on people's self-esteem

    Answer: c   Type: M   Page(s): 184   Key 1: F

32. Jack's marriage to Jill was in jeopardy; the two had been fighting non-stop for weeks. Then Jack began thinking about Mel, whose marriage to Marcia was even worse than his and Jill's. Research suggests that thinking about Mel should make Jack

    a) turn to drugs
    b) develop a more complex self-schema
    c) feel better
    d) feel worse

    Answer: d   Type: M   Page(s): 184   Key 1: A

33. Cancer patients prefer to associate with

    a) strangers who are in perfect health
    b) people who have diseases other than cancer
    c) cancer patients who are doing better than they are
    d) cancer patients who are doing worse than they are

    Answer: c   Type: M   Page(s): 185   Key 1: F

34. Compared to social comparisons that we choose, social comparisons that are thrust on us by other people

    a) have no impact on our self-concept
    b) have, if anything, less impact on our self-concept
    c) have, if anything, more impact on our self-concept
    d) are redundant, since they're the social comparisons we would have chosen in any case

    Answer: c   Type: M   Page(s): 185   Key 1: F

35. Nancy had just struggled to graduate from State U. law school. Now she was applying for a job at a large firm downtown. On the day of her interview, Nancy ran into Pauline, a wildly attractive, outgoing woman Nancy's age who just graduated first in her class at Harvard Law School. Research indicates that meeting Pauline should make Nancy

    a) feel better
    b) feel worse
    c) seek a sideways social comparison
    d) seek a downward social comparison

    Answer: b   Type: M   Page(s): 185   Key 1: A

36. What is the goal of social comparison?

    a) to draw people closer to one another
    b) to distance people from those they dislike
    c) to make people feel better about themselves
    d) to make people feel worse about others

    Answer: c   Type: M   Page(s): 186   Key 1: F

37. Paul and Ned, two promiscuous gay men, have just received the results of their medical tests. Paul has tested positive for HIV; Ned has tested negative. Research indicates that relative to Ned, Paul will estimate that he has

    a) one hundred times the chance of developing AIDS
    b) twice the chance of developing AIDS
    c) the same chance of developing AIDS
    d) less chance of developing AIDS

    Answer: d   Type: M   Page(s): 186   Key 1: A

38. According to _____, cultures develop to help people overcome death anxiety by making them feel better about themselves.

    a) terror management theory
    b) functional world view theory
    c) objective self-awareness theory
    d) subjective self-awareness theory

    Answer: a   Type: M   Page(s): 187   Key 1: F

39. When asked to describe themselves, people usually emphasize

    a) the ways in which they are similar to others
    b) the ways in which they are different from others
    c) the ways in which they are better than others
    d) the ways in which they are worse than others

    Answer: b   Type: M   Page(s): 188   Key 1: F

40. Darlene is the token female in an otherwise all-male engineering firm. Research suggests that Darlene's token status will

    a) make her try harder
    b) allow her to loaf
    c) facilitate her job performance
    d) impair her job performance

    Answer: d   Type: M   Page(s): 188   Key 1: A

41. The most important function of self-presentation is

    a) to delude ourselves into believing that we're someone we're not
    b) to win friends and influence people
    c) to get help from other people in refining our self-concepts
    d) to deceive other people about who we are

    Answer: c   Type: M   Page(s): 190   Key 1: F

42. Identity negotiation refers to the process by which

    a) we come to know a purely private self
    b) we reach agreement with others about who we are
    c) power struggles in a relationship are resolved
    d) the mission of groups is established

    Answer: b   Type: M   Page(s): 191   Key 1: F

43. Your text discusses a number of frequently used self-presentational strategies. Which of the following is NOT one of them?

    a) imitation
    b) intimidation
    c) ingratiation
    d) supplication

    Answer: a   Type: M   Page(s): 191   Key 1: F

44. Yolanda desperately wants others to like her. Which of the following strategies is she most likely to use?

    a) self-promotion
    b) exemplification
    c) supplication
    d) ingratiation

    Answer: d   Type: M   Page(s): 192   Key 1: A

75

45. Which self-presentational strategy is used most frequently?

    a) intimidation
    b) ingratiation
    c) exemplification
    d) supplication

    Answer: b   Type: M   Page(s): 192   Key 1: F

46. To make others feel guilty, Alphonso has a frugal lifestyle, and gives 90% of his salary to starving lepers in Liberia. Alphonso's self-presentational strategy is

    a) self-promotion
    b) supplication
    c) ingratiation
    d) exemplification

    Answer: d   Type: M   Page(s): 192   Key 1: A

47. The self-presentational strategy of supplication is

    a) of special use to people with superb social skills
    b) used as a last resort
    c) designed to make a person appear competent
    d) designed to make a person appear morally worthy

    Answer: b   Type: M   Page(s): 192   Key 1: F

48. Everyone wants an identity that

    a) can help them earn a living
    b) is morally blameless
    c) is socially desirable
    d) other people support

    Answer: d   Type: M   Page(s): 192   Key 1: F

49. _____ consists of getting people to agree with what we believe to be true of ourselves.

    a) Self-definition
    b) Self-verification
    c) Self-enhancement
    d) Self-derogation

    Answer: b   Type: M   Page(s): 194   Key 1: F

50. Self-verification conflicts with self-enhancement

    a) under all circumstances
    b) under no circumstances
    c) for people who have positive self-concepts
    d) for people who have negative self-concepts

    Answer: d   Type: M   Page(s): 192   Key 1: F

51. Debbie thinks of herself as unattractive and stupid. According to research, with which of the following would Debbie most prefer to interact?

    a) Ellen, who regards Debbie as unattractive, but smart
    b) Felicia, who regards Debbie as attractive, but stupid
    c) Gloria, who regards Debbie as unattractive and stupid
    d) Hazel, who regards Debbie as attractive and smart

    Answer: c   Type: M   Page(s): 195   Key 1: F

52. In a study, subjects who had negative self-concepts preferred to interact with a person who viewed them negatively, rather than a person who viewed them positively. When asked about their preference, these subjects said that the interaction with someone who viewed them negatively would

    a) be more harmonious
    b) be more confrontational
    c) focus more on the other person, rather than the subject
    d) focus more on the subject, rather than the other person

    Answer: a   Type: M   Page(s): 195   Key 1: F

53. Individuals who want to have their identities confirmed have two ways to seek self-verification: choosing certain interaction partners and

    a) reflecting on certain of their own characteristics
    b) acting out the roles they want to adopt
    c) structuring interactions in a certain way
    d) terminating interactions they don't like

    Answer: c   Type: M   Page(s): 196   Key 1: F

54. Julie always presents herself as gloomy, whether the people around her are gloomy or not. Julie is

    a) a high self-monitor
    b) a low self-monitor
    c) high in need for uniqueness
    d) low in need for uniqueness

    Answer: b   Type: M   Page(s): 198   Key 1: A

55. High self-monitors

    a) are open-minded
    b) are closed-minded
    c) would be good actors
    d) are introspective

    Answer: c   Type: M   Page(s): 198   Key 1: F

56. Who is most likely to engage in self-verification?

    a) someone who is high in self-monitoring
    b) someone who is moderate in self-monitoring
    c) someone who is low in self-monitoring
    d) self-monitoring is unrelated to self-verification

    Answer: c   Type: M   Page(s): 198   Key 1: A

57. For an assignment in drama class, Larry (a low self-monitor) had to play the role of a cynical, selfish stockbroker. Larry's classmates criticized his acting. They said that Larry was simply too good a person to play this cynical role. Research indicates that the classmates' comments should

    a) make Larry feel bad
    b) make Larry feel good
    c) encourage Larry to be introspective
    d) discourage Larry from being introspective

    Answer: b   Type: M   Page(s): 199   Key 1: A

58. Self-awareness

    a) exaggerates an individual's shortcomings
    b) is a pleasurable state
    c) is another term for self-monitoring
    d) is another term for self-verification

    Answer: a   Type: M   Page(s): 200   Key 1: F

59. People change their behavior to fit ideal standards when they are

    a) high in self-verification
    b) low in self-monitoring
    c) high in self-awareness
    d) low in self-complexity

    Answer: c   Type: M   Page(s): 201   Key 1: F

60. George just had a four-martini lunch. Research indicates that the four martinis will reduce George's

    a) self-verification
    b) self-monitoring
    c) self-distinctiveness
    d) self-awareness

    Answer: d   Type: M   Page(s): 201   Key 1: A

61. Self-evaluation maintenance involves strategically managing three factors. Which of the following is NOT one of them?

    a) closeness of other performers
    b) attributions for performance
    c) quality of performance, relative to others
    d) relevance of performance

    Answer: b   Type: M   Page(s): 203   Key 1: F

62. Betty's self-evaluation maintenance depends on her performance, her closeness to other performers, and

    a) the relevance of the performance to Betty's self-concept
    b) the relevance of the performance to the others' self-concepts
    c) Betty's level of self-consciousness
    d) Betty's level of self-monitoring

    Answer: a   Type: M   Page(s): 203   Key 1: F

63. To Joe, dart playing is important and Scrabble playing ability is trivial. Joe would bask in reflected glory if he was close to

    a) Sam, whom Joe could beat every day in darts
    b) Ted, who is the top dart player in the world
    c) Paul, whom Joe could beat every day in Scrabble
    d) Roger, who is the top Scrabble player in the world

    Answer: d   Type: M   Page(s): 203   Key 1: A

64. Self-evaluation maintenance prompts people to

    a) set up obstacles to their own performance
    b) distract themselves from self-attention
    c) minimize their association with losers
    d) put all their eggs in one basket

    Answer: c   Type: M   Page(s): 203   Key 1: F

65. Aaron, Bob, and Carl all consider themselves to be math whizzes. In the state Mathematics contest, Aaron finished first; Bob finished second; and Carl finished third. Now Bob has to wait for an hour to get his second-place award. There are two couches in the waiting room. Aaron is sitting on one of them; Carl is sitting on the other. Research suggests that Bob will

   a) sit next to Aaron
   b) sit next to Carl
   c) stand equidistant between Aaron and Carl
   d) sit next to Aaron for thirty minutes and next to Carl for thirty minutes

   Answer: b   Type: M   Page(s): 204   Key 1: A

66. _____ involves exaggerating identity symbols when an important aspect of the self-concept has been threatened.

   a) Self-enhancement
   b) Self-derogation
   c) Identity negotiation
   d) Symbolic self-completion

   Answer: d   Type: M   Page(s): 205   Key 1: F

67. Joe, an unattached male heterosexual, has always thought of himself as an introvert. But as part of an experiment, a psychologist just gave Joe false information indicating that he is an extrovert. Joe now has the opportunity to interact with LaVonne, a gorgeous woman who says she loves extroverted guys. Research on symbolic self-completion suggests that Joe will present himself to LaVonne as

   a) self-confident
   b) modest
   c) introverted
   d) extroverted

   Answer: c   Type: M   Page(s): 206   Key 1: A

68. Zelda could engage in self-handicapping in either of two ways: by setting up an obstacle to her performance or

   a) not trying
   b) claiming a disability
   c) cheating
   d) overpracticing

   Answer: b   Type: M   Page(s): 206   Key 1: F

69. When people claim they cannot perform well because of a handicap, they

    a) are engaged in exemplification
    b) are engaged in self-verification
    c) typically perform worse than they would have if they had not made the claim
    d) frequently perform better than they would have if they had not made the claim

    Answer: d   Type: M   Page(s): 207   Key 1: F

70. Self-handicapping is most likely to occur when

    a) people are uncertain about whether or not they will do well
    b) people are certain that they will do poorly
    c) the reason for the self-handicapping will be obvious
    d) the matter at hand is unimportant

    Answer: a   Type: M   Page(s): 208   Key 1: F

ESSAY

71. Discuss the concept of self-schemas. How does this concept differ from other concepts about the self? How is it similar? Illustrate the concept by describing the self-schema of someone you know well.

    Answer:
    Students should begin their answer to this question by summarizing the material on pages 173-175 of the text. As noted there, self-schemas are sets of beliefs that help people organize their knowledge about themselves. Not everyone has a schema about their own standing on every personality dimension. But everyone is "schematic" for one trait or another. People who are schematic for a trait can quickly and confidently answer questions related to that trait, by consulting a trait label for themselves they have stored in memory. After reviewing this material, students should compare and contrast self-schemas with other concepts about the self -- (for example) self-complexity, possible selves, and self-consciousness. They should conclude their answer by discussing the self-schemas of someone they know.

    Type: E   Page(s): 173   Key 1: F

72. At one time or another, everyone has been told "Don't put all your eggs in one basket." Critically evaluate this advice by reviewing social psychological research on self-complexity. Is it ever good to "put all your eggs in one basket"? If so, when?

    Answer:
    It's not a good idea to "put all your eggs in one basket" because people who have simple self-concepts are vulnerable if the one trait by which they define themselves is threatened. Students should note this fact and review some of the research described on page 176. Perhaps it is never good to "put all your eggs in one basket"; however, it would be harmless if the trait by which an individual defined the self was never threatened.

    Type: E   Page(s): 176   Key 1: F

73. Self-discrepancies depend on the fit between three types of self. Identify the three types of self and the discrepancies to which they give rise. Explain the causes and consequences of each type of discrepancy. In your opinion, which type of discrepancy is most harmful? Why?

Answer:
Students could answer this question by reviewing the material on pages 180-183 of the text. As noted there, one can distinguish between the actual self, the ideal self, and the ought self. Discrepancies between the actual self and the ideal self give rise to sadness; discrepancies between the actual self and the ought self give rise to anxiety or agitation.

Type: E   Page(s): 181   Key 1: F

74. Identify five frequently used self-presentational strategies. Describe the goals and risks of pursuing each of these strategies. Which of the strategies would an unscrupulous student be best advised to pursue to get an A in a social psychology course? Which strategy would be most likely to backfire? Explain your answers.

Answer:
Students could answer this question by summarizing the material on page 191 of the text. The five self-presentational strategies are ingratiation, self-promotion, intimidation, exemplification, and supplication. Students should identify the identity sought by each strategy and the associated risks. Students would complete their answer by identifying one strategy that could be successfully used and one that could not be successfully used to get an A in social psychology.

Type: E   Page(s): 191   Key 1: F

75. Psychologists make a distinction between the public self and the private self. The public self is the self that we present to others; the private self is the self known only to ourselves. Consider the following concepts: self-distinctiveness, self-verification, self-monitoring, and self-handicapping. Discuss the relevance of each of these concepts to the public self and the private self. Which concepts concern only the public self? Which concern only the private self? Which concern both? Be sure to explain each of these four concepts as part of your discussion.

Answer:
In answering this question, students would need to explain the concepts of self-distinctiveness (p. 187), self-verification (p. 194), self-monitoring (p. 198), and self-handicapping (p. 206). As discussed in the text, self-distinctiveness and self-verification concern primarily the private self. Self-handicapping and self-monitoring involve both the public and the private self. Students should receive credit if they make informed arguments about each of the four concepts.

Type: E   Page(s): 187-208   Key 1: A

Chapter 6

Attitudes

MULTIPLE CHOICE

1. As noted in your text, researchers have for many years regarded _____ as "the central concept in social psychology".

    a) intrinsic motivation
    b) extrinsic motivation
    c) attitude
    d) personality

    Answer: c   Type: M   Page(s): 215   Key 1: F

2. As originally used in the early 1700s, the term "attitude" referred to a person's

    a) mood or emotion
    b) posture or physical stance
    c) intelligence
    d) complete personality

    Answer: b   Type: M   Page(s): 215   Key 1: F

3. A(n) _____ has been defined as "a psychological tendency that is expressed by evaluating a particular entity with some degree of favor or disfavor".

    a) attitude
    b) motive
    c) judgment
    d) decisional heuristic

    Answer: a   Type: M   Page(s): 216   Key 1: F

4. The major theory of attitudes holds that an attitude consists of _____ components.

    a) two
    b) three
    c) four
    d) five

    Answer: b   Type: M   Page(s): 216   Key 1: F

Attitudes

5. Barbara hates drunk drivers. Barbara's hatred is the _____ component of her attitude.

   a) conative
   b) behavioral
   c) cognitive
   d) affective

   Answer: d   Type: M   Page(s): 216   Key 1: A

6. Ursula has a negative attitude toward sororities. Which of the following is a cognitive component of Ursula's attitude?

   a) her hatred of sororities in general
   b) her hatred of a particular sorority at her University
   c) her belief that sorority members are snobs
   d) her intention to avoid interacting with sorority members

   Answer: c   Type: M   Page(s): 216   Key 1: A

7. 100% of John's feelings about homosexuals are negative, but only 50% of his thoughts, and 20% of his actions toward homosexuals are negative. John

   a) has a wider latitude than longitude of acceptance
   b) has a narrower latitude than longitude of acceptance
   c) has an ambivalent attitude toward homosexuals
   d) doesn't really have an attitude toward homosexuals

   Answer: c   Type: M   Page(s): 218   Key 1: A

8. In assessing attitudes, there is a distinction between

   a) objective and subjective assessments
   b) direct and indirect assessments
   c) inferential and deferential assessments
   d) experimenter-initiated and subject-initiated assessments

   Answer: b   Type: M   Page(s): 218   Key 1: F

9. A researcher asks Barbara three questions about her attitude toward drunk drivers. Barbara answers each question on a scale that ranges from -4 to +4. The researcher adds up Barbara's responses to the three questions. The researcher is using a

   a) Likert scale
   b) Thurstone scale
   c) bogus pipeline scale
   d) projective technique

   Answer: a   Type: M   Page(s): 219   Key 1: A

10. Likert scales, semantic differential scales, and latitudes of acceptance are three

    a) direct methods of measuring attributions
    b) indirect methods of measuring attributions
    c) direct methods of measuring attitudes
    d) indirect methods of measuring attitudes

    Answer: c   Type: M   Page(s): 219   Key 1: F

11. According to _____ theory, the connotative meaning of a word has three aspects: evaluation, potency, and activity.

    a) formal linguistic
    b) informal linguistic
    c) semantic differential
    d) syntactic differential

    Answer: c   Type: M   Page(s): 220   Key 1: F

12. Yolanda was asked to evaluate Rap Music on several dimensions, like DESIRABLE-UNDESIRABLE, GOOD-BAD, and PLEASANT-UNPLEASANT. Yolanda is answering

    a) semantic differential scales
    b) Likert scales
    c) Thurstone scales
    d) Guttman scales

    Answer: a   Type: M   Page(s): 220   Key 1: A

13. Which of the following is NOT an aspect of the connotative meaning of a word?

    a) potency
    b) intent
    c) activity
    d) evaluation

    Answer: b   Type: M   Page(s): 220   Key 1: F

14. The latitude of acceptance is an example of a(n)

    a) direct assessment technique
    b) indirect assessment technique
    c) single-point assessment technique
    d) summated assessment technique

    Answer: a   Type: M   Page(s): 220   Key 1: F

15. Which of the following is an example of an indirect attitude assessment technique?

    a) the semantic differential
    b) the syntactic differential
    c) the Holtzman ink-blot test
    d) the bogus pipeline

    Answer: d   Type: M   Page(s): 221   Key 1: F

16. Karlins, Coffman, and Walters (1969) seemed to find that whites had no negative stereotypes of blacks. Sigall and Page (1971) found that in fact whites retained some negative stereotypes of blacks. Sigall and Page reached their conclusion with

    a) a black experimenter
    b) the bogus pipeline
    c) the randomized-response technique
    d) the theory of reasoned action

    Answer: b   Type: M   Page(s): 221   Key 1: F

17. An indirect assessment technique would be most useful in assessing

    a) a vegetarian's attitude toward vegetarianism
    b) a meat-eater's attitude toward hamburgers
    c) a crack user's attitude toward crack
    d) an aspirin user's attitude toward aspirin

    Answer: c   Type: M   Page(s): 221   Key 1: A

18. The bogus pipeline is successful in getting people to report their attitudes because subjects

    a) are hypnotized prior to the attitude assessment
    b) believe that the experimenter knows their attitude anyway
    c) realize that their responses are anonymous
    d) are convinced that the experimenter is not evaluating them

    Answer: b   Type: M   Page(s): 221   Key 1: F

19. The bogus pipeline is presented to subjects as

    a) a way for them to fool the experimenter
    b) a way for them to make money
    c) a lie detector machine
    d) a shock-generating device

    Answer: c   Type: M   Page(s): 221   Key 1: F

20. The bogus pipeline is most useful in getting truthful answers

    a) that the subject does not consciously know
    b) that would in any case be reported
    c) to questions of opinion
    d) to questions of fact

    Answer: d   Type: M   Page(s): 222   Key 1: F

21. Electromyographic recordings can be used to measure attitudes from changes in

    a) brain-waves
    b) basal body temperature
    c) skin coloration
    d) facial muscles

    Answer: d   Type: M   Page(s): 222   Key 1: F

22. To measure attitudes, some social psychologists assess minute changes in facial muscles. To do so, they use

    a) videotapes that are played back at normal speed
    b) videotapes that are played back frame-by-frame
    c) electromyographic recordings
    d) PET scans

    Answer: d   Type: M   Page(s): 222   Key 1: F

23. What is most likely to shape the cognitive component of an attitude?

    a) inherited prejudices
    b) information
    c) classical conditioning
    d) instrumental conditioning

    Answer: b   Type: M   Page(s): 223   Key 1: F

24. Four-year-old Robby watches 40 hours of TV each week. During 38 of those hours, violence is being portrayed in a positive light. From this positive information about violence, Robby is most likely to develop

    a) positive feelings toward violence
    b) intentions to commit violence
    c) positive thoughts about violence
    d) reservations about committing violence

    Answer: c   Type: M   Page(s): 223   Key 1: A

25. _____ of attitudes involves coming to like or dislike an attitude object because it has been previously associated with pleasurable or unpleasurable events.

    a) Extinction
    b) Spontaneous recovery
    c) Instrumental conditioning
    d) Classical conditioning

    Answer: d   Type: M   Page(s): 224   Key 1: F

26. An experimenter projects a series of pictures of goats on screen in front of you. Just after projecting each picture, the experimenter gives you a strong electric shock. You come to fear goats. This is an example of

    a) first-hand information
    b) second-hand information
    c) classical conditioning
    d) instrumental conditioning

    Answer: c   Type: M   Page(s): 224   Key 1: A

27. Attitudes that are based on classical conditioning are most likely to serve a

    a) knowledge function
    b) social adjustive function
    c) self-presentational function
    d) value-expressive function

    Answer: d   Type: M   Page(s): 225   Key 1: F

28. Research shows that the classical conditioning of attitudes

    a) is the same as the instrumental conditioning of attitudes
    b) does NOT depend on information about the attitude object
    c) applies to dogs, but NOT to people
    d) is especially effective when people have a lot of direct experience with the attitude object

    Answer: b   Type: M   Page(s): 225   Key 1: F

29. A Soviet psychologist named Volkova classically conditioned children to respond to the abstract idea of goodness. She did so by

    a) squirting cranberry juice in their mouths
    b) squirting the children with a hose
    c) having the children suck on lemons
    d) having the children watch their parents respond

    Answer: a   Type: M   Page(s): 225   Key 1: F

30. Al's psychotherapist nods and smiles every time Al makes a positive comment about himself. As a consequence, Al starts to have a better attitude toward himself. This is an example of

    a) the semantic differential
    b) the syntactic differential
    c) classical conditioning
    d) instrumental conditioning

    Answer: d   Type: M   Page(s): 225   Key 1: A

31. Instrumental conditioning contributes most strongly to the _____ component of attitudes.

    a) certainty
    b) actions
    c) thoughts
    d) feelings

    Answer: b   Type: M   Page(s): 226   Key 1: F

32. When Joan was a child, she often saw her parents criticize women who had abortions. Now Joan believes that abortions should be outlawed. This is an example of

    a) modeling
    b) generalization
    c) classical conditioning
    d) instrumental conditioning

    Answer: a   Type: M   Page(s): 226   Key 1: F

33. Attitudes can serve a number of different functions. Which of the following is NOT one of them?

    a) behavior informative
    b) value expressive
    c) social adjustive
    d) knowledge

    Answer: a   Type: M   Page(s): 226   Key 1: F

34. By directing what people pay attention to and how they perceive events, attitudes serve a(n)

    a) reality adjustive function
    b) biasing function
    c) knowledge function
    d) precognitive function

    Answer: c   Type: M   Page(s): 227   Key 1: F

35. People think that their own attitudes are more popular than they actually are. This is evidence that attitudes serve a(n)

    a) algorithmic function
    b) value-expressive function
    c) knowledge function
    d) social adjustive function

    Answer: c Type: M   Page(s): 227   Key 1: F

36. John deeply feels that human life is invaluable. Hence he has a pro-life attitude about the issue of abortion. This attitude serves a(n)

    a) identity defining function
    b) emotional maintenance function
    c) value expressive function
    d) ego defensive function

    Answer: c Type: M   Page(s): 227   Key 1: A

37. Jane favors women's rights to have an abortion, because she had one and couldn't bear to believe that life begins at conception. Jane's attitude serves a(n)

    a) personal adjustive function
    b) social adjustive function
    c) value expressive function
    d) ego defensive function

    Answer: d Type: M   Page(s): 228   Key 1: A

38. Which of the following attitudes most clearly serves a utilitarian function?

    a) Albert's deeply-felt opposition to nuclear weapons
    b) Ben's positive attitude about his boss's new suit
    c) Carla's opposition to her supervisor's new plan
    d) Darlene's enthusiastic attitude about Yoga

    Answer: b Type: M   Page(s): 229   Key 1: A

39. As research has shown, high self-monitors use their attitudes to serve the _____ function.

    a) social adjustive
    b) behavior informative
    c) knowledge
    d) value expressive

    Answer: a Type: M   Page(s): 229   Key 1: F

40. When people want to be "right," they adopt attitudes which serve the

    a) ego-defensive function
    b) value-expressive function
    c) utilitarian function
    d) social adjustive function

    Answer: b   Type: M   Page(s): 230   Key 1: F

41. Attitudes that are based on classical conditioning are most likely to serve a(n)

    a) knowledge function
    b) social adjustive function
    c) utilitarian function
    d) ego defensive function

    Answer: d   Type: M   Page(s): 231   Key 1: F

42. Attitudes sometimes strengthen themselves in the face of disconfirming evidence. This is

    a) affective intensification
    b) the fundamental paradox of social psychology
    c) bolstering
    d) belief perseverance

    Answer: d   Type: M   Page(s): 231   Key 1: F

43. In a research study, an experimenter tells you that you have no ability to distinguish Sanskrit from Arabic. After the study, this same experimenter tells you that s/he deceived you and that your actual performance in distinguishing Sanskrit from Arabic had nothing to do with what you were told. According to research on belief perseverance, you would

    a) never believe the experimenter in the first place
    b) still believe that you couldn't distinguish Sanskrit from Arabic
    c) now believe that you could distinguish Sanskrit from Arabic
    d) never trust an experimenter again

    Answer: b   Type: M   Page(s): 232   Key 1: A

44. A psychologist told Zelda that librarians are smarter than lawyers. He had Zelda give an explanation for why this was true. Later, the psychologist told Zelda that, in fact, lawyers are smarter than librarians. According to research, Zelda would

    a) still believe that librarians are smarter than lawyers
    b) come to believe that librarians and lawyers are equally smart
    c) come to believe that lawyers are smarter than librarians
    d) come to suspend judgment and have no beliefs on this matter

    Answer: a   Type: M   Page(s): 233   Key 1: A

45. Xerxes, who favors the legalization of marijuana, is participating in a psychology experiment on belief perseverance. There, he reads two articles -- one which supports the legalization of marijuana and one which opposes it. After reading the two articles, Xerxes should

   a) be most persuaded by the article he read first
   b) be most persuaded by the article he read last
   c) favor the legalization of marijuana even more than before
   d) neither favor nor oppose the legalization of marijuana

   Answer: c   Type: M   Page(s): 233   Key 1: A

46. According to research, thought-feeling consistency leads to

   a) thought-feeling equilibrium
   b) thought-feeling disequilibrium
   c) person-situation consistency
   d) attitude-behavior consistency

   Answer: d   Type: M   Page(s): 235   Key 1: F

47. Elvira hates snakes and has negative thoughts about them. Fred also hates snakes, but thinks that snakes serve a number of positive functions -- like eating rats. Gloria likes snakes, but thinks that snakes do some bad things -- liking biting people. Of Elvira, Fred, and Gloria, who should show the greatest consistency between their attitude toward snakes and their behavior toward snakes?

   a) Elvira should show the greatest attitude-behavior consistency.
   b) Fred should show the greatest attitude-behavior consistency.
   c) Gloria should show the greatest attitude-behavior consistency.
   d) Fred and Gloria should show the same attitude-behavior consistency; Elvira's should be lower.

   Answer: a   Type: M   Page(s): 235   Key 1: A

48. A number of factors may affect how well attitudes predict behavior. Which of the following is NOT one of them?

   a) subjective norms
   b) specificity matching
   c) statistical artifacts
   d) direct experience

   Answer: c   Type: M   Page(s): 236   Key 1: F

49. The theory of reasoned action concerns

    a) attitude-behavior consistency
    b) the distinction between reason and emotion
    c) attribution of attitudes to others
    d) attribution of attitudes to self

    Answer: a   Type: M   Page(s): 237   Key 1: F

50. Which of the following is NOT an element of the theory of reasoned action?

    a) perceived behavior control
    b) attitude
    c) behavior intention
    d) behavior

    Answer: a   Type: M   Page(s): 237   Key 1: F

51. According to the theory of reasoned action, an attitude consists of a person's

    a) conscience and ego-ideal
    b) feelings about possible outcomes
    c) latitude of acceptance and latitude of rejection
    d) latitude and longitude of acceptance

    Answer: b   Type: M   Page(s): 238   Key 1: F

52. The theory of planned behavior would be best-suited to explaining someone's attitude toward

    a) taking their dog for a walk
    b) capital punishment
    c) alcoholic beverages
    d) a prospective romantic partner

    Answer: a   Type: M   Page(s): 238   Key 1: A

53. In a research study, social psychologists attempted to predict whether new mothers would breast feed their babies. Consistent with the theory of reasoned action, the results of the study showed that breast-feeding behaviors were best predicted by

    a) attitudes alone
    b) attitudes and reinforcement history
    c) attitudes, subjective norms, and behavioral intentions
    d) attitudes, perceptions of control, and behavioral intentions

    Answer: c   Type: M   Page(s): 238   Key 1: F

54. The theory of reasoned action would be LEAST well-suited to explaining

   a) approach behaviors
   b) avoidance behaviors
   c) intentional behaviors
   d) unintentional behaviors

   Answer: d   Type: M   Page(s): 238   Key 1: A

55. What's the difference between the theory of reasoned action and the theory of planned behavior?

   a) There's no difference. They are two different names for the same theory.
   b) The theory of planned behavior does not assume that plans are rational.
   c) The theory of reasoned action is simpler.
   d) The theory of reasoned action is more complex.

   Answer: c   Type: M   Page(s): 239   Key 1: F

56. According to the specificity matching hypothesis,

   a) general measures of attitudes are invariably inaccurate predictors
   b) specific measures of attitudes are invariably inaccurate predictors
   c) specific measures of attitudes are good at predicting multiple-act behaviors
   d) general measures of attitudes are good at predicting multiple-act behaviors

   Answer: d   Type: M   Page(s): 239   Key 1: F

57. The specificity matching hypothesis has been used to

   a) illuminate the situation vs. person debate
   b) predict when attitudes will be consistent with behavior
   c) predict whether or not a couple is well-suited for marriage
   d) construct a rational model of attribution

   Answer: b   Type: M   Page(s): 239   Key 1: F

58. Alice, a pro-life activist, wants to predict whether Zelda will put a pro-life bumper sticker on her car. To make this prediction most accurately, Alice should ask Zelda:

   a) What is your attitude toward putting political bumper stickers on your car?
   b) What is your attitude toward putting a pro-life bumper sticker on your car?
   c) Are you pro-life?
   d) Do you favor a woman's right to have an abortion?

   Answer: b   Type: M   Page(s): 240   Key 1: A

59. In a research study, college students had the opportunity to interact with either a typical or an atypical homosexual. This study concluded that

    a) in general, college students don't like homosexuals
    b) homosexual subjects would rather interact with a typical homosexual; heterosexual subjects would rather interact with an atypical homosexual
    c) general attitudes predict behaviors toward typical, but not atypical, members of categories
    d) there's really no such thing as a "typical" member of any category

    Answer: c   Type: M   Page(s): 241   Key 1: F

60. Behaviors can be predicted better from attitudes that are based on direct experience than attitudes that are not based on direct experience. One reason for this may be that

    a) attitudes which are based on direct experience tend to be highly specific
    b) attitudes which are based on direct experience tend to be highly general
    c) subjective norms have a smaller impact if the subject has had direct experience
    d) subjective norms have a bigger impact if the subject has had direct experience

    Answer: c   Type: M   Page(s): 242   Key 1: F

61. A highly accessible attitude is an attitude that

    a) comes to mind easily
    b) is easy to understand
    c) concerns a topic on which all people have attitudes
    d) concerns a topic on which only a few people have attitudes

    Answer: a   Type: M   Page(s): 243   Key 1: F

62. In some research studies, people who rehearse their attitudes show more attitude-behavior consistency than people who do not. This is most easily explained by

    a) the theory of reasoned action
    b) the theory of planned behavior
    c) latitudes of acceptance and rejection
    d) the concept of attitude accessibility

    Answer: d   Type: M   Page(s): 244   Key 1: F

63. John has a positive attitude toward soft drinks. According to research, he will be most likely to have a soft drink if he introspects about

    a) his feelings toward soft drinks
    b) the reasons for his attitude toward soft drinks
    c) the reasons for his attitude toward other beverages
    d) nothing at all

    Answer: a   Type: M   Page(s): 245   Key 1: A

64. Which of the following is a consummatory behavior?

    a) interviewing for a job
    b) playing with a puzzle for fun
    c) using seat belts to prevent serious injury
    d) studying for exams

    Answer: b Type: M Page(s): 246 Key 1: F

65. Which types of behavior are based primarily on thoughts?

    a) voluntary behaviors
    b) involuntary behaviors
    c) instrumental behaviors
    d) consummatory behaviors

    Answer: c Type: M Page(s): 246 Key 1: F

66. Consummatory behaviors are

    a) unlearned
    b) hard to extinguish
    c) emotionally-driven
    d) thought-driven

    Answer: c Type: M Page(s): 246 Key 1: F

67. The distinction between instrumental and consummatory behaviors is important because it helps to explain

    a) the difference between classical conditioning and instrumental conditioning
    b) the difference between instrumental conditioning and modeling
    c) how introspection can affect attitude-behavior consistency
    d) when indirect attitude measures are better than direct attitude measures

    Answer: c Type: M Page(s): 247 Key 1: F

68. Sometimes, introspection increases attitude-behavior consistency; sometimes, it decreases attitude-behavior consistency. Why?

    a) It depends on the subject's level of extroversion.
    b) It depends on the subject's Machiavellianism.
    c) It depends on whether the behavior is instrumental or consummatory.
    d) It depends on whether the attitude is based on direct experience or on modeling.

    Answer: c Type: M Page(s): 247 Key 1: F

69. John, a high school student, is preparing for the SAT. According to research, John's attitude toward preparing for the SAT will be most consistent with his behavior if John introspects about

    a) his feelings about preparing for the SAT
    b) the reasons for his attitude toward preparing for the SAT
    c) his life in general
    d) nothing at all

    Answer: b   Type: M   Page(s): 247   Key 1: A

70. Introspection has been found to

    a) affect attitudes, but not behaviors
    b) affect behaviors, but not attitudes
    c) affect both attitudes and behaviors
    d) affect neither attitudes nor behaviors

    Answer: a   Type: M   Page(s): 247   Key 1: F

ESSAY

71. You have been hired to assess people's attitudes toward sexual harassment. Discuss at least three techniques that could be used to assess these attitudes. Which of the techniques would you use? Why?

    Answer:
    Students could answer this question by drawing on the material on pages 218-222 of the text. Although attitudes toward sexual harassment could be assessed by a variety of direct techniques (like Likert scales, semantic differential scales, or latitudes of acceptance), indirect assessments might be preferable. These could include the bogus pipeline or electromyographic recordings. The best answer to this question would elaborate on three of these techniques and argue convincingly for the use of one in assessing attitudes toward sexual harassment.

    Type: E   Page(s): 219   Key 1: A

72. In a brief essay, describe five functions that attitudes can serve. Give an example of an attitude that might serve each function.

    Answer:
    In answering this question, students need to summarize the information presented on pages 226-230 of the text. As noted there, attitudes can serve a knowledge function, a value-expressive function, an ego defensive function, a utilitarian function, and a social adjustive function. Students need to define and give an example for each of these five functions.

    Type: E   Page(s): 227   Key 1: F

73. What is belief perseverance? Why does it occur? What are its psychological effects? In answering these questions, be sure to cite psychological research.

    Answer:
    Students can answer this question by drawing on the material on pages 231-234 of the text. As noted there, belief perseverance occurs when attitudes and beliefs actively maintain or strengthen themselves in the face of disconfirming evidence. One explanation for belief perseverance is that people spontaneously explain their beliefs and that these explanations are what make the beliefs hard to undermine. In such circumstances, disconfirming evidence may function to make attitudes more extreme. The best answer to this question would describe the specifics of one or more of the research studies summarized in the text.

    Type: E   Page(s): 231   Key 1: F

74. A critic made the following comment:
    "Attitudes have been called the most central concept in social psychology, but in fact the are trivial. After all, attitudes are one thing, but behavior is totally different. As everyone knows, you can't predict behavior from attitudes."
    In a paragraph or two, react to the critic's comment. Do you agree? Do you disagree? Be sure to justify your answer by citing specifics from psychological research.

    Answer:
    In answering this question, students should draw on the material from pages 235-248 of the text. As noted there, attitudes can predict behavior under certain circumstances -- when, for example, the attitudes display thought-feeling consistency, when they are highly accessible, and when they are based on direct experience. Students should cite several of the factors listed on page 236 of the text and describe some of the research illustrating the importance of each.

    Type: E   Page(s): 236   Key 1: A

75. A skeptic was overheard saying: "Social psychologists claim that there are three components to an attitude, but that's not really true. The distinctions among the so-called components of an attitude have absolutely no real-world importance; and these distinctions are, in any case, artificial."

    In a paragraph or two, comment on the skeptic's comment. Be sure to base your commentary on psychological research.

    Answer:
    Although students could answer this open-ended question in a variety of ways, they would need to identify the three components of an attitude: thoughts, feelings, and actions. They might proceed to note that thoughts are based on information, feelings on classical conditioning, and actions on instrumental conditioning (see page 231 of the text); and that the three different components serve different psychological functions.

    Type: E   Page(s): 216   Key 1: A

Chapter 7

Attitude Change

MULTIPLE CHOICE

1. Experts believe that the battered woman syndrome involves three stages. Which of the following is NOT one of them?

   a) minor abusive incident
   b) contrition
   c) exit
   d) acute battering

   Answer: c   Type: M   Page(s): 252   Key 1: F

2. Melvin, a typical male, and Fran, a typical female, were serving on a jury in which a woman was accused of murdering her husband. The defense attorney was thinking of having an expert witness testify about the battered woman syndrome, since the defendant had been battered. Research indicates that the witness's testimony would affect

   a) neither Melvin nor Fran's decisions about the verdict
   b) Melvin's decision about the verdict, but not Fran's
   c) Fran's decision about the verdict, but not Melvin's
   d) both Melvin and Fran's decision about the verdict

   Answer: c   Type: M   Page(s): 252   Key 1: A

3. To change people's attitudes, you can change their feelings

   a) with rewards
   b) with new information
   c) with modeling
   d) by pairing the attitude object with positive or negative events

   Answer: d   Type: M   Page(s): 252   Key 1: F

4. What makes a communication persuasive? The three most important factors to consider are: the source, the content, and the

   a) modality
   b) audience
   c) payoff
   d) context

   Answer: b   Type: M   Page(s): 253   Key 1: F

99

5 . Communicator credibility involves two factors: expertise and

    a) trustworthiness
    b) personal involvement
    c) familiarity
    d) attractiveness

    Answer: a   Type: M   Page(s): 255   Key 1: F

6 . Alice was an expert on no-fault automobile insurance who had no vested interest in the issue. By definition, Alice is a(n)

    a) central communicator
    b) peripheral communicator
    c) attractive communicator
    d) credible communicator

    Answer: d   Type: M   Page(s): 255   Key 1: A

7 . The sleeper effect is an effect of the

    a) style of a persuasive communication
    b) audience of a persuasive communication
    c) modality of a persuasive communication
    d) source of a persuasive communication

    Answer: d   Type: M   Page(s): 256   Key 1: F

8 . Jack gave a convincing speech against gun control, but he was an ugly man who was very different from his audience. Initially, the audience didn't believe Jack's arguments. But over time, they came to agree with the positions he advocated. This is the

    a) sleeper effect
    b) source-dissociation effect
    c) rebound effect
    d) consolidation effect

    Answer: a   Type: M   Page(s): 256   Key 1: A

9 . A sleeper effect in persuasion does NOT occur if the source

    a) looks unattractive
    b) comes from a totally different background than the audience
    c) is untrustworthy
    d) gives weak arguments

    Answer: d   Type: M   Page(s): 256   Key 1: F

10. Jerome is trying to persuade Isabel to marry him. Research indicates that Jerome will be most persuasive if he gives

    a) one argument
    b) three arguments
    c) five arguments
    d) seven arguments

    Answer: d   Type: M   Page(s): 257   Key 1: A

11. In trying to persuade people to sign a pro-life petition, Hazel included arguments on both sides of the abortion issue; Isabel mentioned only the pro-life arguments. Relative to Isabel, Hazel will be persuasive in convincing

    a) people who are already pro-life
    b) people who are not pro-life
    c) men
    d) women

    Answer: b   Type: M   Page(s): 257   Key 1: A

12. To maximize your persuasive impact, you should

    a) argue AGAINST the position you want audience members to adopt
    b) repeat your arguments at least a dozen times
    c) explicitly draw the conclusion of the argument
    d) let audience members draw conclusions for themselves

    Answer: c   Type: M   Page(s): 257   Key 1: F

13. Fear arousal will facilitate persuasion if

    a) the message shows how fearful consequences can be avoided
    b) the fear is aroused by the communicator's style, rather than argument content
    c) the fear distracts audience members from argument content
    d) the fear is extremely intense

    Answer: a   Type: M   Page(s): 258   Key 1: F

14. Who's most likely to be influenced by a persuasive communication?

    a) Alice, who is mentally retarded
    b) Betty, who (though not retarded) is below average in IQ
    c) Christina, who is average in intelligence
    d) Darlene, who is highly intelligent

    Answer: c   Type: M   Page(s): 259   Key 1: A

15. Persuasive communications have the most influence on people who are average in intelligence. Why?

    a) These people are most likely to agree with the communicator in the first place.
    b) These people are most likely to be similar to the communicator.
    c) These people are most likely to understand and accept the arguments.
    d) Most arguments are written for the average person.

    Answer: c Type: M Page(s): 259 Key 1: F

16. Under what circumstances are women easier to persuade than men?

    a) never
    b) always
    c) on topics that are of more interest to women than men
    d) on topics that are of less interest to women than men

    Answer: d Type: M Page(s): 260 Key 1: F

17. You need to convince one of your four neighbors to sign a petition to get a new political party on the ballot in your state. Based on research, which of the following should be easiest to persuade?

    a) Earl, your 20-year-old neighbor
    b) Fred, your 30-year-old neighbor
    c) Gary, your 40-year-old neighbor
    d) Harry, your 65-year-old neighbor

    Answer: a Type: M Page(s): 261 Key 1: A

18. Some researchers have found that 20-year-olds are easier to persuade than older adults. How did the researchers explain this result?

    a) 20-year-olds are not as intelligent as older adults
    b) 20-year-olds are more likely to be having momentous life experiences
    c) 20-year-olds don't know as many counterarguments
    d) 20-year-olds are more idealistic than older adults

    Answer: b Type: M Page(s): 261 Key 1: F

19. You're designing an ad for TV sets to be shown to Koreans. Research suggests that the ad will be most persuasive if it

    a) appeals to the individual viewer
    b) shows the benefits of the TV to the viewer's whole family
    c) is simple
    d) is complex

    Answer: b Type: M Page(s): 262 Key 1: A

20. According to _____, there are two routes to persuasion: central and peripheral.

    a) the elaboration likelihood model
    b) the affective-cognitive model
    c) cognitive dissonance theory
    d) balance theory

    Answer: a   Type: M   Page(s): 263   Key 1: F

21. The elaboration likelihood model is most useful in explaining

    a) how to change people's attitudes by changing their behavior
    b) how to change people's attitudes by changing their thoughts
    c) how to change people's thoughts by changing their behavior
    d) how to change people's behavior by changing their thoughts

    Answer: b   Type: M   Page(s): 263   Key 1: F

22. When they take the peripheral route to persuasion, people rely on

    a) the most compelling point of the strongest argument
    b) the worst flaw in the weakest argument
    c) the logical consistency of all the arguments
    d) heuristics

    Answer: d   Type: M   Page(s): 263   Key 1: F

23. Which of the following is most closely related to the elaboration likelihood model of persuasion?

    a) cognitive dissonance theory
    b) self-perception theory
    c) the heuristic-systematic model
    d) the perspective-taking model

    Answer: c   Type: M   Page(s): 263   Key 1: F

24. Four people were persuaded by a TV commercial to buy a new car. Which of the following was most likely to have been persuaded along the central route?

    a) Jack, who was attracted to the bikini-clad model who was lying on top of the car
    b) Karl, who solves complex crossword puzzles for fun
    c) Lester, who was impressed by a jingle that was presented during the middle of the commercial
    d) Mark, who wasn't paying much attention

    Answer: b   Type: M   Page(s): 264   Key 1: A

25. The city of Mobile Alabama has just announced that it will be raising property taxes by 50%. Four people heard the announcement. Which of the four is most likely to elaborate on the city's arguments?

    a) Mildred, who owns no property in Mobile
    b) Max, who owns lots of property in Mobile
    c) Mickey, who has high need for cognitive closure
    d) Minnie, who has low need for cognitive closure

    Answer: b   Type: M   Page(s): 265   Key 1: A

26. _____ occurs when people act contrary to external pressure because they believe their freedom is being threatened.

    a) Cognitive dissonance
    b) The negativism heuristic
    c) Inoculation
    d) Psychological reactance

    Answer: d   Type: M   Page(s): 266   Key 1: F

27. Nancy was forewarned that Ned would try to persuade her to do something. This forewarning should

    a) arouse Nancy's psychological reactance
    b) arouse Nancy's cognitive dissonance
    c) have no effect on Ned's ability to persuade Nancy
    d) make it easier for Ned to persuade Nancy

    Answer: a   Type: M   Page(s): 266   Key 1: A

28. You're afraid that Otto the chronic alcoholic might persuade your best friend to drive home drunk. You can inoculate her against this persuasion by

    a) forewarning her that someone will be trying to persuade her to drive home drunk
    b) forewarning her that someone will be trying to persuade her of something
    c) letting her practice refuting weak arguments in favor of drunk driving
    d) arming her with the strongest possible arguments against drunk driving

    Answer: c   Type: M   Page(s): 267   Key 1: F

29. Some people have a high need for cognitive closure. Relative to other people, they're especially likely to resist new evidence when they have

    a) made up their minds
    b) publicly stated that they would resist new evidence
    c) been forewarned that new evidence might be forthcoming
    d) NOT been forewarned that new evidence might be forthcoming

    Answer: a   Type: M   Page(s): 268   Key 1: F

30. Bolstering, differentiation, and transcendence are three strategies for

    a) changing others' attitudes by changing their thoughts
    b) changing others' attitudes by changing their feelings
    c) changing others' attitudes by changing their behavior
    d) retaining one's own attitude

    Answer: d   Type: M   Page(s): 269   Key 1: F

31. Cathy, who uses cocaine, has just heard irrefutable evidence that cocaine is addictive. She tells herself that cocaine is nonetheless worth using, because it's so much fun. Cathy has just engaged in

    a) differentiation
    b) denial
    c) bolstering
    d) inoculation

    Answer: c   Type: M   Page(s): 269   Key 1: A

32. Social psychologists know two ways to change people's feelings: classically condition the attitude or

    a) operantly condition the attitude
    b) provide a model of the attitude
    c) put people in a good mood
    d) provide new information about the attitude object

    Answer: c   Type: M   Page(s): 270   Key 1: F

33. Classical conditioning

    a) takes a central route to attitude change
    b) takes a peripheral route to attitude change
    c) changes attitudes by changing behaviors
    d) changes attitudes by changing thoughts

    Answer: b   Type: M   Page(s): 271   Key 1: F

34. In a psychology experiment, Patty was repeatedly shown neutral words (like "exercise bicycle") paired with negative words (like "dirty"). Patty is most likely in an experiment on

    a) the classical conditioning of attitudes
    b) the operant conditioning of attitudes
    c) the mere exposure effect
    d) cognitive dissonance

    Answer: a   Type: M   Page(s): 271   Key 1: F

35. Paul and Ned attended a sales talk for home water filtration systems. Throughout the talk, Paul was in a positive mood; Ned was in a negative mood. Relative to Ned, Paul is

   a) less likely to attend to the arguments
   b) more likely to attend to the arguments
   c) less likely to experience psychological reactance
   d) more likely to experience psychological reactance

   Answer: a   Type: M   Page(s): 272   Key 1: A

36. Research shows that we have an especially positive emotional reaction to people

   a) whose pupils are dilated
   b) whose pupils are normal in size
   c) whose pupils are constricted
   d) who like the things we dislike

   Answer: a   Type: M   Page(s): 273   Key 1: F

37. Attitude researchers have used subliminal perception to

   a) create an experimental demand for subjects to like a person
   b) make subjects aware that they were being classically conditioned
   c) change attitudes solely by changing feelings
   d) change attitudes along the central route to persuasion

   Answer: c   Type: M   Page(s): 274   Key 1: F

38. In the mere exposure effect, people

   a) come to dislike highly familiar objects
   b) come to like highly familiar objects
   c) are influenced by the mere presence of peers
   d) are influenced by the mere presence of an experimenter

   Answer: b   Type: M   Page(s): 274   Key 1: F

39. Mere exposure effects on attitudes are especially strong when

   a) the subject is high in need for cognitive closure
   b) the subject is low in need for cognitive closure
   c) people are aware that they're receiving the exposures
   d) people are not aware that they're receiving the exposures

   Answer: d   Type: M   Page(s): 274   Key 1: F

40. Classical conditioning would be most effective in

    a) undermining the counterarguments of someone who had high need for cognition
    b) undermining the counterarguments of someone who had low need for cognition
    c) changing an attitude that was initially based on feelings
    d) changing an attitude that was initially based on thoughts

    Answer: c   Type: M   Page(s): 275   Key 1: A

41. According to _____, people change their attitudes to reduce the aversive arousal they experience when they have two thoughts that contradict one another.

    a) self-perception theory
    b) homeostasis theory
    c) arousal reduction theory
    d) cognitive dissonance theory

    Answer: d   Type: M   Page(s): 276   Key 1: F

42. Cognitive dissonance theory concerns

    a) changing people's attitudes by changing their thoughts
    b) changing people's attitudes by changing their behavior
    c) changing people's attitudes by changing their feelings
    d) none of these

    Answer: b   Type: M   Page(s): 276   Key 1: F

43. Olivia had given away her house and abandoned her children to join a cult that predicted that the world would end on January 1. The world did not end. According to research on cognitive dissonance, what is Olivia most likely to do next?

    a) commit suicide
    b) beg her children for forgiveness
    c) develop amnesia for her participation in the cult
    d) try to convince others that her actions had saved the world

    Answer: d   Type: M   Page(s): 277   Key 1: A

44. Three social psychologists joined a doomsday group in order to

    a) convince the group's members that they were acting irrationally
    b) facilitate group morale and decision-making
    c) study the group's reaction when the group's prophecies failed
    d) study the group's methods of recruiting new members

    Answer: c   Type: M   Page(s): 277   Key 1: F

45. Which of the following circumstances is NOT one in which attitudes change because of cognitive dissonance?

   a) effort justification
   b) insufficient effort
   c) insufficient justification
   d) insufficient deterrence

   Answer: b   Type: M   Page(s): 278   Key 1: F

46. How do people react to postdecisional dissonance?

   a) by regretting their choice
   b) by convincing themselves that they didn't really have a choice
   c) by convincing others that they didn't really have a choice
   d) by emphasizing the advantages of their choice over the alternative

   Answer: d   Type: M   Page(s): 278   Key 1: F

47. As the winner on a TV game show, Ramirez got to choose between a boat or a trip to Hawaii. He chose the boat. According to cognitive dissonance theory, Ramirez is now most likely to

   a) give the boat to a relative
   b) sell the boat and give the proceeds to charity
   c) decide that Hawaii would have been boring
   d) decide that Hawaii would have been fun

   Answer: c   Type: M   Page(s): 279   Key 1: A

48. According to cognitive dissonance theory, effort justification occurs when people

   a) justify their worth by putting a lot of effort in everything they do
   b) regulate their effort so that it is commensurate with the rewards they will receive
   c) exert a lot of effort to achieve a disappointing goal
   d) achieve a monumental goal without much effort

   Answer: c   Type: M   Page(s): 279   Key 1: F

49. As part of a fraternity initiation, Sam had a boat oar broken over his thighs. According to cognitive dissonance theory, how should Sam react to this severe initiation?

   a) He should report the fraternity to the police.
   b) He should exaggerate the severity of the initiation.
   c) He should quit the fraternity.
   d) He should like the fraternity more.

   Answer: d   Type: M   Page(s): 280   Key 1: A

50. Sally loves hiking but hates skydiving. Theoretically, Sally would experience cognitive dissonance if she

    a) went hiking for $1000
    b) went hiking for $1
    c) went skydiving for $1000
    d) went skydiving for $1

    Answer: d   Type: M   Page(s): 280   Key 1: A

51. In a famous experiment, subjects were paid $1 to tell someone that a boring task was interesting. This was a study of

    a) cognitive elaboration
    b) cognitive dissonance
    c) classical conditioning
    d) operant conditioning

    Answer: b   Type: M   Page(s): 280   Key 1: F

52. As part of a psychology experiment, Randy ate a fried grasshopper. Theoretically, Randy would be most likely to experience cognitive dissonance if he

    a) had previously liked the taste of grasshoppers
    b) had previously had no opinion about the taste of grasshoppers
    c) ate the grasshopper for a jerk
    d) ate the grasshopper for a nice guy

    Answer: c   Type: M   Page(s): 281   Key 1: A

53. Tracy's Mom told her not to play with the pretty new doll but didn't explain why. Theoretically, Tracy will be most likely to experience cognitive dissonance if she

    a) has no opportunity to play with the doll
    b) has an opportunity to play with the doll, but doesn't
    c) has an opportunity to play with the doll and does
    d) never wanted to play with the doll in the first place

    Answer: b   Type: M   Page(s): 282   Key 1: A

54. For a counterattitudinal action to cause attitude change via cognitive dissonance, it is NOT necessary for

    a) the action to cause aversive consequences
    b) the actor to assume personal responsibility for the consequences of the action
    c) others to blame the actor for the consequences of the action
    d) the actor to experience aversive arousal

    Answer: c   Type: M   Page(s): 283   Key 1: F

55. Ursula, who strongly opposed abortion, wrote an essay opposing abortion which she believed would paradoxically encourage women to get an abortion. Research indicates that this proattitudinal action will

    a) increase Ursula's opposition to abortion
    b) reduce Ursula's opposition to abortion
    c) have no effect on Ursula's attitude toward abortion
    d) be extremely high in credibility

    Answer: b Type: M   Page(s): 284   Key 1: A

56. Van chose to give a speech in favor of a tax increase, even though he personally opposed the increase. At the time, Van thought that his speech would encourage a number of his peers to support the increase. In fact, the speech had no consequences whatsoever. Research indicates this counterattitudinal action will

    a) reduce Van's opposition to a tax increase
    b) increase Van's opposition to a tax increase
    c) have no effect on Van's attitude toward a tax increase
    d) encourage use of a representativeness heuristic

    Answer: a Type: M   Page(s): 285   Key 1: A

57. In a psychology experiment, Wanda took a sugar pill, then chose to write an essay attacking her most cherished beliefs. Research suggests that she's LEAST likely to question these beliefs if

    a) the experimenter was a male
    b) the experimenter was a female
    c) she was told that the sugar pill was a stimulant
    d) she was told that the sugar pill was a relaxant

    Answer: c Type: M   Page(s): 285   Key 1: A

58. In an experiment, subjects took a sugar pill that was described as a stimulant, then chose to write a counterattitudinal essay. Results indicated that the subjects' attitude toward the topic of the essay did not change. How did the researchers explain this result?

    a) The subjects blamed their actions on the pill.
    b) The subjects' essays weren't very convincing.
    c) The subjects perceived that their essays weren't very convincing.
    d) The subjects misattributed their aversive arousal to the pill

    Answer: d Type: M   Page(s): 285   Key 1: F

59. People can reduce aversive arousal by making themselves "look good". This is called

    a) compensatory self-completion
    b) self-abdication
    c) self-affirmation
    d) self-supplication

    Answer: c   Type: M   Page(s): 286   Key 1: F

60. In several experiments, subjects have written counterattitudinal essays, then been hooked up to a "bogus pipeline". The "pipeline" was used to determine whether subjects

    a) would believe that the pipeline was real
    b) thought their essay would have aversive consequences
    c) felt personal responsibility for the essay
    d) had genuinely changed their attitudes toward the essay topic

    Answer: d   Type: M   Page(s): 286   Key 1: F

61. People are most likely to infer their attitudes from their own actions if

    a) the attitudes are strongly held
    b) the attitudes are not strongly held
    c) the actions are directed toward a person they know
    d) the actions are directed toward a stranger

    Answer: b   Type: M   Page(s): 287   Key 1: F

62. According to the two-factor theory of emotion, anger and happiness are different because they

    a) are represented in different parts of the autonomic nervous system
    b) are represented in different parts of the cerebral cortex
    c) correspond to different facial expressions
    d) are experienced in different contexts

    Answer: d   Type: M   Page(s): 288   Key 1: F

63. According to a "two-factor theory", emotions depend on:

    a) the central nervous system and the peripheral nervous system
    b) generalized arousal and a situational context
    c) a specific physiological state and a specific facial expression
    d) cognitive dissonance and elaboration likelihood

    Answer: b   Type: M   Page(s): 288   Key 1: F

64. In a psychology experiment, male subjects thought their heart rate increased as they were viewing certain "centerfold" slides. In fact, the heart rate sounds were bogus. Results showed that the sounds

    a) made the subjects feel more positively about the slides
    b) made the subjects feel more negatively about the slides
    c) distracted the subjects from feeling anything about the slides
    d) induced evaluation apprehension

    Answer: a Type: M Page(s): 289 Key 1: F

65. Self-perception changes attitudes when people

    a) experience aversive arousal
    b) experience pleasant arousal
    c) remember their previous attitudes
    d) do not remember their previous attitudes

    Answer: d Type: M Page(s): 289 Key 1: F

66. In an "interpersonal simulation", Zach read about a subject who was offered $1 to tell someone that a boring task was interesting. Zach then predicted the subject's attitude toward the task. This "simulation" was designed to

    a) test self-perception theory
    b) test self-affirmation theory
    c) see whether Zach would feel vicarious responsibility
    d) see whether Zach would experience vicarious cognitive dissonance

    Answer: a Type: M Page(s): 290 Key 1: A

67. Research shows that people

    a) are most likely to infer their attitudes from actions which they undertake for a large reward
    b) are most likely to infer their attitudes from actions which they undertake to avoid a large punishment
    c) "recall" that they've always had the same attitude that they have now (even if they haven't)
    d) can remember attitudes they held a long time ago better than attitudes they held recently

    Answer: c Type: M Page(s): 291 Key 1: F

68. Attitudes are most likely to be changed via self-perception when

    a) the action is extremely discrepant from the initial attitude
    b) the action is not extremely discrepant from the initial attitude
    c) there are peripheral cues to persuasion
    d) there are no peripheral cues to persuasion

    Answer: b Type: M Page(s): 292 Key 1: F

69. Overjustification occurs when

    a) you're paid too much for doing something you don't like
    b) you're paid too little for doing something you don't like
    c) you're paid just the right amount for doing something you don't like
    d) you're paid for doing something you like

    Answer: d   Type: M   Page(s): 293   Key 1: F

70. Mommy told Alice, a four-year-old, that she would get a soda if she would draw Mommy a picture. Alice likes drawing anyway. Research indicates that Mommy's offer of a soda will

    a) reduce Alice's extrinsic motivation to draw
    b) reduce Alice's intrinsic motivation to draw
    c) reduce Alice's cognitive dissonance
    d) make Alice experience cognitive dissonance

    Answer: b   Type: M   Page(s): 294   Key 1: A

ESSAY

71. What qualities make a communication persuasive? In answering this question, be sure to cite specific factors that bear on the source, the content, and the audience of a persuasive attempt.

    Answer:
    Students should answer this question by summarizing the material on pages 254-262 of the text. As noted in Table 7.1, a source's persuasiveness depends on four factors: credibility, attractiveness, similarity, and a sleeper effect. The persuasiveness of the content of a communication depends on the number and type of arguments, as well as appeals to emotion. Persuasion also depends on four characteristics of the audience: intelligence, sex, age, and culture. The best answer to this question would elaborate on these factors in detail.

    Type: E   Page(s): 254   Key 1: F

72. Describe the elaboration likelihood model of persuasion, focusing on the "two routes to persuasion" and factors that influence which of the two "routes" are followed.

    Answer:
    Students should answer this question by summarizing the material on pages 262-266 of the text. The elaboration likelihood model distinguishes between a central and a peripheral route to persuasion. As noted in Figure 7.3, The central route to persuasion involves an active consideration of the content of arguments; the peripheral route involves the use of heuristics and attention to content-irrelevant cues. Theoretically, the central route is taken only when people are able and motivated to elaborate on the arguments in a persuasive message. The best answer to this question would describe in some detail the implications of and evidence for the elaboration likelihood model.

    Type: E   Page(s): 263   Key 1: F

73. As the parent of a 10-year-old boy, you're afraid that other children will soon try to persuade your son to take drugs. Based on psychological research, what factors would encourage him to resist these persuasive attempts? How can you help him to resist this unwanted persuasion? Be sure to cite specific concepts and the psychological research on which they're based.

Answer:
Students can answer this question by drawing on the material presented on pages 266-269 of the text. As noted there, a boy could be "inoculated" against persuasion and would in any case be resistant to any persuasive attempt of which he had been forewarned. Parents might hope that unwanted attempts at persuasion would arouse the boy's psychological reactance. A boy might defend his anti-drug attitudes by denial, bolstering, or differentiation. The best answer to this question would explain how these techniques could be exploited in childrearing.

Type: E   Page(s): 266   Key 1: A

74. Discuss cognitive dissonance theory. Explain the basic theory and the circumstances under which it is applicable. Explain how the theory might be used to induce people who had never owned a home computer to buy one.

Answer:
Students could answer this question by drawing on the material presented on pages 276-287 of the text. As noted there, cognitive dissonance theory describes conditions under which counterattitudinal actions will cause attitude change. These conditions include postdecisional dissonance, effort justification, insufficient justification, and insufficient deterrence (p. 279). Theoretically, dissonance causes attitude change when a counterattitudinal action 1) causes aversive consequences, 2) for which the actor feels responsible, and 3) induces aversive arousal which 4) the actor attributes to the action, and 5) the actor has no other way to reduce dissonance. These factors are noted on page 283. The theory could be used in several ways to get people to buy their first home computer. One might, for example, get a person who did not like computers to star in a commercial designed to "hook" kids on computer games, but pay the person only $1 to do so. Students should explain how they would structure this experience so that points 1-5 above were satisfied.

Type: E   Page(s): 279   Key 1: A

75. Compare and contrast cognitive dissonance theory with the self-perception theory of persuasion. How are the theories similar? How do they differ? Under what circumstances is persuasion best explained by cognitive dissonance theory? Under what circumstances is it best explained by self-perception theory?

Answer:
Students should answer this question by summarizing the material on pages 287-295 of the text. Students should begin by explaining the rudiments of the two theories. They should note that the two theories have a similar goal: to explain how attitudes can be changed by changing behavior. They should note that the two theories differ in their explanation for this attitude change. Cognitive dissonance theory attributes attitude change to the individual's desire to reduce aversive arousal; self-perception theory attributes this change to a process of rational attribution. Cognitive dissonance theory is the better of the two theories in explaining the effects of actions that are extremely discrepant from an initial attitude that is strongly held. Self-perception theory is the better of the two in explaining the effects of actions that are only slightly discrepant from an initial attitude that is weakly held. Unlike cognitive dissonance theory, self-perception theory can also account for the effects of overjustification for actions that are consistent with an initial attitude (p. 293).

Type: E   Page(s): 287   Key 1: F

Chapter 8

Stereotyping, Prejudice, and Discrimination

MULTIPLE CHOICE

1. Alphonzo, a member of a negatively stigmatized race, was accused of raping Alice. At Alphonzo's trial, the judge instructed the jurors to be free of "sympathy or prejudice." Research shows that this instruction

   a) increases Alphonzo's chances of being found guilty
   b) increases the severity of the sentence Alphonzo will receive, if he is found guilty
   c) reduces racial bias
   d) has all of these effects

   Answer: c   Type: M   Page(s): 298   Key 1: A

2. Stereotypes are biased

   a) behaviors
   b) behavioral intentions
   c) feelings
   d) thoughts

   Answer: d   Type: M   Page(s): 299   Key 1: F

3. Bob, a neo-Nazi, hates Jewish people. His hatred is

   a) a prejudice
   b) discrimination
   c) a prototype
   d) a stereotype

   Answer: a   Type: M   Page(s): 299   Key 1: A

4. There are three components of negative attitudes toward social groups. Which of the following is NOT one of them?

   a) discrimination
   b) tokenism
   c) stereotypes
   d) prejudice

   Answer: b   Type: M   Page(s): 299   Key 1: F

116

5. _____ are beliefs about the characteristics of members of a group.

    a) Discriminations
    b) Prejudices
    c) Ethnocentrics
    d) Stereotypes

    Answer: d   Type: M   Page(s): 299   Key 1: F

6. In response to surveys, today's White college students are most likely to report that Blacks are

    a) ignorant
    b) superstitious
    c) aggressive
    d) physically dirty

    Answer: c   Type: M   Page(s): 299   Key 1: F

7. Research on stereotypes indicates that _____ are assumed to be materialistic.

    a) White males
    b) White females
    c) Hispanic males
    d) Hispanic females

    Answer: a   Type: M   Page(s): 300   Key 1: F

8. Cathy is 6 years old; David is 75. Research suggests that

    a) Cathy will have a negative stereotype of David
    b) Cathy will have a positive stereotype of David
    c) David will have a negative stereotype of Cathy
    d) David will have a positive stereotype of Cathy

    Answer: a   Type: M   Page(s): 301   Key 1: A

9. Edgar is prejudiced against homosexuals. Fred, although not a homosexual himself, hangs out at gay bars. Research shows that Edgar will

    a) have no special feelings toward Fred
    b) have a prejudice against Fred
    c) have especially positive feelings toward Fred
    d) have negative feelings toward Fred when he sees Fred hanging around homosexuals, but positive feelings toward him at other times

    Answer: b   Type: M   Page(s): 302   Key 1: A

10. In response to surveys, Dutch people have reported prejudice toward a number of different immigrant groups. Which of the following is NOT one of them?

    a) Turks
    b) Moroccans
    c) Surinamers
    d) Hispanics

    Answer: d   Type: M   Page(s): 302   Key 1: F

11. Your textbook defines discrimination as

    a) selectively unjustified behavior toward members of a target group -- whether the behavior is positive or negative
    b) selectively unjustified negative behavior toward members of a target group
    c) the process of noting differences among different individuals
    d) the process of reacting differently to different stimuli

    Answer: b   Type: M   Page(s): 302   Key 1: F

12. Research indicates that Whites are most likely to show racial discrimination in helping if the person who needs help

    a) is physically present
    b) is not physically present
    c) is the same gender as the helper
    d) is not the same gender as the helper

    Answer: b   Type: M   Page(s): 303   Key 1: F

13. Prejudice is most likely to be revealed

    a) in what we say
    b) in nonverbal behavior
    c) when we are in a good mood
    d) when we are in a public place

    Answer: b   Type: M   Page(s): 304   Key 1: F

14. Prejudice involves two stages:

    a) a cognitive stage followed by a behavioral stage
    b) a behavioral stage followed by a cognitive stage
    c) a deliberative stage followed by a spontaneous stage
    d) a spontaneous stage followed by a deliberative stage

    Answer: d   Type: M   Page(s): 304   Key 1: F

15. According to the two-stage model of prejudice, we assume that people have characteristics that are stereotypical of their group

    a) before we suppress our negative reactions
    b) at the same time as we suppress our negative reactions
    c) after we suppress our negative reactions
    d) at all times

    Answer: a   Type: M   Page(s): 305   Key 1: F

16. While participating in a psychology experiment, Gloria (a white college student) was asked four questions. To which of the following questions would she have responded most quickly?

    a) Are blacks materialistic?
    b) Are whites materialistic?
    c) Are whites religious?
    d) Are whites lazy?

    Answer: b   Type: M   Page(s): 306   Key 1: A

17. An experimenter asked subjects two questions: 1) Are blacks materialistic? and 2) Are blacks lazy? Which of the following subjects would have given a faster response to the second question than the first question?

    a) Hal, a white who reported that he hated blacks
    b) Henry, a white who reported no hatred for blacks
    c) Homer, a black who reported that he hated whites
    d) All of these subjects would have given a faster response to the second question than the first question.

    Answer: d   Type: M   Page(s): 306   Key 1: A

18. Relative to people in a neutral mood, people _____ are more likely to base their judgments on stereotypes.

    a) who are sad
    b) who are angry
    c) who are anxious
    d) who are in any way feeling bad

    Answer: b   Type: M   Page(s): 307   Key 1: F

19. George, a completely unprejudiced white male, will soon be meeting Ginger, a black female. Research indicates that George will spontaneously note

    a) Ginger's race, but not her gender
    b) Ginger's gender, but not her race
    c) neither Ginger's gender nor her race
    d) both Ginger's gender and her race

    Answer: d   Type: M   Page(s): 306   Key 1: A

20. Stereotypic thinking is

    a) linear
    b) nonlinear
    c) cognitively efficient
    d) cognitively inefficient

    Answer: c   Type: M   Page(s): 307   Key 1: F

21. Gloria, who prides herself on being open-minded, was in charge of hiring counselors for a boys' summer camp. One of the applicants was Hal, who stated that he was gay. Gloria is most likely to respond with prejudice against Hal if Gloria

    a) has just been told that she's subtly prejudiced against gays
    b) has just been told that she's openly prejudiced against gays
    c) is busy and doesn't have time to think
    d) is not busy and has lots of time to think

    Answer: c   Type: M   Page(s): 307   Key 1: A

22. According to the two-stage model presented in your text, people are most likely to act with prejudice if they

    a) react spontaneously
    b) make a small deliberative adjustment
    c) make a moderate-sized deliberative adjustment
    d) make a big deliberative adjustment

    Answer: a   Type: M   Page(s): 307   Key 1: F

23. Henrietta had never thought of herself as prejudiced in any way. But as part of a psychology experiment, she was told that she was subtly prejudiced against obese people. Later, she heard some jokes about fat people. Research indicates that Henrietta will

    a) find these jokes especially funny
    b) find these jokes especially unfunny
    c) be especially likely to pass these jokes along to others
    d) be especially unlikely to pass these jokes along to others

    Answer: b   Type: M   Page(s): 308   Key 1: A

24. You're most likely to show a stereotype rebound effect if you

    a) temporarily suppress your own stereotypes
    b) tell others to suppress their stereotypes
    c) affiliate with people who have no stereotypes
    d) affiliate with people who have stronger stereotypes than you

    Answer: a   Type: M   Page(s): 309   Key 1: A

25. Mommy told 12-year-old Ivan not to say (or even think) anything negative about Hispanics while he was attending Juanita's party. Research on stereotype rebound effects indicates that Ivan will

    a) say negative things about Hispanics at the party anyway
    b) think negative things about Hispanics at the party
    c) say and think very positive things about Hispanics at the party
    d) say and think very negative things about Hispanics after the party is over

    Answer: d   Type: M   Page(s): 309   Key 1: A

26. Your textbook mentions three thought processes that cause stereotyping, prejudice, and discrimination. Which of the following is NOT one of them?

    a) implicit stereotyping
    b) ethnic confabulation
    c) illusory correlation
    d) ignoring covariation

    Answer: b   Type: M   Page(s): 311   Key 1: F

27. The concept of illusory correlation has been used to explain

    a) behavioral confirmation effects
    b) self-verification effects
    c) stereotyping of minority groups
    d) stereotyping of majority groups

    Answer: c   Type: M   Page(s): 311   Key 1: F

28. According to the concept of illusory correlation, we're most likely to associate

    a) a member of a small group with a frequent behavior
    b) a member of a small group with an infrequent behavior
    c) a member of a fictitious group with a behavior we've never seen
    d) a member of a real group with a behavior we've never seen

    Answer: b   Type: M   Page(s): 311   Key 1: F

29. In a psychology experiment, June read about 12 people: 8 of whom belonged to Group A and 4 of whom belonged to group B. June read that 6 of the members of Group A and 3 of the members of Group B were extroverted; while the others were introverted. Research shows that June will tend to recall that these people are

    a) more likely to be introverted if they belong to Group A than Group B
    b) more likely to be introverted if they belong to Group B than Group A
    c) more likely to be introverted than extroverted
    d) equally likely to be introverted whatever their Group

    Answer: b   Type: M   Page(s): 312   Key 1: A

30. In a psychology experiment, Julie read about 18 people: 12 of whom belonged to Group Y and 6 of whom belonged to group Z. Julie read that 8 of the members of Group Y and 4 of the members of group Z were happy-go-lucky; while the others were grim. Julie is participating in an experiment on

    a) explicit stereotyping
    b) implicit stereotyping
    c) the anchoring-and-adjustment heuristic
    d) illusory correlation

    Answer: d   Type: M   Page(s): 312   Key 1: A

31. Illusory correlations

    a) are found only in people who have preexisting stereotypes
    b) call special attention to the unusual actions of majority group members
    c) become more likely if the perceiver has time to deliberate
    d) become less likely if the perceiver has time to deliberate

    Answer: c   Type: M   Page(s): 313   Key 1: F

32. On standardized achievement tests, black children in the United States actually score

    a) higher than white children
    b) just as high as white children
    c) lower than white children
    d) higher than black adults

    Answer: c   Type: M   Page(s): 314   Key 1: F

33. When they ignore covariation, people tend to

    a) ignore simple relationships
    b) take simple relationships at face value
    c) neutralize their stereotypes
    d) overcompensate for their stereotypes

    Answer: b   Type: M   Page(s): 314   Key 1: F

34. Many people believe that men are more famous than women. This belief reflects

    a) reverse stereotyping
    b) implicit stereotyping
    c) illusory correlations
    d) the base rate fallacy

    Answer: b Type: M Page(s): 315 Key 1: F

35. Who engages in the implicit stereotyping of women?

    a) men, but not women
    b) women, but not men
    c) high school dropouts, but not college students
    d) all groups that have been studied to date

    Answer: d Type: M Page(s): 316 Key 1: F

36. The differences between Black Americans and White Americans would seem smallest to

    a) Karlita, a Hispanic American female
    b) Lucinda, a Black American female
    c) Marv, a Black American male
    d) Ned, a White American male

    Answer: a Type: M Page(s): 316 Key 1: A

37. Research shows that people favor the members of their own group over members of another group

    a) only if they have personally met the members of their own group
    b) only if they have personally met the members of the other group
    c) only if the groups are meaningful
    d) even if the groups are meaningless

    Answer: d Type: M Page(s): 317 Key 1: F

38. In talking about the members of a rival sorority, Olivia said "They are all alike, but we are not." Olivia's comment illustrates

    a) the uniform projection bias
    b) the complexity-extremity bias
    c) the outgroup homogeneity effect
    d) the illusory correlation effect

    Answer: c Type: M Page(s): 317 Key 1: A

39. Who is most likely to think that University of Oklahoma students are more similar to one another than University of Nebraska students?

    a) Otto, a University of Oklahoma student who loves his school
    b) Patricia, a University of Nebraska student who loves her school
    c) Quellian, a University of Oklahoma student who knows the college majors of everyone he meets at Oklahoma
    d) Ruby, a University of Nebraska student who knows the college majors of everyone she meets at Nebraska

    Answer: d   Type: M   Page(s): 318   Key 1: A

40. Which of the following is most likely to show an IN-group homogeneity effect?

    a) a huge group
    b) a medium-sized group
    c) a small group
    d) Researchers have never found an IN-group homogeneity effect.

    Answer: c   Type: M   Page(s): 318   Key 1: A

41. An attempt to reconcile personal identity with social identity produces

    a) the outgroup homogeneity effect
    b) implicit stereotyping
    c) illusory correlations
    d) the tendency to ignore complex relationships

    Answer: a   Type: M   Page(s): 318   Key 1: A

42. _____ refers to the belief that policies that benefit blacks are destroying traditional values.

    a) Traditional racism
    b) Old-fashioned racism
    c) Symbolic racism
    d) Contemporary racism

    Answer: c   Type: M   Page(s): 319   Key 1: F

43. You're trying to predict the results of the next mayoral election, which pits a black candidate against a white. For making these predictions, which of the following is the best question to ask prospective voters?

    a) "Do you dislike blacks?"
    b) "Do you like whites more than blacks?"
    c) "Do you think blacks are getting too demanding?"
    d) "Do you think blacks are lazy?"

    Answer: c   Type: M   Page(s): 320   Key 1: A

44. Sandra is a symbolic racist. Trish is a non-racist. Relative to Trish, Sandra is more likely to say

    a) "Racial discrimination is a thing of the past."
    b) "Racial discrimination still exists."
    c) "Blacks are lazy."
    d) "Blacks are not lazy."

    Answer: a   Type: M   Page(s): 320   Key 1: A

45. Ambivalence amplification occurs when

    a) people who had felt positively about a group hear some negative information about that group
    b) people who had felt negatively about a group hear some positive information about that group
    c) people who both like and dislike a group react extremely toward members of the group
    d) people who have both positive and negative thoughts about a group disregard any neutral thoughts they may have

    Answer: c   Type: M   Page(s): 321   Key 1: A

46. Ted, who is highly ambivalent about blacks, is evaluating two law school applicants: Blair (who is black) and Whit (who is white). The two candidates have equal credentials, and both are highly qualified. Research indicates that Ted will

    a) evaluate Blair more favorably than Whit
    b) evaluate Blair less favorably than Whit
    c) give equal evaluations to the two candidates
    d) randomly select one of the two candidates to receive a higher evaluation

    Answer: a   Type: M   Page(s): 321   Key 1: A

47. White Americans who simultaneously like and dislike blacks

    a) react more positively than negatively toward blacks
    b) react more negatively than positively toward blacks
    c) react neutrally toward blacks
    d) have extreme reactions toward blacks

    Answer: d   Type: M   Page(s): 321   Key 1: F

48. Realistic conflict occurs when

    a) two minority groups form a temporary coalition
    b) majority and minority groups compete for scarce resources
    c) the real self is discrepant from the ideal self
    d) the real self is discrepant from the ought self

    Answer: b   Type: M   Page(s): 322   Key 1: F

49. Powerful groups have an investment in maintaining social inequality. This produces

    a) implicit stereotyping
    b) spontaneous outgroup categorization
    c) realistic conflict
    d) illusory correlations

    Answer: c   Type: M   Page(s): 322   Key 1: F

50. The central character in many television commercials is a product user. These users tend to be

    a) men
    b) women
    c) blacks
    d) American Indians

    Answer: b   Type: M   Page(s): 324   Key 1: F

51. Which of the following is least likely to be depicted on television?

    a) an extremely healthy 40-year-old
    b) an extremely healthy 65-year-old
    c) a moderately healthy 65-year-old
    d) an extremely unhealthy 65-year-old

    Answer: c   Type: M   Page(s): 324   Key 1: F

52. Which of the following statements about sex differences is true?

    a) Females in all animal species stay home with the young.
    b) Females in all human cultures stay home with the young.
    c) Males in all human cultures go out of the home to provide for the family.
    d) None of these statements are true.

    Answer: d   Type: M   Page(s): 325   Key 1: F

53. Research shows that on memory tests

    a) young Chinese people score better than young Americans
    b) young Chinese people score worse than young Americans
    c) old Chinese people score better than old Americans
    d) old Chinese people score worse than old Americans

    Answer: c   Type: M   Page(s): 326   Key 1: F

54. Which of the following is most likely to agree that "Some groups of people are simply inferior to others?"

    a) Tom, who scores low on the Social Dominance Orientation scale
    b) Trey, who scores high on the Social Dominance Orientation scale
    c) Sharon, who scores high on the Hierarchical Legitimization scale
    d) Sheila, who scores low on the Hierarchical Legitimization scale

    Answer: b   Type: M   Page(s): 326   Key 1: A

55. Research shows that

    a) men have stronger gender stereotypes than women
    b) men and women subscribe to the same gender stereotypes
    c) Blacks have stronger racial stereotypes than Hispanics
    d) none of these statements are true

    Answer: b   Type: M   Page(s): 327   Key 1: F

56. Wanda is prejudiced against the elderly. According to the contact hypothesis, Wanda's prejudice can be reduced if she

    a) gets in contact with her real self
    b) gets in contact with her ought self
    c) makes contact with elderly people
    d) makes contact with people who aren't prejudiced against the elderly

    Answer: c   Type: M   Page(s): 329   Key 1: A

57. According to the _____, we can reduce stereotyping, prejudice, and discrimination if groups come to know each other better.

    a) acquaintance hypothesis
    b) contact hypothesis
    c) affiliation hypothesis
    d) transcendence hypothesis

    Answer: b   Type: M   Page(s): 329   Key 1: F

58. There are a number of conditions that have to be met before contact between two groups will reduce stereotyping, prejudice, and discrimination. Which of the following is NOT one of them?

    a) positive moods
    b) acquaintance potential
    c) mutual goals
    d) equal status

    Answer: a   Type: M   Page(s): 329   Key 1: F

59. A jigsaw method has been used to reduce prejudice in

    a) the workplace
    b) the Army
    c) sports competitions
    d) classroom learning

    Answer: d   Type: M   Page(s): 330   Key 1: F

60. A third-grade teacher tells three of her students that they'll soon be tested over the geography of North America. She gives Xerxes, a Hispanic boy, all of the material on Canada; Yolanda, a Black girl, all of the material on the U.S.; and Zelda, a White girl, all of the material on Mexico. Each of the children is assigned to teach the material they've been given to the other two children in the group. This teacher is using the

    a) quality circles concept
    b) jigsaw technique
    c) team-teaching method
    d) competitive pressure method

    Answer: b   Type: M   Page(s): 330   Key 1: A

61. The jigsaw method works best when

    a) people's heuristics are already working well
    b) there's an algorithmic solution to the problem
    c) participants are explicitly given equal status
    d) preexisting status differences are reversed

    Answer: c   Type: M   Page(s): 331   Key 1: F

62. A task has acquaintance potential if

    a) you can succeed at the task with no prior experience
    b) you get better at the task the longer you've done it
    c) the two people who are assigned the task can quickly determine who is better at it
    d) the two people doing the task can get to know one another as individuals

    Answer: d   Type: M   Page(s): 332   Key 1: F

63. George, a neo-Nazi, has gotten very acquainted with his coworker David, a Jew. Research suggests that this contact with David will have its biggest effect on George's attitude toward

    a) Jews as a group
    b) David as an individual
    c) neo-Nazis as a group
    d) George himself

    Answer: b   Type: M   Page(s): 333   Key 1: F

64. Social psychologists have considered two general approaches to reducing stereotyping, prejudice, and discrimination. These are contact and

   a) deindividuation
   b) recategorization
   c) isolation
   d) exhortation

   Answer: b   Type: M   Page(s): 334   Key 1: F

65. Relative to citizens of other technologically advanced countries, citizens of the United States

   a) are far more supportive of interracial marriages
   b) have the same feelings toward interracial marriages
   c) have far more ambivalence about interracial marriages
   d) are far more opposed to interracial marriages

   Answer: d   Type: M   Page(s): 334   Key 1: F

66. In espousing a "melting pot" society, White Americans really mean that

   a) minority groups should abandon their cultures and adopt White culture
   b) Whites should abandon their culture and adopt minority cultures
   c) a new culture should be created that draws equally upon all existing cultures
   d) each group should retain its own culture

   Answer: a   Type: M   Page(s): 334   Key 1: F

67. Which of the following is NOT a part of Black culture?

   a) an oral tradition
   b) a focus on the present
   c) a value of personal control
   d) a preference for improvised activities

   Answer: c   Type: M   Page(s): 335   Key 1: F

68. There are two recategorization approaches to reducing prejudice: creating one social category to which everyone belongs and

   a) breaking existing categories into smaller subtypes
   b) emphasizing the similarities among existing categories
   c) emphasizing the differences among existing categories
   d) creating several new categories that overlap with one another

   Answer: a   Type: M   Page(s): 335   Key 1: F

69. Walter had formerly been a member of the Crips gang. Their biggest rival was the Blood gang. Now the two groups have united with one another into a single larger gang -- the Bloody Crips. Research suggests that this development will cause Walter to

    a) think more favorably of the former members of the Blood gang
    b) think more favorably of the former members of the Crips gang
    c) think less favorably of the former members of the Blood gang
    d) think less favorably of the former members of the Crips gang

    Answer: a   Type: M   Page(s): 336   Key 1: A

70. Abigail thought all mental patients were dangerous, but then her mother (who wasn't dangerous at all) checked into a mental hospital. Abigail figured that this was "the exception that proved the rule." Abigail has retained her stereotype of mental patients by a form of

    a) implicit stereotyping
    b) illusory correlation
    c) deindividuation
    d) recategorization

    Answer: d   Type: M   Page(s): 337   Key 1: A

ESSAY

71. Describe the two-stage model of stereotyping, prejudice, and discrimination, noting the stages and substages of the model. Use the model to explain an instance in which you were the victim of stereotyping, prejudice, or discrimination.

    Answer:
    Students can answer this question by drawing on the material in Table 8.1 of the text (p. 305). As noted there, this model proposes that tendencies toward stereotyping, prejudice, and discrimination occur spontaneously upon a person's being categorized as a member of a group. Afterwards, there is a deliberative stage in which more information is gathered. Depending of the nature of the new information, the person might be placed into a less negative category, might make a larger adjustment to avoid guilt, and might avoid displaying any negative reactions. The student would need to note how someone had progressed through some of these stages and substages in subjecting them to stereotyping, prejudice, or discrimination.

    Type: E   Page(s): 305   Key 1: F

72. Identify and discuss three thought processes that cause stereotyping, prejudice, and discrimination. Be sure to summarize relevant research.

    Answer:
    Students could answer this question by summarizing the material on pages 311-316 of the textbook. As noted there, negative reactions to group members can be caused by illusory correlations, ignoring covariation, and implicit stereotyping. The best answer to this question would carefully define each of these processes and summarize supportive research.

    Type: E   Page(s): 311   Key 1: F

73. Present-day social psychologists seem to assume that Americans are not as prejudiced as they once were. Identify at least three concepts that have been inspired by this assumption. Be sure to describe each of the concepts in detail. Do you agree that Americans are not as prejudiced as they once were? Why or why not?

Answer:
Social psychologists seem to assume that Americans are not as prejudiced as they once were in the notion of a deliberative adjustment to prejudice (p. 305), the notion of Symbolic Racism (p. 319), and the notion of ambivalence amplification (p. 321). The best answer to this question would describe three such notions in detail, and indicate why the student believes (or doesn't believe) that prejudice in the United States has declined.

Type: E   Page(s): 335   Key 1: F

74. You've been hired by the Human Relations Commission to reduce racial prejudice in the New York City public schools. How will you go about this task? What factors will determine the likelihood of your success? In answering these questions, be sure to draw on social psychological concepts and research.

Answer:
Students should answer this question by drawing on the material on pages 329-337 of the text. They should mention that contact between races can reduce prejudice under conditions of mutual goals, equal status, and acquaintance potential; but that positive feelings toward individuals of a different race may not generalize to the race as a whole. They might require teachers to use the "jigsaw technique" (p. 330) of teaching; or get students to think of themselves as one huge group (p. 334). Another possibility is to get schoolchildren to notice finer and finer differences within each racial group -- so that each person is seen as a unique individual (p. 336). The best answer would combine these concepts in a creative fashion.

Type: E   Page(s): 329   Key 1: A

75. Is it likely that the world will ever be free of stereotyping, prejudice, and discrimination? Why or why not? In answering this question, draw on social psychological concepts and research.

Answer:
Although students could answer this open-ended question in a variety of ways, they should justify their answers by drawing on the material presented in Chapter 8 of the text. They might argue that the world will never be free of stereotyping, prejudice, and discrimination -- because stereotyping occurs spontaneously (p. 305); because minority group members will inevitably be associated with deviant acts (p. 312); and because people will inevitably derive part of their self-concept from a social identity (p. 316). They might, on the other hand, envision a world in which stereotyping, prejudice, and discrimination have ended. This might occur if there were sufficient contact (p. 329) among the different peoples of the world, if people could regard themselves as members of a single huge group (p. 334) or if they could regard each person they met as a unique individual (p. 336).

Type: E   Page(s): 305   Key 1: A

131

Chapter 9

Interpersonal Attraction

MULTIPLE CHOICE

1. In studies of personal and "lonely hearts" newspaper ads, women most often seek

   a) good-looking men
   b) financially secure men
   c) happy-go-lucky men
   d) serious men

   Answer: b   Type: M   Page(s): 340   Key 1: F

2. The most successful personal ads are placed in newspapers by

   a) young men and young women
   b) young men and old women
   c) old men and young women
   d) old men and old women

   Answer: c   Type: M   Page(s): 340   Key 1: F

3. Alice is beautiful and poor. Betty is rich and ugly. According to research on personal ads in U.S. newspapers, how easy should it be for these two women to find male romantic partners?

   a) Neither of the women should have any trouble finding a partner.
   b) Both of the women should have a lot of trouble finding a partner.
   c) It should be easier for Alice than for Betty.
   d) It should be easier for Betty than for Alice.

   Answer: c   Type: M   Page(s): 340   Key 1: A

4. The females of many species maximize their reproductive success by

   a) grooming
   b) flirting
   c) mating
   d) parenting

   Answer: d   Type: M   Page(s): 342   Key 1: F

5. The gender differences reflected in modern newspaper personal ads can be explained by three factors: cultural standards, a need to belong, and

    a) evolutionary pressures
    b) societal expectations
    c) the desire to give love
    d) newspaper policies

    Answer: a   Type: M   Page(s): 342   Key 1: F

6. Charlie is a male. Carla is a female. Theoretically, evolution should pressure both Charlie and Carla to

    a) maximize their investment in their children
    b) maximize the number of partners with whom they have sex
    c) maximize their reproductive success
    d) maximize the length of their lives

    Answer: c   Type: M   Page(s): 342   Key 1: A

7. From an evolutionary perspective, who exercises more choice in finding a mate?

    a) males
    b) females
    c) the two sexes exercise the same degree of choice
    d) males in primate species, females in other species

    Answer: b   Type: M   Page(s): 343   Key 1: F

8. According to evolutionary theory, why are women more likely than men to pursue a parenting strategy in reproduction?

    a) Cultural expectations explain this gender difference.
    b) Biologically, women aren't built to enjoy sex.
    c) Women prefer close associations with a small number of people.
    d) Women have a bigger investment in each child.

    Answer: d   Type: M   Page(s): 343   Key 1: F

9. Research indicates that close attachments

    a) are needed by women but not men
    b) are needed by men but not women
    c) are needed by both women and men
    d) aren't really needed by anyone

    Answer: c   Type: M   Page(s): 344   Key 1: F

133

10. David is a typical American male. Most of David's relationships are probably

    a) equality matching relationships
    b) authority ranking relationships
    c) communal sharing relationships
    d) market pricing relationships

    Answer: d   Type: M   Page(s): 345   Key 1: A

11. There are four types of interpersonal relationships. Which of the following is NOT one of them?

    a) communal sharing
    b) exchange
    c) equality matching
    d) culture maintaining

    Answer: d   Type: M   Page(s): 345   Key 1: F

12. In Eastern nations,

    a) exchange-based relationships are emphasized
    b) communal sharing relationships are emphasized
    c) family ties are more important than individual marriages
    d) marriages are based almost exclusively on love

    Answer: c   Type: M   Page(s): 345   Key 1: F

13. The nations of Asia and the Pacific rim emphasize

    a) authority-ranking relationships
    b) market-pricing relationships
    c) communal sharing relationships
    d) equality matching relationships

    Answer: a   Type: M   Page(s): 345   Key 1: F

14. If only traditional cultural standards were operating,

    a) women would have control over men in market-pricing cultures
    b) women would have control over men in authority-ranking cultures
    c) men would have control over women
    d) neither gender would have control over the other

    Answer: c   Type: M   Page(s): 346   Key 1: F

15. Most people are probably aware of the effect on their sexual behavior of

    a) evolutionary pressures, but not cultural standards
    b) cultural standards, but not evolutionary pressures
    c) both evolutionary pressures and cultural standards
    d) neither evolutionary pressures nor cultural standards

    Answer: d   Type: M   Page(s): 346   Key 1: F

16. Accounts of interpersonal attraction in earlier centuries were almost all written by

    a) religious people
    b) atheists
    c) women
    d) men

    Answer: d   Type: M   Page(s): 347   Key 1: F

17. In which of the following historical eras have men been most attracted to prostitutes?

    a) in Athenian Greece
    b) in 11th century Europe
    c) in the Puritan era
    d) in the modern era

    Answer: a   Type: M   Page(s): 348   Key 1: F

18. Onanna, a well-educated woman of ancient Greece, often invited men into her home for a fee to have dinner, discuss politics, and enjoy physical pleasure. Onanna would have been known as a(n)

    a) concubine
    b) heavenly angel
    c) hetaera
    d) acajou

    Answer: c   Type: M   Page(s): 348   Key 1: A

19. Men were attracted to hetaerae in ancient

    a) Rome
    b) Greece
    c) China
    d) India

    Answer: b   Type: M   Page(s): 348   Key 1: F

20. Yerxes was a resident of ancient Rome, To Yerxes, the highest form of love would have been

    a) sex with his wife
    b) sex with a prostitute
    c) adultery with a virgin
    d) adultery with another man's wife

    Answer: d   Type: M   Page(s): 349   Key 1: A

21. The concept of "courtly love" arose

    a) during the early Christian era
    b) in 11th-century Europe
    c) in Renaissance Italy
    d) during the Age of Reason

    Answer: b   Type: M   Page(s): 349   Key 1: F

22. During the "courtship" of a certain man and a certain woman, lawyers for the two parties argued over the marriage contract. This "courtship" most likely took place

    a) in ancient Rome
    b) in Athenian Greece
    c) during the early Christian era
    d) during the Age of Reason

    Answer: d   Type: M   Page(s): 350   Key 1: F

23. Love in the modern era

    a) is utterly different from love in any earlier era
    b) is somewhat less passionate than in the early Christian era
    c) incorporates trends from all previous eras
    d) emphasizes self-denial

    Answer: c   Type: M   Page(s): 350   Key 1: F

24. Cross-cultural research shows that passionate love is found

    a) only in the United States and western Europe
    b) only in modern cultures
    c) only in the countries of the Northern hemisphere
    d) in virtually every culture

    Answer: d   Type: M   Page(s): 350   Key 1: F

25. Silwa Egyptians surgically alter young girls' genitals in order to

    a) encourage them to have sex
    b) prevent them from enjoying sex
    c) make them look like young men
    d) make them look like older women

    Answer: b   Type: M   Page(s): 351   Key 1: F

26. In virtually every culture, women believe that their ideal mate would be older than they are. From an evolutionary perspective, what's the best explanation for this belief?

    a) Old men make lots of money.
    b) Young men have problems with premature ejaculation.
    c) Old men are inclined to be monogamous.
    d) Young men are prone to violence.

    Answer: a   Type: M   Page(s): 351   Key 1: F

27. A study of customs in 37 cultures revealed that

    a) in most cultures husbands and wives are the same age
    b) in many cultures wives are older than husbands
    c) in many cultures the average husband is older than his wife's parents
    d) none of these statements are true

    Answer: d   Type: M   Page(s): 352   Key 1: F

28. The tendency for men to prefer women younger than themselves is strongest in

    a) technologically advanced cultures
    b) undeveloped cultures
    c) horizontal cultures
    d) vertical cultures

    Answer: b   Type: M   Page(s): 352   Key 1: F

29. Fred is a typical 1990s male. Gloria is a typical 1990s female. Emotional stability would be considered one of the top requirements for an ideal mate by

    a) Fred, but not Gloria
    b) Gloria, but not Fred
    c) both Fred and Gloria
    d) neither Gloria nor Fred

    Answer: c   Type: M   Page(s): 352   Key 1: A

30. Having been married for 20 years, Hal and Hazel felt that their lives were deeply intertwined. Hal and Hazel are most likely experiencing

    a) comparative love
    b) superlative love
    c) passionate love
    d) companionate love

    Answer: d   Type: M   Page(s): 353   Key 1: A

31. Companionate love involves all of the following EXCEPT

    a) closeness
    b) excitement
    c) concern
    d) self-disclosure

    Answer: b   Type: M   Page(s): 353   Key 1: F

32. According to a triangular theory, love involves three dimensions. Which of the following is NOT one of them?

    a) intimacy
    b) commitment
    c) shared responsibilities
    d) passion

    Answer: c   Type: M   Page(s): 354   Key 1: F

33. Having just met, Isaac and Joan feel enormous passion for one another, but no commitment or intimacy. According to the triangular theory of love, Isaac and Joan have

    a) empty love
    b) companionate love
    c) fatuous love
    d) romantic love

    Answer: c   Type: M   Page(s): 355   Key 1: A

34. The most powerful predictor of people's satisfaction with long-term relationships is

    a) passion
    b) commitment
    c) complementarity
    d) intimacy

    Answer: b   Type: M   Page(s): 355   Key 1: F

35. G-PLACE stands for

    a) a certain female erogenous zone
    b) a theory of homosexual attraction
    c) six gender differences in interpersonal attraction
    d) six love styles

    Answer: d   Type: M   Page(s): 355   Key 1: F

36. Kathy is a typical American woman. Larry is a typical American man. Research shows that Kathy is more likely than Larry to be

    a) an altruistic lover
    b) an erotic lover
    c) a game-playing lover
    d) a possessive lover

    Answer: d   Type: M   Page(s): 357   Key 1: A

37. As a handsome multi-millionaire, Marv had the opportunity to marry any one of four women According to research, Marv will be most satisfied if he marries

    a) Mandy, an altruistic lover
    b) Michelle, a possessive lover
    c) Mindy, an erotic lover
    d) Monica, a companionate lover

    Answer: c   Type: M   Page(s): 357   Key 1: A

38. Which of the following is a distal cause of interpersonal attraction?

    a) the need to belong
    b) attachment
    c) physiological arousal
    d) loneliness

    Answer: a   Type: M   Page(s): 358   Key 1: F

39. Ned found himself strongly attracted to Nel. A proximal cause of Ned's attraction was

    a) evolutionary pressure
    b) Ned's loneliness
    c) the standards of Ned's culture
    d) the need to belong

    Answer: b   Type: M   Page(s): 358   Key 1: A

40. Research shows that fear causes men to be

    a) more attracted to ugly women than they would otherwise be
    b) more attracted to beautiful women than they would otherwise be
    c) less attracted to beautiful women than they would otherwise be
    d) more receptive to children than they would otherwise be

    Answer: b   Type: M   Page(s): 359   Key 1: F

41. Oscar and Otto participated in an experiment one at a time. Oscar ran in place for a long time, then saw a videotape of Pauline, who looked extremely unattractive. Otto saw the same videotape without doing any exercise. If these men are typical, Otto should

    a) be less attracted to Pauline than Oscar is
    b) be more attracted to Pauline than Oscar is
    c) be precisely as attracted to Pauline as Oscar is
    d) be faster in answering the experimenter's questions than Oscar is

    Answer: b   Type: M   Page(s): 360   Key 1: A

42. What is the evolutionary function of affectional bonding in human beings?

    a) to provide a prelude to sex
    b) to promote long-term monogamous relationships in the nuclear family
    c) to promote good relationships between married adults and the parents of their spouses
    d) to protect infants from threats to their survival

    Answer: d   Type: M   Page(s): 361   Key 1: F

43. Investigators have found three styles of parent-child attachment. Which of the following is NOT one of them?

    a) anxious/ambivalent attachment
    b) secure attachment
    c) defensive attachment
    d) avoidant attachment

    Answer: c   Type: M   Page(s): 361   Key 1: F

44. Two-year-old Ron gets extremely upset when his mother is absent and clings to her when she returns. Ron has

    a) anxious/ambivalent attachment
    b) avoidant attachment
    c) overattachment
    d) underattachment

    Answer: a   Type: M   Page(s): 361   Key 1: A

45. Sara, who is 18 months old, gets extremely upset when her mother is absent but acts as if she doesn't care when her mother returns. Sara has

    a) easy attachment
    b) avoidant attachment
    c) secure attachment
    d) anxious/ambivalent attachment

    Answer: b   Type: M   Page(s): 361   Key 1: A

46. The most common style of infant-mother attachment is

    a) avoidant
    b) anxious/ambivalent
    c) secure
    d) easy

    Answer: c   Type: M   Page(s): 361   Key 1: F

47. As a child, Ted had a secure attachment to his mother. Research suggests that this early infant-mother attachment will

    a) have no effect on Ted's adult romantic relationships
    b) tend to make Ted secure in his adult romantic relationships
    c) tend to make Ted critical of his adult romantic partners (since they won't measure up to his mother)
    d) tend to make Ted avoid adult romantic relationships

    Answer: b   Type: M   Page(s): 362   Key 1: F

48. 28-year-old Teresa finds that men are reluctant to get as close as she would like. She often feels that no one really loves her. Teresa would be classified as having a(n)

    a) anxious/ambivalent attachment style
    b) avoidant attachment style
    c) hovering attachment style
    d) secure attachment style

    Answer: a   Type: M   Page(s): 363   Key 1: A

49. People who have an avoidant attachment style are most likely to have a(n)

    a) erotic love style
    b) logical love style
    c) companionate love style
    d) game playing love style

    Answer: d   Type: M   Page(s): 365   Key 1: F

50. 25-year-old Ulysses finds it easy to get close to women and is comfortable depending on them and having them depend on him. Ulysses is most likely to have a(n)

    a) companionate love style
    b) altruistic love style
    c) aggressive love style
    d) logical love style

    Answer: b   Type: M   Page(s): 365   Key 1: A

51. Loneliness is associated with all of the following EXCEPT

    a) high blood pressure
    b) low self-esteem
    c) headaches
    d) low IQ

    Answer: d   Type: M   Page(s): 366   Key 1: F

52. LaVonne is extremely lonely. If she's like most lonely people, LaVonne is

    a) unlikely to remember what others say about her
    b) overly eager to introduce herself to others
    c) too critical
    d) egotistical

    Answer: c   Type: M   Page(s): 367   Key 1: A

53. Chronically lonely people have two characteristics that contribute to their lack of popularity. They are socially inept and

    a) too intelligent
    b) too involved in solitary hobbies
    c) too accepting
    d) too critical

    Answer: d   Type: M   Page(s): 367   Key 1: F

54. Self-disclosure refers to

    a) how often we get in touch with our own true feelings
    b) how much we tell others about ourselves
    c) how much of our bodies we allow others to see
    d) how often we look at our own bodies

    Answer: b   Type: M   Page(s): 367   Key 1: F

55. Wanda, an extremely lonely woman, is scheduled to meet Alice next Monday and Bill next Tuesday. Based on research, we would expect Wanda to disclose

    a) more about herself to Alice than to Bill
    b) more about herself to Bill than to Alice
    c) virtually nothing about herself to either Alice or Bill
    d) far too much about herself to both Alice and Bill

    Answer: a   Type: M   Page(s): 368   Key 1: A

56. According to the mere exposure effect,

    a) the more you meet someone, the more you'll like them
    b) the more you meet someone, the less you'll like them
    c) exposure to highly attractive people in movies makes the people we meet in everyday life seem unattractive
    d) mere exposure to the HIV virus is sufficient for a person to contract AIDS

    Answer: a   Type: M   Page(s): 369   Key 1: F

57. People like mirror-images of their faces more than true images of their faces. This illustrates

    a) the matching hypothesis
    b) the similarity-attraction effect
    c) the misattribution of emotional expression
    d) the mere exposure effect

    Answer: d   Type: M   Page(s): 370   Key 1: F

58. Zelda lives in the end apartment on a U-shaped courtyard community. All of the other apartments face in toward the courtyard; while hers faces away. Based on research, we would expect Zelda to be

    a) the most physically attractive resident in the community
    b) the most physically unattractive resident in the community
    c) the most popular resident in the community
    d) the least popular resident in the community

    Answer: d   Type: M   Page(s): 371   Key 1: A

59. For the past 10 years, Alphonzo (a handsome man) has been married to Betty (an ugly woman). For those same 10 years, Carl (an ugly man) has been married to Dawn (a beautiful woman). Based on research, who would we expect to be LEAST satisfied with their marriage?

    a) Alphonzo
    b) Betty
    c) Carl
    d) Dawn

    Answer: c   Type: M   Page(s): 371   Key 1: A

60. In judgments of the physical attractiveness of members of the opposite sex,

    a) men (but not women) are influenced by what others think
    b) women (but not men) are influenced by what others think
    c) both women and men are influenced by what others think
    d) neither men nor women are influenced by that others think

    Answer: b   Type: M   Page(s): 372   Key 1: F

61. Elvira and Fred had been dating for several months. Then as part of a market research project, both saw a series of photographs of highly attractive members of the opposite sex (Elvira seeing handsome men, Fred seeing beautiful women). We would expect this to reduce

    a) both Elvira and Fred's commitment to their relationship
    b) neither Elvira nor Fred's commitment to their relationship
    c) Elvira's commitment to the relationship, but not Fred's
    d) Fred's commitment to the relationship, but not Elvira's

    Answer: d   Type: M   Page(s): 372   Key 1: A

62. Gloria had been dating Hal for a year. Then as part of her job at the local TV station, she had to look through the photographs of a large number of men who had applied for a position as news anchor. Research indicates that this will reduce Gloria's commitment to her relationship with Hal if the photographs depict

    a) handsome men
    b) ugly men
    c) dominant men
    d) submissive men

    Answer: c   Type: M   Page(s): 372   Key 1: A

63. Physically attractive people are assumed to be

   a) intelligent
   b) sociable
   c) interesting
   d) all of these

   Answer: d   Type: M   Page(s): 373   Key 1: F

64. According to the matching hypothesis,

   a) men seek female partners who match their ideal for sexual gratification
   b) women seek male partners who match their ideal for financial security
   c) people seek partners who match their own physical attractiveness
   d) all of these statements are true

   Answer: c   Type: M   Page(s): 373   Key 1: F

65. People prefer romantic partners who are similar to themselves in

   a) length of ear lobes
   b) age
   c) preferred tactics in strategic games
   d) all of these

   Answer: d   Type: M   Page(s): 374   Key 1: F

66. Irving is always sad. With whom is he most likely to have a relationship?

   a) Joan, who is always sad
   b) Kathy, who is always happy
   c) Lorrie, who is sad half of the time and happy half of the time
   d) Mona, who is always in a neutral mood

   Answer: a   Type: M   Page(s): 374   Key 1: A

67. Social psychological research shows that

   a) opposites attract
   b) birds of a feather flock together
   c) there's no truth in either of these sayings
   d) both of these sayings are true, but under different circumstances

   Answer: b   Type: M   Page(s): 375   Key 1: F

68. Why do we choose friends who are similar to ourselves?

    a) by conscious calculation
    b) to resolve intrapsychic conflicts
    c) because we assume that others will like us if they are similar to us
    d) all of these factors play a role

    Answer: c   Type: M   Page(s): 375   Key 1: F

69. According to the repulsion hypothesis,

    a) men have a stronger reaction to physically unattractive women than physically attractive women
    b) women have a stronger reaction to physically unattractive men than physically attractive men
    c) people are spontaneously repulsed by strangers who are dissimilar to themselves
    d) people come over time to be repulsed by people who are too similar to themselves

    Answer: c   Type: M   Page(s): 376   Key 1: F

70. Research shows that similarity is important in

    a) dating relationships, but not marriages
    b) marriages, but not dating relationships
    c) both marriages and dating relationships
    d) neither marriages nor dating relationships

    Answer: c   Type: M   Page(s): 376   Key 1: F

ESSAY

71. How do the two genders differ in what they want in an opposite-sex partner? How can these gender differences be explained? Review relevant research on gender differences in newspaper personal ads, and identify three factors that can account for these differences.

    Answer:
    Students should answer this question by reviewing the material on pages 340-347 of the text. As noted there, men look for physically attractive women and offer financial resources; women look for financially successful men and offer physical attractiveness. These differences may be explained by three factors: 1) evolutionary pressures that encourage men to pursue a mating strategy and women a parenting strategy (p. 342), 2) the strong human need to belong in a close relationship (p. 344), and 3) cultural standards that have traditionally encouraged women to care for children and men to work outside the home (p. 345).

    Type: E   Page(s): 342   Key 1: F

72. Are patterns of heterosexual attraction in the United States today unique? Or are these the same patterns found in all historical eras and in all cultures? Answer this question by describing heterosexual attraction in different cultures and different ages.

Answer:
Students could answer this question by summarizing some of the material on pages 347-352 of the text. They should draw on the history of love in Table 9.1 (p. 348) and the cross-cultural descriptions on page 351. Although there are differences in patterns of attraction across time and cultures, some common themes emerge. Men usually control financial resources, and women are left at home to rear children.

Type: E   Page(s): 348   Key 1: F

73. Your textbook describes two theories of love: a triangular theory and theory of six love styles. Summarize these two theories; then compare and contrast the theories. Which theory do you think offers the better description of love? Why?

Answer:
To answer this question, students should begin by summarizing the material on pages 354-357 of the text. According to the triangular theory, love involves passion, intimacy, and commitment. According to the other theory, there are six styles of love: game-playing, possessive, logical, altruistic, companionate, and erotic. The two theories differ in an important respect: while the triangular theory holds that love is not balanced unless it includes an equal mix of three different elements, the other theory holds that each individual will inevitably emphasize one style of love over another.

Type: E   Page(s): 356   Key 1: A

74. A critic recently stated, "I don't care what social psychologists say. It's crazy to believe that a two-year-old boy's attachment to his mother is the same thing as a thirty-five-old man's love for his wife."
    In a paragraph or two, reply to the critic's remark by noting similarities between infant attachment and adult love. Be sure to identify three different attachment styles, and note how they function in infancy and adulthood.

Answer:
Students could answer this question by drawing on the material on pages 361-365 of the text. They should describe the secure, avoidant, and anxious/ambivalent attachment styles (p. 364), and summarize some of the parallels between infant attachment and adult romantic love (on pages 362-363).

Type: E   Page(s): 362   Key 1: A

147

75. Why do we find some people more attractive than others? Identify at least three factors that make an individual attractive to others, and explain WHY these factors make the individual attractive. Be sure to cite relevant research.

Answer:
Students could answer this question by drawing on the material on pages 369-376 of the text. As noted there, we are attracted to people who are familiar, physically attractive, and similar to ourselves. The impact of familiarity is adaptive, and is evident in animals as well as humans. The impact of physical attractiveness may reflect either evolutionary pressures or cultural standards. The impact of similarity may reflect people's usual high level of self-esteem and their implicit assumption that others who resemble the self will be likable. Or it may reflect the assumption that similar others will be attracted to the self.

Type: E   Page(s): 369   Key 1: F

Chapter 10

Close Relationships

MULTIPLE CHOICE

1. When asked by an attractive opposite-sex stranger to go to bed, men

   a) are less likely than women to agree to the request
   b) are just as likely as women to agree to the request
   c) are more likely than women to agree to the request
   d) were more likely than women to agree to the request in the 1970s, but are no more likely than women to agree in the 1990s

   Answer: c   Type: M   Page(s): 380   Key 1: F

2. Alice and Albert were both attractive undergraduates, but they didn't know one another. Alice asked Albert out on a date. Research suggests that Albert

   a) will almost certainly refuse
   b) is more likely to refuse than Alice would have been, if Albert had asked her out
   c) has about a 50-50 chance of accepting
   d) will almost certainly accept

   Answer: c   Type: M   Page(s): 380   Key 1: A

3. Bob, an attractive undergraduate, had a strong sex drive. One day he considered walking up to a random female he didn't know, and asking if she would go to bed with him. What are the chances that she would agree?

   a) 0%
   b) about 25%
   c) about 50%
   d) about 75%

   Answer: a   Type: M   Page(s): 380   Key 1: A

4. In the 1990s, undergraduate females almost always refuse invitations for sex offered by male strangers. According to research, which reason are they most likely to give?

   a) They're afraid of getting AIDS.
   b) They have boyfriends.
   c) They're afraid of being physically assaulted.
   d) They're afraid of getting a bad reputation.

   Answer: b   Type: M   Page(s): 381   Key 1: F

5. Carl, an attractive undergraduate, walked up to a random female he didn't know, and asked if she would go to bed with him. She refused. He asked why. Of the following, which is LEAST likely to give as her excuse?

   a) "I already have a boyfriend."
   b) "I don't know you well enough."
   c) "I don't like being approached like that."
   d) "I'm scared of getting AIDS."

   Answer: d Type: M   Page(s): 382   Key 1: A

6. David was thinking about having a one-night stand with one of three different women: Elvira (who's beautiful), Fran (who is intelligent), or Gloria (who has a pleasant personality). All other things being equal, with whom would David most prefer to have his one-night stand?

   a) Elvira
   b) Fran
   c) Gloria
   d) He'd be equally interested in having a one-night stand with any of these three women.

   Answer: a Type: M   Page(s): 382   Key 1: A

7. When considering marriage, men are LESS interested than women in

   a) their partner's intellect
   b) their partner's agreeableness
   c) both their partner's intellect and their partner's agreeableness
   d) neither their partner's intellect nor their partner's agreeableness

   Answer: d Type: M   Page(s): 382   Key 1: F

8. When trying to make themselves attractive to the opposite sex, men and women are equally likely to

   a) brag about their accomplishments
   b) wear fashionable clothes
   c) go on a diet to lose weight
   d) increase their exposure to members of the opposite sex

   Answer: d Type: M   Page(s): 383   Key 1: F

9. When trying to make themselves attractive to members of the opposite sex, women are more likely than men to

   a) talk openly about having sex
   b) be sympathetic
   c) buy dinner at a fancy restaurant
   d) brag about accomplishments

   Answer: b Type: M   Page(s): 383   Key 1: F

10. On their first date, Ed and Felicia were trying to make themselves attractive to one another. Research suggests that Ed is more likely than Felicia to

a) have spent a lot of time making himself look good
b) wear cologne
c) brag about accomplishments
d) be sympathetic

Answer: c   Type: M   Page(s): 383   Key 1: A

11. When trying to make themselves attractive to men, women perform a number of specific actions. Research shows that, in fact, these actions make the women

a) more attractive to men
b) less attractive to men
c) more attractive to other women
d) less attractive to other women

Answer: a   Type: M   Page(s): 384   Key 1: F

12. As your textbook notes, deep commitment to a relationship depends on three factors: belief in the relationship, mutual support, and

a) interdependence
b) respect for the partner's separate identity
c) matching levels of physical attractiveness
d) a match between the man's accomplishments and the woman's attractiveness

Answer: a   Type: M   Page(s): 384   Key 1: F

13. To measure a couple's interdependence, researchers use the

a) Depth-of-Relationship Questionnaire
b) Relationship Closeness Inventory
c) Interdependence Orientation Survey
d) Independence-Interdependence Scale

Answer: b   Type: M   Page(s): 384   Key 1: F

14. Interdependence and mutual influence characterize close relationships

a) only among adolescents
b) only among the middle-aged
c) only among the elderly
d) among all age groups

Answer: d   Type: M   Page(s): 384   Key 1: F

15. Which of the following couples is most likely to break up in the next nine months?

    a) Irv and Isabel, whose lives are completely independent
    b) Jack and June, who have a moderate degree of interdependence
    c) Kathy and Kurt, who are highly interdependent
    d) Larry and Laurie, who lead completely independent professional lives but are highly interdependent in their social lives

    Answer: a   Type: M   Page(s): 385   Key 1: A

16. Marv and Mary are happily married and have just celebrated their 40th anniversary. Marv and Mary are most likely to have

    a) been independent of one another early in their marriage
    b) become more interdependent over the years
    c) become less interdependent over the years
    d) each had several extramarital affairs

    Answer: b   Type: M   Page(s): 385   Key 1: A

17. Which of the following couples is most likely to stay together?

    a) Ned and Nan, who frankly confront one another's faults
    b) Oscar and Olivia, who overlook one another's faults
    c) Paul and Patricia. He confronts her about her faults. She overlooks his.
    d) Roger and Roxie. She confronts him about his faults. He overlooks hers.

    Answer: b   Type: M   Page(s): 386   Key 1: A

18. Perceptions of social support are most important in

    a) young men's satisfaction with their marriages
    b) middle-aged men's satisfaction with their marriages
    c) old men's satisfaction with their marriages
    d) women's satisfaction with their marriages

    Answer: d   Type: M   Page(s): 387   Key 1: F

19. Sandy and Stan are happily married. Teresa and Ted's marriage is on the skids. According to research, who is most likely to be in bad health?

    a) Sandy
    b) Stan
    c) Teresa
    d) Ted

    Answer: c   Type: M   Page(s): 387   Key 1: A

20. Who is least likely to snap at their spouse when things go wrong?

    a) a psychologically masculine woman
    b) a psychologically feminine man
    c) an absent-minded genius
    d) a moron with lots of common sense

    Answer: b   Type: M   Page(s): 387   Key 1: F

21. Terri, a woman with traditional sex-role attitudes, just had her first baby. She's now discovered that she'll be having to do more work than she ever imagined. According to research, this should

    a) change Terri's sex-role attitude
    b) have no effect on Terri's commitment to her marriage
    c) reduce Terri's commitment to her marriage
    d) increase Terri's commitment to her marriage

    Answer: d   Type: M   Page(s): 387   Key 1: A

22. Based on research, which of the following is LEAST likely to get divorced?

    a) Ursula, a traditional woman who married her childhood sweetheart
    b) Vanessa, a liberated woman who married her childhood sweetheart
    c) Wanda, a traditional woman who married a man she barely knew
    d) Xanadu, a liberated woman who married a man she barely knew

    Answer: a   Type: M   Page(s): 388   Key 1: A

23. Which of the following has a collectivistic culture?

    a) the United States
    b) China
    c) New Zealand
    d) the Netherlands

    Answer: b   Type: M   Page(s): 389   Key 1: F

24. Your textbook discusses four types of relationships that people have with one another. Which of the following is NOT one of them?

    a) market pricing
    b) equality matching
    c) role enacting
    d) authority ranking

    Answer: c   Type: M   Page(s): 390   Key 1: F

25. The residents of a certain South Pacific island follow a norm in being extremely loyal to one another. The Islanders' culture is most likely based on

    a) market pricing relationships
    b) authority ranking relationships
    c) equality matching relationships
    d) communal sharing relationships

    Answer: d   Type: M   Page(s): 391   Key 1: A

26. Social identity is emphasized in

    a) authority ranking relationships
    b) market pricing relationships
    c) equality matching relationships
    d) none of these types of relationships

    Answer: a   Type: M   Page(s): 391   Key 1: F

27. In a certain ancient culture, people were expected to return favors in kind, but not in excess. This culture was based on

    a) market pricing relationships
    b) authority ranking relationships
    c) communal sharing relationships
    d) none of these

    Answer: d   Type: M   Page(s): 391   Key 1: A

28. Personal identity is emphasized in

    a) authority ranking relationships
    b) communal sharing relationships
    c) market pricing relationships
    d) all of these types of relationships

    Answer: c   Type: M   Page(s): 391   Key 1: F

29. Which type of relationship has been LEAST frequent in most societies throughout most of history?

    a) authority ranking relationships
    b) market pricing relationships
    c) communal sharing relationships
    d) equality matching relationships

    Answer: b   Type: M   Page(s): 392   Key 1: F

154

30. Your textbook discusses four types of marriages: communal sharing, equality matching, market pricing, and

    a) culture transmitting
    b) society enhancing
    c) role enacting
    d) authority ranking

    Answer: d   Type: M   Page(s): 392   Key 1: F

31. Alex and Barbara will soon be wed. They are both extremely traditional. Theirs is most likely to be a(n)

    a) communal sharing marriage
    b) equality matching marriage
    c) authority ranking marriage
    d) market pricing marriage

    Answer: c   Type: M   Page(s): 392   Key 1: A

32. Charlie and Dawn, who have been married for 5 years, have the same bank account. Theirs is most likely to be a(n)

    a) communal sharing marriage
    b) equality matching marriage
    c) authority ranking marriage
    d) market pricing marriage

    Answer: a   Type: M   Page(s): 392   Key 1: A

33. We could best tell that Earl and Fran have a market pricing marriage by knowing that they

    a) have the same bank account
    b) do everything possible to save money
    c) follow the traditional roles of husband and wife
    d) have drawn up a prenuptial agreement

    Answer: d   Type: M   Page(s): 392   Key 1: A

34. In "lonely hearts" ads, women who consider themselves attractive demand male partners who are financially successful. This is most consistent with a(n)

    a) ranking orientation
    b) egoistic orientation
    c) communal orientation
    d) exchange orientation

    Answer: d   Type: M   Page(s): 393   Key 1: F

35. When Gloria is in a relationship, she doesn't bother to keep tabs on how much she's putting into the relationship and how much she's getting out. For her, being together is what matters. Gloria's orientation to relationships is called a(n)

    a) exchange orientation
    b) altruistic orientation
    c) communal orientation
    d) androgenous orientation

    Answer: c   Type: M   Page(s): 393   Key 1: A

36. Hap told his wife Hazel, "If you let me watch the basketball game on TV tonight, I'll let you go to your bridge club tomorrow." Hap's orientation to his marriage is called a(n)

    a) egoistic orientation
    b) contractual orientation
    c) exchange orientation
    d) communal orientation

    Answer: c   Type: M   Page(s): 393   Key 1: A

37. In exchange relationships, people

    a) feel that being in the relationship is worth it -- no matter what
    b) keep track of how much they contribute
    c) exchange their personal identity for a social identity
    d) move quickly from partner to partner

    Answer: b   Type: M   Page(s): 394   Key 1: F

38. Research indicates that men are most likely to signal that they want a communal relationship with

    a) other men in business settings
    b) other men in social settings
    c) romantically available women
    d) romantically unavailable women

    Answer: c   Type: M   Page(s): 394   Key 1: F

39. Who's most likely to hide their emotions?

    a) people in an authority-ranking relationship
    b) people in a culture-transmitting relationship
    c) people in an exchange relationship
    d) people in a communal relationship

    Answer: c   Type: M   Page(s): 394   Key 1: F

40. As research shows, you're more likely to help someone who will later be in a position to help you UNLESS

    a) that person takes an exchange orientation toward their relationship with you
    b) you take an exchange orientation toward your relationship with that person
    c) that person takes a communal orientation toward their relationship with you
    d) you take a communal orientation toward your relationship with that person

    Answer: d   Type: M   Page(s): 395   Key 1: F

41. Relative to people with a communal orientation, those with an exchange orientation are

    a) generally more satisfied with their marriages
    b) generally less satisfied with their marriages
    c) more satisfied with their marriages only if they're getting more out of the marriage than they're putting in
    c) less satisfied with their marriages only if they're putting more into the marriage than they're getting out

    Answer: b   Type: M   Page(s): 395   Key 1: F

42. Irene (an exchange-oriented woman) had been married to Xavier for five years, and had always felt that she was getting more out of her marriage than she put in. Research indicates that relative to women with a communal orientation, Irene will be

    a) more satisfied with her marriage
    b) less satisfied with her marriage
    c) just as satisfied with her marriage
    d) either more satisfied or less satisfied with her marriage, depending on whether Xavier has an exchange or a communal orientation

    Answer: b   Type: M   Page(s): 396   Key 1: A

43. When people who have recently been divorced are asked why they got divorced, they most frequently blame

    a) themselves
    b) their ex-spouse
    c) an external influence
    d) getting married in the first place

    Answer: b   Type: M   Page(s): 398   Key 1: F

44. In a study of people in close relationships, subjects were asked to list specific actions of their partner that upset and angered them. These actions fell into four categories. Which of the following is NOT one of them?

    a) possessive actions
    b) inconsiderate actions
    c) flirtatious actions
    d) abusive actions

    Answer: c   Type: M   Page(s): 398   Key 1: F

45. In newlywed couples, men are more upset than women about their spouses'

    a) neglect
    b) abusive actions
    c) inconsiderate actions
    d) possessive actions

    Answer: d   Type: M   Page(s): 398   Key 1: F

46. Jack and Jill are dating. Karen and Karl have been married for six months. Based on research, who is most likely to be upset about their partner's inconsiderate behavior?

    a) Jack
    b) Jill
    c) Karen
    d) Karl

    Answer: c   Type: M   Page(s): 399   Key 1: A

47. By taking a "macho" attitude and not talking about their marriages, men

    a) upset their wives
    b) keep their wives from getting even more upset than they already are
    c) improve their relationships with their male friends
    d) impair their relationships with their male friends

    Answer: a   Type: M   Page(s): 400   Key 1: F

48. As your textbook notes, Americans are

    a) more willing to consider divorce than people in any other country
    b) more willing to consider divorce than Brazilians
    c) less willing to consider divorce than people in any other country
    d) less willing to consider divorce than Brazilians

    Answer: d   Type: M   Page(s): 400   Key 1: F

49. As your textbook notes, jealousy

    a) doesn't really pose a danger to any relationships
    b) doesn't pose a danger to long-term marriages
    c) is basically the same as other negative emotions
    d) is different from other negative emotions

    Answer: d   Type: M   Page(s): 400   Key 1: F

50. What makes people the most jealous throughout the world?

    a) their partner's having sexual fantasies about someone else
    b) their partner's dancing with someone else
    c) their partner's flirting with someone else
    d) It varies from culture to culture.

    Answer: d   Type: M   Page(s): 401   Key 1: F

51. In _____, men get most jealous when they suspect that their wives are having a sexual affair with another man.

    a) the United States
    b) all individualistic countries
    c) all communal countries
    d) all countries

    Answer: a   Type: M   Page(s): 401   Key 1: F

52. In married couples,

    a) wives do most of the complaining
    b) husbands do most of the complaining
    c) wives are most likely to show sarcasm
    d) husbands are most likely to show sarcasm

    Answer: a   Type: M   Page(s): 401   Key 1: F

53. Your textbook discusses four behaviors that corrode marital satisfaction, calling them the "four horsemen of the apocalypse." Which of the following is NOT one of them?

    a) complaining
    b) stonewalling
    c) complacency
    d) contempt

    Answer: c   Type: M   Page(s): 402   Key 1: F

54. Researchers have found that when couples have serious disagreements, many engage in a series of four destructive behaviors. Which is the last behavior displayed in this sequence?

    a) contempt
    b) stonewalling
    c) defensiveness
    d) complaining

    Answer: b   Type: M   Page(s): 402   Key 1: F

55. Ivan and Zelda had been married for six years, but never could agree on where to live. Research shows that when disagreeing over this issue, Ivan is more likely than Zelda to

    a) be defensive
    b) criticize
    c) stonewall
    d) show contempt

    Answer: c   Type: M   Page(s): 402   Key 1: A

56. Research shows that when discussing areas of disagreement,

    a) husbands are demanding while wives withdraw
    b) wives are demanding while husbands withdraw
    c) husbands are philosophical while wives are practical
    d) wives are philosophical while husbands are practical

    Answer: b   Type: M   Page(s): 403   Key 1: F

57. As parents of a hyperactive child, Joan and Larry had a lot of disagreements. As research suggests, Joan's approach to these disagreements is most likely to differ from Larry's when the disagreement concerns

    a) their child's education
    b) their child's social life
    c) something Larry wants Joan to change
    d) something Joan wants Larry to change

    Answer: d   Type: M   Page(s): 403   Key 1: A

58. In close relationships, women tend to confront problems; men tend to withdraw. What causes this sex difference?

    a) social pressure from same-sex peers
    b) social pressure from parents
    c) sex differences in reactions to stress
    d) sex differences in opportunities for an alternative relationship

    Answer: c   Type: M   Page(s): 403   Key 1: F

59. There are differences in the way men and women deal with problems in close relationships. These result from

    a) men's greater tendency to become aversively aroused
    b) women's greater tendency to become aversively aroused
    c) men's greater ability to turn off aversive arousal
    d) women's greater ability to turn off aversive arousal

    Answer: d   Type: M   Page(s): 404   Key 1: F

60. Men cannot shut down their aversive arousal as quickly as women. This causes husbands to

    a) be verbally abusive toward their wives
    b) withdraw from problems raised by their wives
    c) think through marital problems more carefully than their wives
    d) bring up more areas of disagreement than their wives

    Answer: b   Type: M   Page(s): 404   Key 1: F

61. People report one of four reactions to dissatisfaction in their romantic relationships: exit, neglect, loyalty, and

    a) interest
    b) disinterest
    c) voice
    d) objectivity

    Answer: c   Type: M   Page(s): 405   Key 1: F

62. Otto and Olivia had been fighting ever since they moved in together. But last week Otto told Olivia that he couldn't take it any more, so he was moving out. Theoretically, how did Otto react to dissatisfaction with his relationship with Olivia?

    a) exit
    b) voice
    c) disloyalty
    d) neglect

    Answer: a   Type: M   Page(s): 405   Key 1: A

63. Your text discusses four reactions to dissatisfaction with romantic relationships. Which is the constructive-passive reaction?

    a) neglect
    b) loyalty
    c) empathy
    d) exit

    Answer: b   Type: M   Page(s): 405   Key 1: F

64. Minnie told her long-time boyfriend Max "I can't stand the way you ignore me!" Research shows that Max is more likely to respond constructively to this remark if he

    a) responds immediately
    b) waits before responding
    c) is external in locus of control
    d) is internal in locus of control

    Answer: b   Type: M   Page(s): 406   Key 1: A

65. After a romantic relationship ends, who feels the worst?

    a) the man
    b) the woman
    c) the person who initiated the break-up
    d) the person who was rejected

    Answer: c   Type: M   Page(s): 406   Key 1: F

66. Who is most likely to take an active approach in dealing with problems in a romantic relationship?

    a) a person who is satisfied with the relationship
    b) a person who is dissatisfied with the relationship
    c) a person who has a good alternative to the relationship
    d) a person who has no alternative to the relationship

    Answer: c   Type: M   Page(s): 407   Key 1: F

67. Jane had been dating Jerry for 4 years, and had no other romantic prospects. Jane's lack of other opportunities will predispose her to take a(n) _____ approach to dealing with problems that arise with Jerry.

    a) active
    b) passive
    c) constructive
    d) destructive

    Answer: b   Type: M   Page(s): 407   Key 1: A

68. Psychologists believe that volatile marriages are

    a) inherently unstable
    b) stable
    c) inherently one-sided
    d) equitable

    Answer: b   Type: M   Page(s): 408   Key 1: F

69. Your text discusses three types of stable marriages. Which of the following is NOT one of them?

    a) validating
    b) avoiding
    c) detached
    d) volatile

    Answer: c   Type: M   Page(s): 408   Key 1: F

70. How many types of unstable marriages were discussed in the text?

    a) one
    b) two
    c) five
    d) ten

    Answer: b   Type: M   Page(s): 409   Key 1: F

ESSAY

71. What do people do when they want to attract members of the opposite sex? Do men and women do different things? Be specific in identifying actions that people take to signal that they want a close relationship.

    Answer:
    Students could answer this question by identifying some of the actions listed on page 383. When they want a new relationship, both men and women tell jokes, display their sophistication, increase their exposure to members of the opposite sex, and touch them. To make themselves attractive to a woman, men pay her a lot of attention, brag about their accomplishments, and make it clear that they want sex. To make themselves attractive to a man, women smile, express sympathy, and try to look physically attractive.

    Type: E   Page(s): 383   Key 1: F

72. Once a relationship has progressed beyond the initial stage, deeper commitment depends on at least three factors, as your textbook notes. Identify these three factors, and explain why they are important to relationships. Be sure to describe relevant research.

    Answer:
    As noted on page 384 of the text, couples deepen their commitment to one another by becoming interdependent, by providing one another with mutual support, and by believing in the relationship. The best answer to this question would explain the impact of each of these factors and summarize several of the research studies described on pages 384-388.

    Type: E   Page(s): 384   Key 1: F

73. Your textbook describes four "structures of social life" -- that is, four types of social relationships that people around the world have with each other. Describe each of the four types of relationships, noting the prevalence of each in individualistic and communal cultures. Which type of relationship would, in your opinion, be the best to have in a marriage? Why?

    Answer:
    To answer this question, students should describe the four types of relationships listed in Table 10.1 (p. 390) of the textbook. These are: communal sharing, authority ranking, equality matching, and market pricing relationships. As the textbook notes, communal sharing relationships are most common in collectivistic cultures, while market pricing relationships are most common in individualistic cultures. Students should also indicate which type of marriage they think would be best, by drawing on the material on page 392 of the text.

    Type: E   Page(s): 390   Key 1: F

74. Psychologists have described "four horsemen of the apocalypse" -- that is, a sequence of four destructive behaviors that some couples display when they discuss topics of continuing disagreement. Describe this sequence of behaviors, noting the role typically played by men and women in each stage.

    Answer:
    As noted on page 402 of the text, the "four horsemen of the apocalypse" are: 1) complaining and criticizing, 2) contempt, 3) defensiveness, and 4) stonewalling. Women are more likely than men to complain and criticize (that is, demand that something be done to resolve a disagreement). Men are more likely than women to stonewall (that is, psychologically withdraw from the problem). A complete answer to this question would include physiological reasons for these gender differences.

    Type: E   Page(s): 402   Key 1: F

75. Alvin and Betty, your good friends, have been dating for several years. Now they're having serious problems in their relationship. Having heard that you're taking a course in social psychology, they've come to you to help understand the problems couples usually face and to seek advice for mending their own relationship. What will you tell them? Be sure to cite specific concepts and research evidence that you've learned in this course.

Answer:
Students could answer this open-ended question in a variety of ways. They might begin by summarizing the actions that upset people in close relationships (p. 399), noting that women are usually upset by men's lack of consideration and that men are usually upset by women's possessiveness. They might describe the sequence of four behaviors (on p. 402) that harm relationships: complaining, contempt, defensiveness, and stonewalling. They might note that women usually demand resolution of disagreements, while men usually stonewall because men have a harder time turning off aversive arousal (p. 404). They might tell Alvin and Betty about the four reactions that people have to problems in close relationships: exit, voice, loyalty, and neglect (p. 405); and recommend that the couple attempt constructive reactions (voice and loyalty), rather than destructive reactions (exit and neglect). They might even note that volatile marriages can be highly stable (p. 408). Although students need not review all of these facts when answering this question, they should clearly demonstrate knowledge learned from the text.

Type: E   Page(s): 397   Key 1: A

Chapter 11

Social Influence Through Social Interaction

MULTIPLE CHOICE

1. The first social psychology experiment concerned

   a) children reeling fishing lines
   b) a social dilemma of resource usage
   c) the deleterious effects of stereotypes
   d) competition in a two-person game

   Answer: a   Type: M   Page(s): 418   Key 1: F

2. In studying the records of a league of bicyclists, the early social psychologist Norman Triplett noted that

   a) most bicycle racers were middle-aged males
   b) most bicycle racers were teenage males
   c) bicyclists raced fastest when racing against one another
   d) bicyclists raced fastest when racing by themselves against the clock

   Answer: c   Type: M   Page(s): 418   Key 1: F

3. Animals and human beings intensify their behavior when others of their species are present. This is known as

   a) social loafing
   b) social contagion
   c) social facilitation
   d) psychopresence

   Answer: d   Type: M   Page(s): 419   Key 1: F

4. Research has shown that the presence of others causes people to

   a) eat less
   b) buy less when they are shopping
   c) perform difficult tasks more poorly
   d) wind fishing reels more slowly

   Answer: c   Type: M   Page(s): 420   Key 1: F

5. Albert is trying to learn Swahili, a language he doesn't know. According to research on social facilitation, Albert would be best advised to study Swahili

   a) in the presence of someone who knows Swahili but does not help
   b) in the presence of someone who doesn't know Swahili
   c) in the presence of as many other people as possible
   d) alone

   Answer: d   Type: M   Page(s): 420   Key 1: A

6. Your text discusses a number of factors that cause social facilitation and impairment. Which of the following is NOT one of these factors?

   a) self-presentation
   b) distraction
   c) social identity
   d) evaluation apprehension

   Answer: c   Type: M   Page(s): 420   Key 1: F

7. Research has shown that cockroaches take longer to escape from a lighted maze when

   a) other cockroaches are present
   b) it is in the interest of a group of cockroaches for them not to escape
   c) the maze has been coated with perfume
   d) the maze has been coated with insecticide

   Answer: a   Type: M   Page(s): 420   Key 1: F

8. Because the presence of another person is arousing, it intensifies

   a) the correct response
   b) the incorrect response
   c) any response that would otherwise be inhibited
   d) the easiest, best-learned response

   Answer: d   Type: M   Page(s): 420   Key 1: F

9. Research has shown that the psychological presence of computer monitoring

   a) facilitates the performance of complex tasks
   b) impairs the performance of complex tasks
   c) induces social loafing on complex tasks
   d) has no effect on the performance of complex tasks

   Answer: b   Type: M   Page(s): 421   Key 1: F

10. In a psychology experiment, Barbara was trying to learn a list of words while seated in front of a student who was blindfolded and wearing headphones. Barbara found that she had more difficulty learning the words than she would have had if she had been alone. What is the most likely explanation for this effect?

    a) Barbara felt apprehension over being evaluated.
    b) Barbara was distracted.
    c) Barbara was concerned about her self-presentation.
    d) Barbara felt that she was in competition with the other person.

    Answer: b   Type: M   Page(s): 422   Key 1: A

11. Carla was reviewing for her final exam in social psychology. She had learned the course material quite well, having studied it over and over. Carla was forced to conduct her review session in the presence of distracting bells and buzzers. According to research, these distractions should

    a) make Carla's review slower but more accurate
    b) make Carla's review faster but less accurate
    c) make Carla's review slower and less accurate
    d) facilitate Carla's review

    Answer: b   Type: M   Page(s): 422   Key 1: F

12. When attempting a complex task, people who are highly self-conscious

    a) try as hard as they possibly can
    b) quit trying when they conclude that they're not doing well
    c) complete the task as quickly as possible -- even if this means making a lot of mistakes
    d) avoid making any mistakes -- even if this means performing very slowly

    Answer: b   Type: M   Page(s): 424   Key 1: F

13. As your textbook notes, social loafing is the opposite of

    a) social interaction
    b) social interdependence
    c) social facilitation and impairment
    d) social intensification

    Answer: c   Type: M   Page(s): 424   Key 1: F

14. Social loafing occurs when people

    a) have nothing to do
    b) are more concerned with socializing than with working
    c) are given a task that's impossibly hard
    d) work collectively as part of a team

    Answer: d   Type: M   Page(s): 424   Key 1: F

15. Research has shown that people clap and cheer least loudly when they are clapping and cheering

    a) alone
    b) with one other person
    c) with two other people
    d) in front of a large audience

    Answer: c   Type: M   Page(s): 424   Key 1: F

16. David was helping three other people push Elvira's car out of a ditch. David didn't push very hard because he figured the other guys would push the car out of the ditch anyway. David's behavior is an example of a

    a) free-rider effect
    b) sucker effect
    c) collectivity effect
    d) deindividuation effect

    Answer: a   Type: M   Page(s): 426   Key 1: A

17. Unlike the free-rider effect, the sucker effect

    a) facilitates performance on simple tasks
    b) impairs performance on complex tasks
    c) results when individuals rely on others' contributions
    d) results when individuals worry that others will be relying on their contribution

    Answer: d   Type: M   Page(s): 426   Key 1: F

18. Social loafing seems to reflect all of the following factors EXCEPT

    a) increases in drive
    b) freedom from negative evaluation
    c) the sucker effect
    d) the free-rider effect

    Answer: a   Type: M   Page(s): 426   Key 1: F

19. When performing a task that's meaningful and important, people are especially likely to

    a) show a free-rider effect
    b) show a sucker effect
    c) match the level of effort exerted by their coworkers
    d) compensate for their coworkers' lack of effort

    Answer: d   Type: M   Page(s): 427   Key 1: F

20. Consistent with the notion of social facilitation, intercollegiate swimmers swim faster in relays than in individual events when

    a) individual lap times are announced
    b) only team times are announced
    c) the swimmers are novices
    d) there's no audience watching the swim meet

    Answer: a Type: M Page(s): 426   Key 1: F

21. When people feel that their contribution to a task is dispensable, the result is

    a) social impairment of performance
    b) social loafing
    c) deindividuation
    d) a sucker effect

    Answer: b Type: M Page(s): 426   Key 1: F

22. Fred, a corporate executive, needed his workers to brainstorm about ideas for marketing the company's product. In order to minimize social loafing on this brainstorming task, Fred should

    a) present the task as unimportant
    b) minimize each worker's fear of being evaluated
    c) make sure that each worker feels individually evaluated
    d) make sure that the brainstorming group as a whole feels evaluated

    Answer: c Type: M Page(s): 426   Key 1: A

23. Social impact theory attributes social loafing to

    a) the number and status of influence targets
    b) the number and status of influence sources
    c) one's desire to free-ride on others' contributions
    d) the fear of others taking a free-ride on you

    Answer: a Type: M Page(s): 428   Key 1: F

24. According to _____, the greater the number and status of people who are present, the more they influence our behavior.

    a) social facilitation theory
    b) social impact theory
    c) evaluation apprehension theory
    d) learned drive theory

    Answer: b Type: M Page(s): 428   Key 1: F

25. Conformity to an incorrect answer is greatest when

    a) there's only one person present and s/he gives the incorrect answer
    b) there are many people present and they all give the incorrect answer
    c) there are many people present and exactly half give the incorrect answer
    d) there are many people present and only one gives the incorrect answer

    Answer: b Type: M   Page(s): 429   Key 1: F

26. Gloria was giving a public speech. At first, only one person was watching the speech. A minute later, a second person walked into the room and began watching. Later, a third person walked in and began watching. As Gloria's speech progressed, more and more people filed into the room one at a time and began watching Gloria speak.
    Theoretically, Gloria should have experienced the greatest increase in social impact when the number of spectators

    a) increased from 1 to 2
    b) increased from 2 to 3
    c) increased from 3 to 4
    d) increased from 9 to 10

    Answer: a Type: M   Page(s): 429   Key 1: A

27. Research has shown that people are most likely to stop and stare at a tall building when

    a) it's a warm day
    b) it's a cool day
    c) one person is already staring at the building
    d) ten people are already staring at the building

    Answer: d Type: M   Page(s): 429   Key 1: F

28. The effects of crowding are most easily explained by

    a) social facilitation theory
    b) social impairment theory
    c) social impact theory
    d) social loafing theory

    Answer: c Type: M   Page(s): 430   Key 1: F

29. Research has shown that crowding

    a) has surprisingly positive effects on physical health
    b) makes rats less aggressive
    c) makes enjoyable experiences more enjoyable
    d) makes enjoyable experiences less enjoyable

    Answer: c Type: M   Page(s): 430   Key 1: F

30. To get the biggest tip that she can for each diner that she serves, a waitress should serve

    a) 6 solitary diners who are seated at 6 separate tables
    b) 3 couples who are seated at 3 separate tables
    c) 2 dining trios who are seated at 2 separate tables
    d) 1 group of six diners all seated at the same table

    Answer: a   Type: M   Page(s): 431   Key 1: A

31. Research has shown that people have the highest blood pressure if they must perform a task

    a) in front of a high school student
    b) in front of a Ph.D.
    c) in front of a high school student and a Ph.D.
    d) alone

    Answer: b   Type: M   Page(s): 431   Key 1: F

32. A self-fulfilling prophecy

    a) is initially true
    b) is initially false
    c) concerns the self-image of the person making the prophecy
    d) concerns the self-restraint of the person about whom the prophecy is made

    Answer: b   Type: M   Page(s): 433   Key 1: F

33. The concept of behavioral confirmation has been used to explain

    a) the prisoner's dilemma
    b) social dilemmas
    c) compresence effects
    d) self-fulfilling prophecies

    Answer: d   Type: M   Page(s): 433   Key 1: F

34. In a classic study, college men talked to college women who they didn't know. This research showed that the men made a self-fulfilling prophecy about the women when given

    a) bogus photographs of the women
    b) notes that had supposedly been written by the women
    c) bogus information about the women's intelligence
    d) bogus information about the women's sexual mores

    Answer: a   Type: M   Page(s): 433   Key 1: F

35. Irving is talking on the telephone to Julie. Although Irving has never met Julie, he believes that she's beautiful. As research has shown, Irving's belief will affect

    a) Irving's behavior, but not Julie's behavior
    b) Julie's behavior, but not Irving's behavior
    c) both Irving's behavior and Julie's behavior
    d) neither Irving's behavior nor Julie's behavior

    Answer: c   Type: M   Page(s): 433   Key 1: A

36. A woman is talking on the telephone to a man who believes she's ugly. According to research, the woman is likely to

    a) sound especially warm -- but only if the man states that he believes she's ugly
    b) sound especially warm -- even if the man never says anything about his belief
    c) sound especially uncomfortable -- but only if the man states that he believes she's ugly
    d) sound especially uncomfortable -- even if the man never says anything about his belief

    Answer: d   Type: M   Page(s): 434   Key 1: A

37. In a social psychology experiment, Kathy's job was to find out whether Lynette was intelligent. Which of the following questions would Kathy be most likely to ask Lynette?

    a) How many courses have you failed here at college?
    b) What's your greatest intellectual strength?
    c) What do you dislike about loud parties?
    d) In what situations are you most talkative?

    Answer: b   Type: M   Page(s): 435   Key 1: A

38. Research has shown that information seems most useful when it

    a) confirms our expectations
    b) disconfirms our expectations
    c) concerns an issue about which we have no expectations
    d) concerns an issue about which we are just beginning to develop expectations

    Answer: a   Type: M   Page(s): 435   Key 1: F

39. Behavioral confirmation is most likely to occur when the targets of behavioral confirmation want to

    a) be likable
    b) be right
    c) get to know the other person
    d) disconfirm the other person's stereotypes

    Answer: a   Type: M   Page(s): 435   Key 1: F

173

Social Influence Through Social Interaction

40. Otto talked to four different women who had placed personal ads. Otto believed that all four of these women were beautiful. Which of these women is LEAST likely to show a behavioral confirmation of Otto's belief about her beauty?

   a) Pam -- who desperately wants Otto to like her
   b) Qualinda -- who wants the phone conversation to go smoothly
   c) Rosalind -- who wants to get to know Otto
   d) Sharon -- who is from a lower status background than Otto

   Answer: c   Type: M   Page(s): 435   Key 1: A

41. The distinction between "getting along" and "getting to know" has been used to explain

   a) competition and cooperation in two-person games
   b) behavioral confirmation of expectations
   c) social loafing
   d) social facilitation and impairment

   Answer: b   Type: M   Page(s): 435   Key 1: F

42. In many everyday social interactions, perceivers who hold expectations _____ than the targets of those expectations.

   a) are less likely to initiate social interaction
   b) are less intelligent
   c) are more concerned with being liked
   d) have higher status

   Answer: d   Type: M   Page(s): 436   Key 1: F

43. Max believed that Minnie wasn't very creative. In fact, she was. Minnie would be most likely to disconfirm Max's belief if she

   a) genuinely liked Max
   b) want to impress Max
   c) was highly motivated to express her true identity
   d) wasn't overly concerned about interacting with Max

   Answer: c   Type: M   Page(s): 437   Key 1: A

44. In a classic study, teachers were told that certain of their students would be "late bloomers". This expectation

   a) lowered the IQ scores of students who were relatively unintelligent
   b) had no effect on the IQ scores of students who were relatively unintelligent
   c) raised the IQ scores of students who were relatively unintelligent
   d) had highly inconsistent effects

   Answer: c   Type: M   Page(s): 438   Key 1: F

45. In a classic study, teachers were told that certain of their students would be "late bloomers". Which students did they hear this about?

    a) Students who had performed unusually well on a test of creativity.
    b) Students who had performed unusually poorly on a test of creativity.
    c) Students who had better mathematical skills than verbal skills.
    d) A set of students who had been chosen at random.

    Answer: d   Type: M   Page(s): 438   Key 1: F

46. In a study on teacher expectations, Nellie heard that Hanna was from a poor family. Later, she saw Hanna perform inconsistently on an achievement test, giving some right answers and some wrong answers. After seeing Hanna's test performance, Nellie is likely to be

    a) more biased in her evaluation of Hanna than before
    b) less biased in her evaluation of Hanna than before
    c) more eager to interact with Hanna than before
    d) less eager to interact with Hanna than before

    Answer: a   Type: M   Page(s): 439   Key 1: A

47. Mr. Williams, a third-grade teacher, believes that Oliver is smart and that Paul is not. Research has shown that Mr. Williams is likely to

    a) give longer explanations to Paul than to Oliver
    b) wait longer for an answer from Oliver than for an answer from Paul
    c) praise Paul more than Oliver
    d) smile more at Paul than Oliver

    Answer: b   Type: M   Page(s): 440   Key 1: A

48. Research has uncovered several reasons why teachers treat children differently, based on their expectations about the child's ability. Which of the following is NOT one of them?

    a) Teachers believe that they must compensate to overcome their expectations.
    b) Teachers believe that low expectation children would not do school work unless closely supervised.
    c) Teachers like children who are similar to them better than children who are dissimilar to them.
    d) Teachers believe that low expectation children could not improve no matter what.

    Answer: a   Type: M   Page(s): 440   Key 1: F

49. According to research, what should teachers do if they want to avoid treating students differentially based on their expectations about the students?

   a) acknowledge their own biases
   b) pat low-ability students on the head
   c) try to get to know the students
   d) concentrate on getting students to like them

   Answer: d   Type: M   Page(s): 441   Key 1: F

50. Your textbook presents a three-stage model for self-fulfilling prophecies. Which of the following is NOT one of the stages?

   a) perceiver's initial expectations
   b) target's initial expectations
   c) target's reaction
   d) differential treatment

   Answer: b   Type: M   Page(s): 439   Key 1: F

51. In response to low teacher expectations, students

   a) compensate and try harder to impress the teacher
   b) try to find other adults who have high expectations about them
   c) develop low expectations about their teacher's ability
   d) fail to develop intrinsic interest in learning

   Answer: d   Type: M   Page(s): 442   Key 1: F

52. The "Prisoner's Dilemma" involves

   a) one prisoner
   b) two prisoners
   c) three prisoners
   d) more than three prisoners

   Answer: b   Type: M   Page(s): 444   Key 1: F

53. In the Prisoner's Dilemma,

   a) cooperating is clearly in each individual's interest
   b) people are almost never competitive
   c) consistent competition would, in the long run, be most beneficial
   d) consistent cooperation would, in the long run, be most beneficial

   Answer: d   Type: M   Page(s): 446   Key 1: F

54. In the Prisoner's Dilemma game, cooperators are most interested in maximizing

    a) joint payoffs
    b) their own payoff
    c) the other player's payoff
    d) their own payoff, relative to the other player's

    Answer: a   Type: M   Page(s): 446   Key 1: F

55. In the Prisoner's Dilemma game, a self-fulfilling prophecy leads to

    a) intelligent play
    b) flexible play
    c) cooperative play
    d) competitive play

    Answer: d   Type: M   Page(s): 446   Key 1: F

56. Ted is playing Ursula in the Prisoner's Dilemma. Research on gender differences suggests that

    a) Ted will be more cooperative than Ursula.
    b) Ted will care more about interpersonal relationships.
    c) Ursula will care more about equality.
    d) Prisoner's Dilemma play is unaffected by the gender of the players involved.

    Answer: c   Type: M   Page(s): 447   Key 1: A

57. Dyadic competition refers to competition in which

    a) each player gets only two turns
    b) on each turn there are only two choices
    c) there are only two players
    d) each player has two different objectives

    Answer: c   Type: M   Page(s): 444   Key 1: F

58. Scholars have speculated that human beings spurted ahead of other animals when they developed the ability to

    a) blame their problems on others
    b) blame others' problems on themselves
    c) cooperate
    d) compete

    Answer: c   Type: M   Page(s): 444   Key 1: F

59. At a party next Saturday night, Vanessa plans to have her guests play the Prisoner's Dilemma game. Who is most likely to take a competitive approach to this game?

    a) Wanda, a female extrovert
    b) Xerxes, a male extrovert
    c) Yolanda, Zelda, and Amanda -- a team of highly intelligent women
    d) Bob, Charlie, and Dan -- a team of highly intelligent men

    Answer: d   Type: M   Page(s): 447   Key 1: F

60. Relative to individuals, groups are more likely to maximize

    a) their own payoff without respect to an opponent's payoff
    b) their own payoff relative to an opponent's payoff
    c) the combined payoff of themselves and an opponent
    d) an opponent's payoff without respect to their own payoff

    Answer: b   Type: M   Page(s): 447   Key 1: F

61. GRIT refers to

    a) a method of negotiation
    b) a widely-used two-person game
    c) a public-goods dilemma
    d) a resource dilemma

    Answer: a   Type: M   Page(s): 448   Key 1: F

62. Negotiators are LEAST likely to notice that they agree on an issue if they

    a) agree on a large number of other issues
    b) expect to participate in other similar negotiations later
    c) take the perspective of disinterested observers
    d) perceive that their interests are basically compatible

    Answer: b   Type: M   Page(s): 448   Key 1: F

63. In a social dilemma, the immediate payoff to each participant favors

    a) the development of a relationship over the pursuit of a career
    b) the pursuit of a career over the development of a relationship
    c) cooperation over competition
    d) competition over cooperation

    Answer: d   Type: M   Page(s): 449   Key 1: F

64. The Nuts Game has been used to illustrate

    a) the value of mediation in resolving conflicts
    b) a resource dilemma
    c) the free rider effect
    d) the sucker effect

    Answer: b   Type: M   Page(s): 450   Key 1: F

65. What is the usual result of the Nuts Game?

    a) All of the nuts are gone within the first 10 seconds.
    b) Everyone gets as many nuts as they want.
    c) Women get a larger number of nuts than men.
    d) No one really cares about the game.

    Answer: a   Type: M   Page(s): 450   Key 1: F

66. Research indicates that people are likely to choose a dictatorial leader when

    a) they themselves have a dictatorial personality
    b) others oppose the leader
    c) they fear personal evaluation from an audience
    d) they see that a resource is dwindling away

    Answer: d   Type: M   Page(s): 451   Key 1: F

67. In a drought last summer, the residents of Zuba City Texas didn't have enough water to go
    around. Based on social dilemmas research, what could the mayor of Zuba City have done to
    promote water conservation?

    a) entrust water conservation to the citizens of Zuba City as a whole
    b) entrust water conservation to small groups of citizens
    c) make sure that citizens never talk about the drought
    d) make sure that citizens don't really know how much water is left

    Answer: b   Type: M   Page(s): 452   Key 1: A

68. Trust is important in

    a) preventing the social impairment of performance
    b) maximizing the social facilitation of performance
    c) maximizing cooperation in social dilemmas
    d) preventing the behavioral confirmation of expectations

    Answer: c   Type: M   Page(s): 452   Key 1: F

69. Later this afternoon, Elvira, Fanny, Gary, and Hal will be participating in a social dilemma. Just before the dilemma begins, they will be having a talk. Which of the following comments are they most likely to make?

    a) "I'm going to get what I can while it's still available."
    b) "Everybody should do whatever they want."
    c) "Let me take everything; then I'll give it all back to you."
    d) "Don't anybody be greedy."

    Answer: d   Type: M   Page(s): 452   Key 1: A

70. Just before a social dilemma, an experimenter gave subjects a lecture about moral values. What effect did the lecture have?

    a) It had no effect.
    b) It worked and increased people's tendency to cooperate.
    c) It backfired and increased people's tendency to compete.
    d) It made cooperators more likely to cooperate and competitors more likely to compete.

    Answer: b   Type: M   Page(s): 452   Key 1: F

ESSAY

71. Sometimes the presence of other people facilitates a person's performance; sometimes it impairs a person's performance. Why? Discuss five different factors involved in social facilitation and impairment. Which factor do you think is most important and why?

    Answer:
    Social facilitation and impairment involve: 1) increased "drive" and arousal, 2) evaluation apprehension, 3) distraction, 4) self-presentation, and 5) self-awareness, as noted on pages 420-424. The best answer would explain all these factors, cite one as the most important, and discuss this "most important factor" at greater length.

    Type: E   Page(s): 421   Key 1: F

72. You are designing the workplace of the future. In this workplace, people will be assembling widgets. This is a very easy task. What social factors will have an impact on people's productivity in this setting, and how can you design the work setting to maximize the favorable impact that these factors will have? Be sure to draw on research about social loafing, social facilitation, and social impairment.

    Answer:
    Productivity on this easy task would be maximized if individuals worked in the presence of one another so that there could be a social facilitation of performance (p. 418). Social loafing could be minimized by arranging for each worker's productivity to be evaluated separately from other workers' (p. 426). The best answer would elaborate on these points.

    Type: E   Page(s): 418   Key 1: A

73. A social psychologist recently asserted: "The concepts of social impact theory can be applied to every single phenomenon in social psychology."

    Based on everything that you know about social psychology at this point, do you agree with this assertion? Why or why not? Be sure to support your answer with specifics.

    Answer:
    Although this open-ended question could be answered either affirmatively or negatively, a good answer would demonstrate knowledge of the specifics of social impact theory (as described on pp. 427-431 of the text). The student should note that impact depends on the number and status of social influence sources, as well as the number and status of social influence targets.

    Type: E   Page(s): 427   Key 1: A

74. As a teacher, you don't want your expectations to have any influence on how well your students learn in school. What can you do to prevent your expectations from having any effect? Be sure to describe research in answering this question.

    Answer:
    Expectations might have a smaller impact if teachers tried to "get along" with their students, rather than to "get to know" them. A student who presents this answer might wish to describe the study summarized on p. 435 of the text. In any case, students should show familiarity with some of the material on teacher expectations (pp. 438-443).

    Type: E   Page(s): 438   Key 1: A

75. On certain days of the year, it's better for everyone if no one drives a car. What are the most effective strategies for reducing the number of people who drive on these "pollution alert" days? In answering this question, be sure to use research on social dilemmas.

    Answer:
    The most effective strategies for dealing with this problem would be ones that made people knowledgeable (p. 451) about the social dilemma, and instilled feelings of morality and trust (p. 452). The best answer to this question would elaborate on these points and describe research.

    Type: E   Page(s): 449   Key 1: A

Chapter 12

Helping

MULTIPLE CHOICE

1. As an unwitting subject in a classic social psychology experiment, Billy (a seminary student) is on his way to give a speech about the parable of the Good Samaritan when he sees a man slumped over in a doorway. If he is similar to other subjects in this study, Billy will be LEAST likely to help the man if Billy

   a) has an extroverted personality
   b) has an introverted personality
   c) is late for the appointment to give the speech
   d) is being paid to give the speech

   Answer: c   Type: M   Page(s): 457   Key 1: A

2. Your textbook defines altruism as helping in which

   a) there is absolutely no prospect of reward
   b) the primary benefit sought is an improvement in the other person's condition
   c) the only goal is empathetic joy
   d) the only goal is relief from empathetic distress

   Answer: b   Type: M   Page(s): 457   Key 1: F

3. Your textbook discusses three factors that might create unselfish helping. Which of the following is NOT one of them?

   a) economic conditions
   b) socialization of empathy
   c) the principle of inclusive fitness
   d) people's spontaneous communication of motives and emotions

   Answer: a   Type: M   Page(s): 458   Key 1: F

4. The Carnegie Hero Commission, which recognizes individuals for acts of heroism, almost never recognizes people who rescue a close relative. From the principle of inclusive fitness, what's the best explanation for the Commission's policy?

   a) Recognition would undermine the unselfish nature of such rescues.
   b) Recognition would call attention to the nepotism implicit in such acts.
   c) The Commission simply does not want to include such individuals.
   d) People would rescue their close relatives in any case.

   Answer: d   Type: M   Page(s): 459   Key 1: F

5. Jack, a 45-year-old male, when bailing out a sinking ship, notes that he has room in his lifeboat for only one other person. According to the principle of inclusive fitness, which of the following should he let in the lifeboat?

   a) Alice, a gorgeous 43-year-old female, whom he's never met.
   b) Betty, Jack's 41-year-old wife
   c) Carla, Jack's 69-year-old mother
   d) Darlene, Jack's 12-year-old daughter

   Answer: d Type: M   Page(s): 458   Key 1: A

6. To survive long enough to pass on their genetic characteristics, individuals must excel at two tasks: coping with the environment as individuals and

   a) maintaining the quality of the environment
   b) contributing to a group whose members help each other
   c) coping with their own personality conflicts
   d) attracting a mate

   Answer: b Type: M   Page(s): 458   Key 1: F

7. According to the principle of inclusive fitness, which of the following individuals would, over the course of evolution, have been most likely to pass his characteristics on to succeeding generations?

   a) Zach, a hard-driving hunter
   b) Yang, a pensive loner
   c) Xerxes, who acted for the best interests of others
   d) Ulysses, who looked out only for himself

   Answer: c Type: M   Page(s): 458   Key 1: A

8. People are more likely to help close relatives than distant relatives. This is best explained by

   a) social communication patterns
   b) the spontaneous communication of emotions
   c) the socialization of empathy
   d) the principle of inclusive fitness

   Answer: d Type: M   Page(s): 458   Key 1: F

9. According to the theory of spontaneous communication, people help each other because they

   a) become aversively aroused by the aversive arousal of other group members
   b) know that their act of helping is likely to be spontaneously communicated to others
   c) want others to say good things about them
   d) don't want others to say bad things about them

   Answer: a Type: M   Page(s): 460   Key 1: F

10. Unselfish helping may be created by spontaneous communication, which is

    a) otherwise known as telepathy
    b) completely unprompted by external factors
    c) a strategic display of apparent sincerity to an unwitting receiver
    d) a non-intentional leakage of emotion from one person to another through facial, body, and vocal cues

    Answer: d   Type: M   Page(s): 460   Key 1: F

11. Henrietta, a two-day-old infant, started crying when her diaper got wet. Ingrid, Henrietta's twin sister, was in the adjoining crib. According to the principle of spontaneous communication, Ingrid will

    a) ignore Henrietta.
    b) laugh at Henrietta.
    c) start crying because she shares Henrietta's distress
    d) start crying so that Henrietta won't get all the attention

    Answer: c   Type: M   Page(s): 460   Key 1: A

12. _____ is a likely candidate for an evolutionarily adaptive, biological characteristic that might promote helping within social groups.

    a) Spontaneous communication
    b) Compresence
    c) Camouflage
    d) Mimicry

    Answer: a   Type: M   Page(s): 460   Key 1: F

13. Children have the greatest empathetic arousal for

    a) members of their own sex
    b) members of the opposite sex
    c) adult males
    d) adult females

    Answer: a   Type: M   Page(s): 461   Key 1: F

14. Young infants mimic the facial expressions of adults. This is most likely due to

    a) a spontaneous communication of emotion
    b) the socialization of empathy
    c) a special adult-child attachment
    d) the infant's unique temperament

    Answer: a   Type: M   Page(s): 460   Key 1: F

15. All of the following are types of attachment EXCEPT

    a) anxious/ambivalent
    b) avoidant
    c) sibilant
    d) secure

    Answer: c   Type: M   Page(s): 461   Key 1: F

16. Which of the following children is most likely to develop into an empathetic adult?

    a) Teresa, who has an anxious/ambivalent attachment to her mom
    b) Sarah, who has a secure attachment to her mom
    c) Roganda, who has a sibilant attachment to her mom
    d) Quillian, who has an avoidant attachment to her mom

    Answer: b   Type: M   Page(s): 461   Key 1: A

17. In a study, monkeys could avoid shock if they pressed a lever in response to another monkey's display of distress. Results indicated that this avoidance task could NOT be mastered

    a) unless the distressed monkey could be heard
    b) unless the distressed monkey could be smelled
    c) by monkeys who were raised in isolation
    d) by monkeys who were raised in overcrowded cages

    Answer: c   Type: M   Page(s): 461   Key 1: F

18. Children who have been abused by their caretakers are likely to react to another child's distress with

    a) anger
    b) true empathetic concern
    c) a false appearance of empathetic concern
    d) empathetic concern which may or may not be genuine

    Answer: a   Type: M   Page(s): 462   Key 1: F

19. By rewarding their child's helping behavior, parents

    a) have little effect on the child's social development
    b) increase the child's subsequent likelihood of helping others
    c) paradoxically decrease the child's subsequent likelihood of helping others
    d) will have an effect on the child's helping behavior only if the child has an anxious/ambivalent attachment style

    Answer: b   Type: M   Page(s): 462   Key 1: F

20. In cultures that practice _____, there is a norm of social responsibility, in which people are expected to help those who depend on them.

    a) market pricing
    b) communal sharing
    c) authority ranking
    d) equality matching

    Answer: c   Type: M   Page(s): 463   Key 1: F

21. A norm of equity is imposed in cultures that practice

    a) market pricing
    b) communal sharing
    c) authority ranking
    d) equality matching

    Answer: a   Type: M   Page(s): 463   Key 1: F

22. Barbara lives in a culture that practices communal sharing. Barbara is likely to

    a) refuse to help Carla unless Carla has previously helped her
    b) help Darlene only because it won't involve much effort
    c) help Elvira because she values Elvira's friendship
    d) help Fredericia to precisely the extent that she expects Fredericia will later help her

    Answer: c   Type: M   Page(s): 463   Key 1: A

23. Collectivistic orientations prevail in

    a) rich countries
    b) poor countries
    c) the Southern Hemisphere
    d) the Northern Hemisphere

    Answer: b   Type: M   Page(s): 464   Key 1: F

24. Relative to people who live in collectivistic cultures, those who live in individualistic cultures

    a) are less likely to get divorced
    b) are less likely to be victimized by crime
    c) make friends more easily
    d) have a harder time making friends

    Answer: c   Type: M   Page(s): 464   Key 1: F

25. In dealing with people who are not members of their own group, the members of a collectivistic culture practice

    a) communal sharing
    b) market pricing
    c) authority ranking
    d) empathetic altruism

    Answer: b   Type: M   Page(s): 465   Key 1: F

26. In one study, subjects overheard a woman who was being attacked by her husband. Most of the subjects failed to help the woman. They said that they

    a) thought that the woman could call the police if she wanted to
    b) thought that the "attack" was only part of the experiment
    c) were afraid the husband might attack them
    d) didn't help anybody

    Answer: c   Type: M   Page(s): 467   Key 1: F

27. In a study conducted in the New York City subway system, a victim was unlikely to get help if he looked

    a) effeminate because of the clothes he was wearing
    b) masculine because of his muscular physique
    c) repulsive because of a large birthmark
    d) attractive in his clothes and grooming

    Answer: c   Type: M   Page(s): 468   Key 1: F

28. An experimenter tells Bob that he can go into the room next door. He doesn't mention anything about the room to Charlie. Later, Bob and Charlie overhear a call for help coming from the room next door. Bob goes to see if he can help; Charlie doesn't. The most likely explanation for Bob's greater willingness to help is that

    a) Bob has been socialized to help others
    b) Bob has been cued to feel empathy
    c) Charlie would have to violate an implicit "rule of conduct" to leave the room he's in
    d) Charlie feels slighted by the experimenter

    Answer: c   Type: M   Page(s): 468   Key 1: A

29. In a study, people who felt guilty over touching statues in the Portland Art Museum

    a) objected to being reminded not to touch the statues again
    b) reminded others that they shouldn't touch the statues
    c) helped an art student pick up her pencils
    d) touched other statues when they weren't being watched

    Answer: c   Type: M   Page(s): 469   Key 1: F

Helping

30. You need your roommate's help for a class assignment. The roommate already feels guilty because she misplaced a letter from your parents. According to research, what should you do maximize the probability that your roommate will agree to help you?

    a) nothing
    b) pay her $10 for being a great roommate
    c) praise her profusely in a way that she's not expecting
    d) make sure that she forgets about her guilt

    Answer: a   Type: M   Page(s): 470   Key 1: A

31. On Wednesday, George smashed into his neighbor's car. That made him feel guilty. As a consequence, George

    a) is more likely to give help -- but only to his neighbor
    b) is more likely to give help to anyone
    c) will try to make his neighbor feel guilty
    d) will try to make everyone feel guilty

    Answer: b   Type: M   Page(s): 470   Key 1: A

32. After witnessing someone being harmed, people are

    a) more likely to help others only if they caused the harm
    b) more likely to help others even if they didn't cause the harm
    c) less likely to help others only if they caused the harm
    d) less likely to help others even if they didn't cause the harm

    Answer: b   Type: M   Page(s): 471   Key 1: F

33. Joseph sees Mary drop her books on the sidewalk. Research indicates that Joseph will be most likely to help Mary if

    a) it's a cloudy day
    b) it's a cold day
    c) he wasn't expecting to see anyone
    d) he's just found a quarter in the return slot of a pay phone

    Answer: d   Type: M   Page(s): 472   Key 1: A

34. Subjects who have just received an unexpected gift of cookies are more likely than subjects who haven't received such a gift to

    a) cooperate with an experimenter by annoying people
    b) cooperate with an experimenter by helping people
    c) cooperate with any request
    d) refuse an experimenter's requests

    Answer: b   Type: M   Page(s): 472   Key 1: F

35. People are more likely to answer an experimenter's survey questions on a sunny day than a cloudy day. Why?

    a) Sunshine puts them in a good mood.
    b) On cloudy days, they're afraid they'll get caught in the rain.
    c) Sunny days are warmer.
    d) Cloudy days are windier.

    Answer: a   Type: M   Page(s): 472   Key 1: F

36. Researchers use the phrase "the warm glow of success" to refer to the tendency for

    a) highly successful people to be sexually promiscuous
    b) highly successful people to be extroverted
    c) high temperatures to facilitate performance
    d) positive mood to increase helping

    Answer: d   Type: M   Page(s): 473   Key 1: F

37. Positive mood increases helping EXCEPT when

    a) helping would make the mood even more positive
    b) the mood was induced by an earlier instance of helping
    c) the mood was induced by others' good fortune
    d) the mood was induced by others' bad fortune

    Answer: c   Type: M   Page(s): 473   Key 1: F

38. Researchers have proposed several explanations for the effects of positive mood on helping. Which of the following is NOT one of these explanations?

    a) People who are in a good mood are more likely to notice that others need help.
    b) People who are in a good mood become self-conscious about looking good.
    c) People who are in a good mood exaggerate the likelihood of being rewarded for helping.
    d) People who are in a good mood are more likely to believe that they would get help if they needed it.

    Answer: a   Type: M   Page(s): 473   Key 1: F

39. In an experiment, a drug that was said to "chemically fix" the subject's mood decreased helping by

    a) subjects who were in a positive mood
    b) subjects who were in a negative mood
    c) subjects who were in a neutral mood
    d) all subjects

    Answer: b   Type: M   Page(s): 474   Key 1: F

40. Research shows that helping is

    a) increased by positive mood and decreased by negative mood
    b) increased by negative mood and decreased by positive mood
    c) increased by positive and negative mood
    d) decreased by positive and negative mood

    Answer: c   Type: M   Page(s): 474   Key 1: F

41. People who are in a positive mood help others

    a) only if they think that helping will put them in an even better mood
    b) only if they think that helping won't put them in a worse mood
    c) only for social approval
    d) regardless of the anticipated effects of helping on their mood

    Answer: d   Type: M   Page(s): 474   Key 1: F

42. As part of an experiment, you've just watched another student receive electric shock. Now you're asked whether you would be willing to receive shock, so that the student doesn't have to. Research shows that you're most likely to take shocks in the student's behalf if the student is

    a) a male
    b) a female
    c) similar to you
    d) different from you

    Answer: c   Type: M   Page(s): 476   Key 1: A

43. In an experiment, a subject was given the opportunity to trade places with a student who had been receiving electric shock. The subject's decision was influenced by whether

    a) the subject would have to witness the student being shocked
    b) the experimenter would know the subject's decision
    c) the student would know the subject's decision
    d) the student had demanded that the subject take her place

    Answer: a   Type: M   Page(s): 477   Key 1: F

44. Which of the following leads to unselfish helping?

    a) a feeling of empathetic distress
    b) a feeling of vicarious eustress
    c) a feeling of compassion
    d) a feeling of obligation

    Answer: c   Type: M   Page(s): 477   Key 1: F

45. Four people witnessed Albert get hit by a motorcyclist. Which of these bystanders is least likely to be feeling empathetic distress?

   a) Barb, who is moved by Albert's pain
   b) Cylinda, who doesn't care to know whether Albert will get better
   c) Danielle, who feels sympathy for Albert
   d) Ellen, who will later feel joy simply from knowing that Albert has recovered

   Answer: b   Type: M   Page(s): 478   Key 1: A

46. Empathetic joy results from

   a) merely knowing that another person is no longer suffering
   b) personally giving help to others in need
   c) trying to give help to others in need, even if they don't accept it
   d) reducing one's own empathetic distress

   Answer: a   Type: M   Page(s): 478   Key 1: F

47. People who experience _____ can't regulate their emotional reactions.

   a) empathetic distress
   b) empathetic eustress
   c) empathetic concern
   d) empathetic joy

   Answer: a   Type: M   Page(s): 478   Key 1: F

48. Julie feels soft-hearted and tender every time her younger sister needs help. Julie is experiencing

   a) empathetic eustress
   b) empathetic relief
   c) empathetic concern
   d) primitive passive sympathy

   Answer: c   Type: M   Page(s): 478   Key 1: A

49. Empathetic concern

   a) is motivated by the desire to maintain a good mood
   b) is motivated by the desire to improve a bad mood
   c) can be alleviated by "looking the other way"
   d) cannot be alleviated by "looking the other way"

   Answer: d   Type: M   Page(s): 478   Key 1: F

50. The decision-tree model of helping mentions a number of factors that influence whether or not a bystander helps a person in need. Which of the following is NOT one of these factors?

    a) whether the bystander feels competent to help
    b) whether the bystander expects to feel better by helping
    c) whether the bystander notices the person in need
    d) whether the bystander assumes personal responsibility

    Answer: b   Type: M   Page(s): 481   Key 1: F

51. According to the decision tree model of helping, why do so many people fail to help in emergencies?

    a) emergencies happen so quickly that people don't have time to make good decisions
    b) emergencies arouse so much stress that people aren't able to make good decisions
    c) before deciding to help, people must make a whole sequence of decisions affirmatively
    d) most people decide that they'd rather not get involved

    Answer: c   Type: M   Page(s): 481   Key 1: F

52. According to one model, a bystander decides to help in an emergency situation after following a certain sequence of steps. In order, these steps are

    a) notice the event, feel competent, take responsibility, interpret the event
    b) feel competent, interpret the event, notice the event, take responsibility
    c) notice the event, interpret the event, feel competent, take responsibility
    d) notice the event, interpret the event, take responsibility, feel competent

    Answer: d   Type: M   Page(s): 481   Key 1: F

53. People are more likely to notice an emergency and interpret it as an emergency if they are

    a) alone
    b) in the presence of members of their own sex
    c) in the presence of members of the opposite sex
    d) in a large mixed-sex group

    Answer: a   Type: M   Page(s): 482   Key 1: F

54. Lavonne, an introductory psychology student, is sitting in a psychology laboratory with Marlene and Nancy. Smoke starts pouring into the room. Research suggests that Lavonne will

    a) notice the smoke immediately but not consider it dangerous
    b) notice the smoke immediately and consider it dangerous
    c) not notice the smoke for a while but consider it dangerous when she does notice it
    d) not notice the smoke for a while and not consider it dangerous

    Answer: d   Type: M   Page(s): 482   Key 1: A

55. The diffusion of responsibility principle concerns the effect of

   a) group structure on rules for arriving at group decisions
   b) group structure on the outcome of group decisions
   c) group structure on acceptance of responsibility for group decisions
   d) number of bystanders on helping in emergencies

   Answer: d   Type: M   Page(s): 483   Key 1: F

56. Paul, who suffers from epilepsy, is afraid that he may have a seizure while he's at work. To maximize the likelihood that he'll get help, Paul should try to ensure that

   a) no one is around when he has the seizure
   b) one person is around when he has the seizure
   c) exactly five people are around when he has the seizure
   d) as many people as possible are around when he has the seizure

   Answer: b   Type: M   Page(s): 483   Key 1: A

57. Many of the subjects in a famous experiment didn't help a person who seemed to be having an epileptic seizure. Why?

   a) They didn't notice anything unusual.
   b) They didn't believe that it was a seizure.
   c) They didn't want to ruin the good mood they were in.
   d) They didn't feel personal responsibility to help.

   Answer: d   Type: M   Page(s): 484   Key 1: F

58. In a well-known study, subjects overheard a person who seemed to be having an epileptic seizure. The results of the study showed that

   a) all of the subjects tried to help the seizure victim
   b) none of the subjects tried to help the seizure victim
   c) subjects who didn't try to help within the first three minutes never tried to help
   d) subjects who tried to help but found out that the seizure was fake experienced psychological reactance

   Answer: c   Type: M   Page(s): 484   Key 1: F

59. On Monday Gary, an undergraduate, saw a car accident while he was with Hal, an 8-year-old boy scout. On Tuesday Irv, also an undergraduate, saw a similar accident while he was with Jake, a physician's assistant. On Wednesday, Karl, yet another undergraduate, saw a car accident alone. Who is least likely try to help?

a) Gary
b) Irv
c) Jake
d) Karl

Answer: b   Type: M   Page(s): 484   Key 1: A

60. In a study, Registered Nurses witnessed an accident either alone or in the presence of another student. The student's presence

a) increased the RNs' tendency to help
b) distracted the RNs from noticing the accident
c) decreased the RNs' willingness to take responsibility to help
d) had no effect on the RNs' tendency to help

Answer: d   Type: M   Page(s): 485   Key 1: F

61. Research shows that males are more likely

a) to help a male than a female victim
b) to help a female than a male victim
c) than females to put the needs of others before their own
d) than females to give people long-term emotional support

Answer: b   Type: M   Page(s): 486   Key 1: F

62. In social psychological experiments, males are more likely to help than females. Outraged by this gender difference, Yolanda, a rabid feminist, is determined to design an experiment in which females will be more likely to help than males. What is the biggest challenge Yolanda will face?

a) Females are intimidated when they participate in social psychological experiments.
b) Females give the sort of spectacular, heroic help that's hard to isolate in an experiment.
c) Females give the sort of long-term help that's hard to isolate in an experiment.
d) Females have been socialized to receive help, not give it.

Answer: c   Type: M   Page(s): 486   Key 1: A

63. In most experimental studies, males are more likely to help than are females. Why?

    a) Men are, by nature, more helpful than women.
    b) Most experiments have been designed by male researchers.
    c) Most of the "victims" in experimental studies are women.
    d) Experiments study immediate helping that involves seizing the initiative.

    Answer: d   Type: M   Page(s): 486   Key 1: F

64. In general, females are socialized

    a) to take the initiative to help others
    b) to feel themselves competent to help emergency victims
    c) to be sympathetic
    d) not to help others

    Answer: c   Type: M   Page(s): 486   Key 1: F

65. You have just fallen off a ladder and broken your leg. You are least likely to get help if your accident was overheard by

    a) a group of four strangers
    b) a group of two strangers
    c) a group of four friends
    d) a group of two friends

    Answer: a   Type: M   Page(s): 487   Key 1: A

66. In a research study, an accident was overheard by a group of either two or four students who either had or had not gotten to know one another. The accident victim was least likely to get help from the group

    a) of two students who had gotten to know one another
    b) of four students who had gotten to know one another
    c) of two students who had not gotten to know one another
    d) of four students who had not gotten to know one another

    Answer: d   Type: M   Page(s): 488   Key 1: F

67. In their studies of helping, researchers have found a reverse diffusion of responsibility in

    a) groups of strangers
    b) groups of people who know one another
    c) children
    d) the elderly

    Answer: b   Type: M   Page(s): 488   Key 1: F

68. A comprehensive study conducted in 36 cities across the United States showed that helping was most likely in cities

   a) of lowest population density
   b) of highest population density
   c) that had the warmest climates
   d) that had the coldest climates

   Answer: a   Type: M   Page(s): 489   Key 1: F

69. People are more likely to receive help in a rural area than an urban area. Why?

   a) urban residents have selfish personalities
   b) rural residents have empathetic personalities
   c) urban residents have a false sense of comfort with their surroundings
   d) rural residents are less likely to be distracted

   Answer: d   Type: M   Page(s): 489   Key 1: F

70. You are diabolically plotting to poison your mother, from whom you will inherit $10 million. To minimize the likelihood that a bystander will foil your plot by saving your mother, you should arrange for the poison to take effect when your mother is

   a) in a busy airport
   b) in the small town in which she grew up
   c) with her closest friend, in the friend's home
   d) with her 3 closest friends, in one of the friend's homes

   Answer: a   Type: M   Page(s): 489   Key 1: A

ESSAY

71. Is helping ever unselfish? Answer this question by citing social psychological concepts and research.

   Answer:
   This question can be answered with material drawn from pp. 457-466 of the text. Unselfish helping may reflect the principle of inclusive fitness, the spontaneous communication of arousal, the socialization of empathy, communal sharing relationships, and empathetic concern. The best answer to this essay question would describe research to illustrate each of these factors.

   Type: E   Page(s): 458   Key 1: F

72. Discuss the effects of mood on people's tendency to help. Do positive and negative moods have the same effect? Why?

Answer:
Although positive and negative mood both increase helping, they may do so for different reasons. People who are in a positive mood help for the reasons cited on page 473 of the text. People who are in a negative mood help to improve their mood. The best answer to this question would describe some of the studies summarized in the text.

Type: E   Page(s): 472   Key 1: F

73. Discuss the decision-tree model of helping. Be sure to describe research studies that illustrate the various aspects of the model.

Answer:
This model says that before people decide to help in an emergency, they must: 1) notice the event, 2) interpret it as an emergency, 3) assume personal responsibility, and 4) believe themselves competent to help. The best answer to this question would summarize research to illustrate each of these four decision-points. See pp. 481-486 of the text.

Type: E   Page(s): 481   Key 1: F

74. You suffer from epilepsy. Miraculously, however, you can arrange to have your next seizure whenever and wherever you want. If your goal is to maximize the chance of receiving help from others, when and where will you arrange to have the seizure? Be sure to base your answer on psychological research.

Answer:
This question could be answered in a variety of ways. One might, for example, arrange to have one's seizure around people who know one another (p. 488), who feel familiar with their surroundings (p. 488), and who have medical expertise (p. 485). One might wish to have the seizure while in a rural area (p. 489) and in the presence of only one bystander (p. 483).

Type: E   Page(s): 481   Key 1: A

75. As a benevolent dictator, you want to arrange a society in which people will always help one another. How will you set up your society? In answering this question, be sure to cite psychological research.

Answer:
This question could be answered in a variety of ways. A benevolent dictator might, for example, try to set up a collectivistic culture (p. 464) in which relationships were based on communal sharing (p. 462). The dictator might design a rural society (p. 489) in which everyone knew one another (p. 488) and felt familiar with their surroundings (p. 488). Children would be socialized to feel empathetic concern (pp. 478 and 486).

Type: E   Page(s): 463   Key 1: A

197

Chapter 13

Aggression

MULTIPLE CHOICE

1. Surveys show that _____ of college students have had fantasies of killing someone at least once in their lives.

   a) about 1%
   b) about one-third
   c) about two-thirds
   d) over 98%

   Answer: c   Type: M   Page(s): 491   Key 1: F

2. Jack, a typical male college student, has just had a fantasy about killing Jill. Survey research indicates that this fantasy was most likely to have been prompted by

   a) a roadway run-in with Jill
   b) a dispute at work with Jill
   c) the lover's quarrel Jack and Jill recently had
   d) Jill's public humiliation of Jack

   Answer: d   Type: M   Page(s): 492   Key 1: A

3. Women are more likely than men to have homicidal fantasies about

   a) family arguments
   b) work disputes
   c) roadway hassles
   d) personal threats

   Answer: a   Type: M   Page(s): 492   Key 1: F

4. Which of the following is NOT aggression, as social psychologists define aggression?

   a) John's screaming at his wife Elaine. He did it to make her feel bad.
   b) Jerry's drunk driving accident, in which he killed a bus load of schoolchildren. He didn't mean to hurt anyone.
   c) Jean's suicide. She did it to traumatize her parents.
   d) Joan's attempt to knife Edward. She botched the attempt and "knifed" the couch instead.

   Answer: b   Type: M   Page(s): 492   Key 1: A

198

5. Social psychologists define aggression as

    a) any unprovoked act of violence
    b) any unprovoked act that is designed to inflict harm
    c) any form of behavior that causes physical or psychological injury to someone
    d) any form of behavior that is intended to injure someone physically or psychologically

    Answer: d   Type: M   Page(s): 492   Key 1: F

6. According to the _____, people are "naturally" predisposed to fight and hurt each other, whether in individual conflicts or in wars.

    a) doctrine of automatic aggression
    b) doctrine of inevitable intra-species competition
    c) myth of homo aggressitus
    d) myth of the beast within

    Answer: d   Type: M   Page(s): 492   Key 1: F

7. In 1986, 20 scientists from around the world issued a joint statement declaring that human beings

    a) have inherited a tendency to make war
    b) have not inherited a tendency to make war
    c) should have the right to view sado-masochistic pornography
    d) should not have the right to view sado-masochistic pornography

    Answer: b   Type: M   Page(s): 493   Key 1: F

8. The animals most likely to survive long enough to have children are those who

    a) act aggressively the most often
    b) threaten aggression the most often
    c) act cooperatively the most often
    d) strike the best balance between competition and cooperation

    Answer: d   Type: M   Page(s): 494   Key 1: F

9. George the geneticist selectively bred his dog Fido to be aggressive. Research shows that Fido will be aggressive

    a) against all animals
    b) against dogs, but not other animals
    c) until he loses a fight
    d) throughout his life

    Answer: c   Type: M   Page(s): 494   Key 1: A

Aggression

10. The dominant animal in a group is the one who

   a) controls scarce resources
   b) fights others within the group most often
   c) fights animals outside the group most often
   d) defers to others the most often

   Answer: a Type: M Page(s): 494 Key 1: F

11. The XYY chromosome configuration is more common among _____ than in the population at large.

   a) Nobel prize winners
   b) female wrestlers
   c) prison inmates
   d) all of these groups

   Answer: c Type: M Page(s): 495 Key 1: F

12. Ulysses, a newborn male, inherited an extra Y chromosome from his father. Based on research, what's the likelihood that Ulysses will commit a crime at some point in his life?

   a) About 3%
   b) About one-third
   c) About two-thirds
   d) About 97%

   Answer: a Type: M Page(s): 495 Key 1: A

13. Testosterone is a

   a) female sex hormone
   b) male sex hormone
   c) neurotransmitter that seems to cause aggression
   d) neurotransmitter that seems to inhibit aggression

   Answer: b Type: M Page(s): 496 Key 1: F

14. Ted and Alice just learned that their three-year-old son Bob has unusually high levels of testosterone. From research, Ted and Alice could predict that Bob will grow up to be

   a) unusually intelligent
   b) unusually non-muscular
   c) unusually short
   d) unusually sensitive to frustration

   Answer: d Type: M Page(s): 496 Key 1: A

15. Testosterone levels typically decrease when

    a) an animal wins a fight
    b) an animal loses a fight
    c) a person takes stimulants
    d) a person takes tranquilizers

    Answer: b   Type: M   Page(s): 496   Key 1: F

16. Two-year-old Anna has just seen her mother and father fighting angrily with one another. What's Anna most likely to do just after the fight?

    a) fight with her brother Albert
    b) avoid fighting at all costs
    c) ask for a snack
    d) nothing in particular -- two-year-olds are too young to be affected by their parents fighting

    Answer: a   Type: M   Page(s): 497   Key 1: A

17. Hal, a 42-year-old father, routinely beats his kids. When Hal's kids grow up, they are likely to

    a) be well-mannered
    b) be introverted
    c) be extroverted
    d) beat their own kids

    Answer: d   Type: M   Page(s): 497   Key 1: A

18. In a classic study, nursery-school children saw an adult hit a plastic "punching doll." Later, these children

    a) ate far more ice cream than they should have
    b) refused to eat ice cream even though they loved it
    c) hit the adult who had attacked the "punching doll"
    d) hit a "punching doll" themselves

    Answer: d   Type: M   Page(s): 499   Key 1: F

19. Relative to children who saw a real person attack a plastic "punching doll", those who saw a cartoon of "Herman the Cat" attacking the doll were subsequently

    a) far less aggressive toward a punching doll
    b) far more aggressive toward a punching doll
    c) just as aggressive toward a punching doll
    d) far more aggressive in playing with cats

    Answer: c   Type: M   Page(s): 499   Key 1: F

Aggression

20. Research shows that rates of aggression

    a) are remarkably similar in all human cultures
    b) differ widely from one culture to another
    c) depend almost exclusively on genetic factors
    d) are much lower than rates of pacifism

    Answer: b   Type: M   Page(s): 501   Key 1: F

21. Among the Yanomamo Indians of the Amazon region, approximately 30% of adult deaths are due to violence. Why?

    a) As children, these Indians are taught to be aggressive.
    b) As children, these Indians are not allowed to compete with one another.
    c) These Indians live in extreme poverty.
    d) These Indians must continually combat animal predators.

    Answer: a   Type: M   Page(s): 501   Key 1: F

22. In the United States and other Western cultures, men are

    a) more aggressive than women
    b) less aggressive than women
    c) more empathetic than women
    d) less likely than women to express aggression physically

    Answer: a   Type: M   Page(s): 501   Key 1: F

23. In the United States, boys are more likely than girls

    a) to be taught to empathize with other people
    b) to be taught to empathize with animals
    c) to be picked up and actively handled by adults
    d) none of these

    Answer: c   Type: M   Page(s): 501   Key 1: F

24. Carla is the 10-year-old daughter of Kate. Doug is the 10-year-old son of David. In light of recent trends in American culture, which of the following statements is most likely to be true?

    a) Doug is less aggressive than David was when David was 10.
    b) Doug is more aggressive than David was when David was 10.
    c) Carla is less aggressive than Kate was when Kate was 10.
    d) Carla is more aggressive than Kate was when Kate was 10.

    Answer: d   Type: M   Page(s): 502   Key 1: A

25. Girls are just as aggressive as boys

    a) in competitive sports
    b) in using verbal abuse
    c) at home, but not at school
    d) at school, but not at home

    Answer: b   Type: M   Page(s): 502   Key 1: F

26. Which of the following is most clearly an act of instrumental aggression?

    a) Larry vandalizes Mike's new car to hurt Mike's feelings.
    b) Nick kills Otto for $2 million.
    c) In a fit of anger, Sam whacks Tom over the head with a blunt instrument.
    d) All of these are acts of instrumental aggression.

    Answer: b   Type: M   Page(s): 503   Key 1: A

27. Hostile aggression is

    a) aggression performed in anger -- even if it's for a noble cause
    b) aggression performed in anger -- even if it's for money
    c) aggression engaged in during wartime hostilities
    d) aggression in which the only purpose is to injure and punish

    Answer: d   Type: M   Page(s): 503   Key 1: F

28. In a psychology experiment, male college students were shocked nine times by an experimental confederate. In return, they were most likely to shock the confederate

    a) if the confederate was a young boy
    b) if the confederate was a young girl
    c) if they could see that the confederate was in pain
    d) if they could not see that the confederate was in pain

    Answer: c   Type: M   Page(s): 505   Key 1: F

29. Doug just attacked Ulysses. Psychological research indicates that Doug can minimize the likelihood that Ulysses will attack him back if Doug

    a) pretends that he's in pain
    b) makes sure that Ulysses doesn't know how much pain Doug's experiencing
    c) makes sure that Ulysses knows that Doug's attack was intentional
    d) refuses to apologize

    Answer: b   Type: M   Page(s): 505   Key 1: F

Aggression

30. Laura just made Meagan angry. Meagan is likely to see this incident as

    a) predestined
    b) justified under the circumstances
    c) likely to have long-term consequences
    d) incomprehensible

    Answer: d   Type: M   Page(s): 507   Key 1: A

31. Bob just screamed at Charlie. Bob is likely to see this incident as

    a) having strengthened his relationship with Charlie
    b) having caused long-term damage to his relationship with Charlie
    c) unjustified
    d) incomprehensible

    Answer: a   Type: M   Page(s): 507   Key 1: A

32. In a study, a monkey picked up a cup expecting to find a banana, but found a piece of lettuce Results of the study supported

    a) the notion that aggression is modelled
    b) the frustration-aggression hypothesis
    c) the notion of catharsis
    d) the theory of aggressive instincts

    Answer: b   Type: M   Page(s): 507   Key 1: F

33. Fred plans to break into a line of 400 people who are trying to get tickets for a rock concert. Fred will be most likely to be punched out by the person behind him in line if he

    a) cuts into the front of the line
    b) cuts into the middle of the line
    c) cuts into the back of the line
    d) cuts anywhere into the line -- it doesn't matter where

    Answer: a   Type: M   Page(s): 508   Key 1: F

34. In one study, subjects could turn off a loud noise either by pressing a button or punching a cushion. They punched the cushion

    a) if they'd been drinking alcohol
    b) if they'd been smoking marijuana
    c) if they were paid to punch the cushion
    d) if a machine stopped giving them free coins

    Answer: d   Type: M   Page(s): 508   Key 1: F

204

35. According to a myth called _____, behaving aggressively prevents a later "explosion" of anger.

    a) the frustration-aggression hypothesis
    b) the aggressive cues hypothesis
    c) catharsis
    d) the disinhibition of aggression

    Answer: c Type: M Page(s): 508   Key 1: F

36. The notion of catharsis is that

    a) behaving aggressively increases subsequent aggression
    b) behaving aggressively releases pent-up anger
    c) frustration invariably leads to aggression
    d) aggression is invariably caused by frustration

    Answer: b Type: M Page(s): 508   Key 1: F

37. Research shows that the opportunity to act aggressively

    a) raises a person's blood pressure
    b) raises a person's heart rate
    c) reduces subsequent aggression
    d) increases subsequent aggression

    Answer: d Type: M Page(s): 508   Key 1: F

38. Jess has just been laid off from his job at the auto assembly plant. Research shows that in the end Jess will be most critical of his former employer if he

    a) gets re-employed immediately
    b) has to wait a week before being re-employed
    c) has a chance to talk about his hostility toward the employer
    d) doesn't talk about his hostility toward the employer

    Answer: c Type: M Page(s): 508   Key 1: A

39. In a study, subjects got the chance to shock an experimental confederate while seated beside guns. The presence of the guns

    a) reduced aggression under all circumstances
    b) reduced aggression unless the confederate had a facial scar
    c) increased aggression under all circumstances
    d) increased aggression when the confederate had evaluated the subject negatively

    Answer: d Type: M Page(s): 509   Key 1: F

Aggression

40. Anger is more likely to result in overt aggression when some characteristic of the surrounding context reminds people of aggression, according to the

    a) aggressive cues hypothesis
    b) frustration-aggression hypothesis
    c) theory of instigating situations
    d) theory of cathartic stimuli

    Answer: a   Type: M   Page(s): 509   Key 1: F

41. You've just had a roadway run-in with an ex-marine. The marine is most likely to punch you out if it's

    a) winter
    b) spring
    c) summer
    d) fall

    Answer: c   Type: M   Page(s): 510   Key 1: A

42. In a local bar, Jason insulted Big Ed, a surly 300 pound ex-boxer. Ed is most likely to get violent with Jason if it's

    a) extremely cold in the bar
    b) moderately cold in the bar
    c) moderately hot in the bar
    d) extremely hot in the bar

    Answer: c   Type: M   Page(s): 511   Key 1: A

43. According to excitation-transfer theory, physiological excitation can be transferred from

    a) the sympathetic nervous system to the parasympathetic nervous system
    b) its actual cause to a different object
    c) hostile aggression to instrumental aggression
    d) the victim of an aggressive act to the aggressor

    Answer: b   Type: M   Page(s): 512   Key 1: F

44. Fifteen minutes after riding his bike into work, Lucien was insulted by Max, an obnoxious co-worker. According to excitation-transfer theory, the bike-riding

    a) increases the likelihood that Lucien will punch Max
    b) decreases the likelihood that Lucien will punch Max
    c) increases the likelihood that Lucien will comprehend the insult
    d) decreases the likelihood that Lucien will comprehend the insult

    Answer: a   Type: M   Page(s): 513   Key 1: A

45. Excitation transfer occurs only if people

   a) know why they are excited
   b) don't know why they are excited
   c) have gotten enough sleep the night before
   d) haven't gotten enough sleep the night before

   Answer: b   Type: M   Page(s): 513   Key 1: F

46. As research shows, sexual arousal can increase

   a) men's aggression against men
   b) women's aggression against men
   c) women's aggression against women
   d) all of these

   Answer: d   Type: M   Page(s): 514   Key 1: F

47. Alcohol increases aggression by

   a) making people think about themselves
   b) making people brood over insults and provocations
   c) lowering restraints against aggression
   d) creating an illusion of energy which gets transferred into aggression

   Answer: c   Type: M   Page(s): 515   Key 1: F

48. Alcohol has the biggest effect on aggression if

   a) bystanders would disapprove of the aggression
   b) the aggression was strongly provoked
   c) there was no excuse for the provocation
   d) it's hot, uncomfortable, and the potential aggressor has been exercising

   Answer: a   Type: M   Page(s): 516   Key 1: F

49. Deindividuation refers to

   a) losing track of personal identity
   b) losing track of group affiliations
   c) the cognitive stereotyping of ethnic minorities
   d) the cognitive stereotyping of ethnic majorities

   Answer: a   Type: M   Page(s): 517   Key 1: F

50. Like alcohol consumption, deindividuation

    a) makes people more aware of their negative characteristics
    b) makes people more aware of their positive characteristics
    c) reduces people's inhibitions
    d) increases people's inhibitions

    Answer: c   Type: M   Page(s): 518   Key 1: F

51. Crime is _____ as common in the real world as it is on TV.

    a) ten times
    b) twice
    c) one-half
    d) one-tenth

    Answer: d   Type: M   Page(s): 520   Key 1: F

52. Media violence _____ aggression.

    a) increases
    b) decreases
    c) has no effect on
    d) has inconsistent effects on

    Answer: a   Type: M   Page(s): 521   Key 1: F

53. Just after watching a prizefight on TV, Nick is outraged to learn that his wife Nancy has been having an affair with her boss. Watching the prizefight

    a) increases the likelihood that Nick will murder Nancy.
    b) decreases the likelihood that Nick will murder Nancy.
    c) will have no effect on Nick's likelihood of murdering Nancy.
    d) increases the likelihood of murder if Nick is a college graduate and decreases the likelihood of murder if Nick is not.

    Answer: a   Type: M   Page(s): 521   Key 1: A

54. As laboratory studies show,

    a) media violence increases aggression
    b) behaving aggressively promotes watching media violence
    c) behaving aggressively promotes playing violent video games
    d) all of these statements are true

    Answer: d   Type: M   Page(s): 521   Key 1: F

55. Hanna, the homeowner, shot a masked trick-or-treater, believing that the trick-or-treater was there to rob her. This is an example of

    a) instrumental aggression
    b) hostile aggression
    c) proactive aggression
    d) reactive aggression

    Answer: d   Type: M   Page(s): 522   Key 1: A

56. Thirteen-year-old Johnny was watching a violent show when his little brother broke one of Johnny's toys. Johnny is most likely to react aggressively if the aggressor on the show

    a) was 20 years older than Johnny
    b) was 5 years older than Johnny
    c) was the same age as Johnny
    d) was 5 years younger than Johnny

    Answer: c   Type: M   Page(s): 522   Key 1: A

57. Hal's just been watching an MTV clip that portrayed people trashing homes and stealing cars. Now Hal sees Irving, but not James, give "the finger" to a teacher. Research suggests that Hal

    a) will like Irving more than James
    b) will like James more than Irving
    c) will tell the teacher that Hal gave her "the finger"
    d) will tell the teacher that Irving gave her "the finger"

    Answer: a   Type: M   Page(s): 523   Key 1: A

58. In one study, boys were especially violent in playing floor hockey if the referee used a walkie talkie just before the game. Why?

    a) Earlier, the boys had seen a movie in which violent SWAT team members were using walkie-talkies.
    b) The boys realized that the person on the other end of the walkie-talkie wouldn't be able to see their violence.
    c) The walkie-talkie hadn't been working right, so the referee had screamed at the boys.
    d) The walkie-talkie had emitted a loud screeching sound that irritated the boys.

    Answer: a   Type: M   Page(s): 523   Key 1: F

59. Al, Bob, Carl, and David went to see an intensely violent movie. Which of the four was most aroused by the film?

    a) Al who never watches any media violence
    b) Bob who watches two hours of media violence a day
    c) Carl who watches four hours of media violence a day
    d) David who watches eight hours of media violence a day

    Answer: a   Type: M   Page(s): 524   Key 1: A

60. In one study, subjects watched a fight between two men. Later, subjects who thought that the fight was real were more likely to act aggressively than subjects who thought that the fight was staged. Why?

    a) Those who thought that the fight was real were more physiologically aroused.
    b) Those who thought that the fight was real were not as physiologically aroused.
    c) Those who thought that the fight was real believed that their own aggression was real.
    d) Those who thought that the fight was real did not believe that their own aggression was real.

    Answer: a   Type: M   Page(s): 524   Key 1: F

61. People who watch a lot of TV violence get used to it. This is

    a) deindividuation
    b) disinhibition
    c) desensitization
    d) disacclimation

    Answer: c   Type: M   Page(s): 524   Key 1: F

62. TV viewing doesn't seem to increase aggression in Japan. Why?

    a) Violence is rarely portrayed on Japanese TV.
    b) Japanese audiences view TV violence as mythological.
    c) Japanese programs almost never show the victim suffering.
    d) All of these statements are true.

    Answer: b   Type: M   Page(s): 524   Key 1: F

63. To understand the effect of pornography, it is critical to distinguish between

    a) heterosexual pornography and homosexual pornography
    b) erotic pornography and violent pornography
    c) magazine pornography and videotape pornography
    d) written pornography and pictorial pornography

    Answer: b   Type: M   Page(s): 525   Key 1: F

64. Your textbook defines erotic pornography as pornography that

   a) has serious artistic value
   b) does not involve violence
   c) does not depict full frontal nudity
   d) depicts nude individuals, but not couples in the act of sex

   Answer: b   Type: M   Page(s): 525   Key 1: F

65. In a study, male subjects saw a sexually exploitative cartoon in which men exploited women. Relative to males who saw non-erotic cartoons, these subjects later

   a) were more willing to help a female by taking shocks in her place
   b) were less willing to help a female by taking shocks in her place
   c) gave stronger shocks to a male attacker
   d) gave weaker shocks to a male attacker

   Answer: d   Type: M   Page(s): 525   Key 1: F

66. George was blocked at an intersection when he saw a woman walk across the road. Ten seconds later, George saw the traffic light turn green. George will be most likely to scream at the motorist blocking his path if the woman George saw was

   a) virtually nude
   b) wearing a ridiculous hat
   c) in a wheelchair
   d) in a business suit

   Answer: d   Type: M   Page(s): 526   Key 1: A

67. The rape myth is that

   a) every woman is raped sooner or later
   b) women are sexually aroused by being raped
   c) men cannot be raped
   d) rape is an act of violence

   Answer: b   Type: M   Page(s): 527   Key 1: F

68. In a study, male subjects saw one of two movies about rape. Relative to a movie in which a woman resisted rape, one in which a woman came to be aroused by rape caused the male subjects to

   a) contemplate raping someone themselves
   b) become sexually aroused
   c) give strong shocks to a woman
   d) avoid shocking a woman

   Answer: c   Type: M   Page(s): 528   Key 1: F

Aggression

69. Surveys indicate that about _____ of male college students have used violent pornography.

    a) 1%
    b) one-third
    c) two-thirds
    d) 99%

    Answer: b   Type: M   Page(s): 528   Key 1: F

70. As part of a social psychology experiment, Zack saw a movie in which a woman who was being raped came to enjoy the experience. Later, Zack was carefully debriefed by the experimenter. Participation in this experiment is likely to

    a) increase Zack's acceptance of the rape myth
    b) decrease Zack's acceptance of the rape myth
    c) increase Zack's acceptance of the rape myth if the experimenter was male; decrease it if the experimenter was female
    d) increase Zack's acceptance of the rape myth if the experimenter was female; decrease it if the experimenter was male

    Answer: b   Type: M   Page(s): 528   Key 1: F

ESSAY

71. Are human beings preprogrammed to be aggressive? Cite specific research studies to answer this question.

    Answer:
    Notwithstanding the myth of the beast within (p. 492), human beings are not preprogrammed to be aggressive. In support of this position, students should cite evolutionary considerations, selective breeding studies, and observations on animal aggression (p. 494).

    Type: E   Page(s): 492   Key 1: F

212

72. A scholar recently observed:

"Aggression is just the flip side of altruism. Although social psychologists treat aggression and altruism as though they were unrelated topics, they are actually 'two sides of the same coin.' Every factor that increases altruism decreases aggression, and vice versa. So if you could really understand altruism, you wouldn't need to learn anything else to understand aggression."

In a paragraph or two, comment on the scholar's observation. Do you agree or disagree In your answer, be sure to cite research studies on factors that influence aggression and altruism.

Answer:
Although aggression and altruism may in many respects be "two sides of the same coin," it is not true that "every factor that increases altruism decreases aggression." A bad mood can, for example, increase both altruism and aggression. Males offer more help (of the sort studied in laboratory experiments) than females; and they are also more aggressive. Moreover, potential costs and gains have a big effect on people's willingness to help, yet they have little to do with acts of hostile aggression. The best answer to this open-ended question might cite these asymmetries between aggression and altruism; and would (more generally) use the question as a vehicle for covering several of the major topics in Chapters 12 and 13.

Type: E   Page(s): 504   Key 1: A

73. As a parent, you would like your children to avoid violence whenever possible. What can you do to achieve this goal? How likely is it that your efforts will succeed? Be sure to cite research studies in answering this question.

Answer:
Parents who wish to raise non-violent children should avoid fighting in front of their kids, and should also (of course) refrain from any form of child abuse. By serving as role models, they should teach their children non-violent ways of dealing with life's frustrations. They would also be well-advised to teach their children to empathize with others' problems; and encourage their children not to watch media violence. The best answer to this question would cite research studies to support these points.

Type: E   Page(s): 497   Key 1: A

74. A legislator in your state has called for a complete ban on media violence of any sort, stating that "90% of violent crimes are directly caused by media violence". Do you agree with the legislator's efforts? Why or why not? Be sure to cite research studies in support of your position.

Answer:
In answering this question, students should review experimental and observational studies which indicate that media violence increases aggression. They might also note, however, that it does not increase aggression by females or aggression in Japan or aggression among viewers who focus on the artistic quality of the media depiction (p. 524).

Type: E   Page(s): 520   Key 1: A

75. What are the effects of pornography on aggression? Be sure to cite evidence to support the various effects you describe.

    Answer:
    Erotic pornography does not increase aggression and may in some circumstances reduce it, as various studies show (p. 525). Violent pornography, on the other hand, does increase aggression -- by providing role models of aggression, by arousing excitation that can be transferred into aggression, and by encouraging belief in the rape myth (p. 527). The best answer to this question would cite research studies to support these various points.

    Type: E   Page(s): 525   Key 1: F

Chapter 14

Interpersonal Power

MULTIPLE CHOICE

1. What is the danger to a group if all of the members of the group think alike?

   a) There is no danger.
   b) The group won't be efficient in executing its task.
   c) The group won't define the goals that it's trying to reach.
   d) The group won't be innovative.

   Answer: d   Type: M   Page(s): 532   Key 1: F

2. When the majority of members in a group initially disagree with a minority of members, power is exerted in a number of ways. Which of the following is NOT one of them?

   a) the majority exerts normative influence on the minority
   b) the minority exerts normative influence on the majority
   c) the majority exerts informational influence on the minority
   d) the minority exerts informational influence on the majority

   Answer: b   Type: M   Page(s): 533   Key 1: F

3. In response to informational influence exerted by the majority of people in a group, a minority

   a) complies publicly, but doesn't accept the information privately
   b) complies publicly and accepts the information privately
   c) privately experiences psychological reactance, but doesn't show it
   d) privately experiences psychological reactance and shows it

   Answer: b   Type: M   Page(s): 533   Key 1: F

4. In order to avoid rejection and restore social harmony, a minority

   a) complies with normative influence exerted by a majority
   b) privately accepts normative influence exerted by a majority
   c) offers no resistance to normative influence exerted by a majority
   d) all of these statements are true

   Answer: a   Type: M   Page(s): 533   Key 1: F

5 . Compliance is

   a) cognitive
   b) affective
   c) private
   d) public

   Answer: d   Type: M   Page(s): 534   Key 1: F

6 . As part of a psychology experiment, you must identify the colors of slides being projected
   onto a screen at the front of the room. At the beginning of one particular trial, you were quite
   sure that the slide being projected was yellow. But then you heard four other subjects say
   that it was red. Research shows that you will most likely

   a) say that the slide is red, and believe that it's red
   b) say that the slide is red, but believe that it's yellow
   c) say that the slide is yellow, and believe that it's yellow
   d) say that the slide is yellow, but believe that it's red

   Answer: b   Type: M   Page(s): 535   Key 1: A

7 . In a classic study of conformity, Solomon Asch had subjects judge the lengths of lines.
   Subjects overheard some of their peers give incorrect responses. This study showed that

   a) the minority publicly complied with the majority
   b) the minority privately accepted the judgments of the majority
   c) the majority publicly complied with the minority
   d) the majority privately accepted the judgments of the minority

   Answer: a   Type: M   Page(s): 535   Key 1: F

8 . Tammy, Betty, and Susan were the three members of a college quiz bowl team. In response
   to a question about leaders during World War II, Tammy was absolutely
   sure that the answer was Hitler, but Betty and Susan both stated (incorrectly) that the answer
   was Mussolini. Research shows that Tammy is most likely to go along with Betty and
   Susan's answer if

   a) Tammy doesn't fear rejection
   b) Tammy, Betty, and Susan are similar to one another
   c) Susan is similar to Betty, but Tammy is different
   d) Tammy is similar to Betty, but Susan is different

   Answer: b   Type: M   Page(s): 536   Key 1: A

9. Bob knew that he was right not to smoke marijuana, but was afraid that if he didn't try it he would never get a fraternity bid. Bob is

    a) experiencing psychological reactance
    b) motivated to engage in symbolic self-completion
    c) being subjected to normative influence
    d) being subjected to informational influence

    Answer: c   Type: M   Page(s): 536   Key 1: A

10. Sally was sure that she was right not to let Albert drive her home, because Albert was completely drunk. But Sally's date and her friends said Albert could drive just fine. Sally is least likely to ride home with Albert if

    a) she's scared of being rejected
    b) everyone is in a big hurry
    c) everyone stops talking to Sally
    d) Teresa agrees that Albert should not drive

    Answer: d   Type: M   Page(s): 536   Key 1: A

11. In a famous experiment, Sherif used the visual hallucination known as the autokinetic effect in order to

    a) demonstrate normative influence
    b) demonstrate informational influence
    c) show that minorities can convert majorities
    d) show that majorities reject minorities who refuse to go along

    Answer: b   Type: M   Page(s): 536   Key 1: F

12. Because people want to understand and perceive reality correctly, they are subject to

    a) normative influence
    b) epistemic influence
    c) informational influence
    d) none of the above

    Answer: c   Type: M   Page(s): 536   Key 1: F

13. With informational influence, majorities

    a) break up into minorities
    b) form coalitions with competing groups
    c) establish norms
    d) motivate compliance

    Answer: c   Type: M   Page(s): 537   Key 1: F

14. As a subject in a psychology experiment, you're asked to judge how far a light has moved. You're not really sure, but you think it moved about 2 inches. Now you hear one subject say that it moved 6 inches and a second subject say that it moved 4 inches. Research indicates that you are most likely to

    a) say that the light moved 2 inches and believe that it moved 2 inches
    b) say that the light moved 2 inches, but believe that it moved 3 inches
    c) say that the light moved 3 inches, but believe that it moved 2 inches
    d) say that the light moved 3 inches and believe that it moved 3 inches

    Answer: d   Type: M   Page(s): 537   Key 1: A

15. The norms produced by informational influence

    a) are temporary
    b) can last for generations
    c) involve the action, but not the feeling component of attitudes
    d) involve the feeling, but not the action component of attitudes

    Answer: b   Type: M   Page(s): 537   Key 1: F

16. Informational influence is strongest when

    a) group members are similar to one another
    b) group members are different from one another
    c) the task is difficult
    d) the task is easy

    Answer: c   Type: M   Page(s): 538   Key 1: F

17. The sheer number of people in a majority

    a) has a big effect on both informational and normative influence
    b) has little effect of either informational or normative influence
    c) has a bigger effect on normative influence than informational influence
    d) has a bigger effect on informational influence than normative influence

    Answer: c   Type: M   Page(s): 538   Key 1: F

18. Carl and David were attending the same physics class. Neither one was doing well in the class, and both were considering whether or not to get some tutoring. Two friends told Carl that they had gotten tutored. Twenty friends told David that they had gotten tutored. Relative to Carl, David is more likely to

    a) say that tutoring would be good for him, and believe it
    b) say that tutoring would be good for him, but not believe it
    c) believe that tutoring would be good for him, but not say it
    d) neither say nor believe that tutoring would be good for him

    Answer: b   Type: M   Page(s): 538   Key 1: A

19. Most instances of conformity involve

    a) informational influence, but not normative influence
    b) normative influence, but not informational influence
    c) both normative and informational influence
    d) neither normative nor informational influence

    Answer: c   Type: M   Page(s): 539   Key 1: F

20. Private acceptance is also known as

    a) projection
    b) compliance
    c) reification
    d) internalization

    Answer: d   Type: M   Page(s): 539   Key 1: F

21. Earl was drafted into the Army and hated it. But over time he began to identify with the guys in his unit. This is most likely to change Earl's

    a) private compliance into public acceptance
    b) private acceptance into public compliance
    c) public compliance into private acceptance
    d) public acceptance into private compliance

    Answer: c   Type: M   Page(s): 539   Key 1: A

22. Research shows that minorities

    a) don't really have any effects
    b) affect other minorities, but not majorities
    c) influence majorities who wonder whether they may be wrong
    d) influence majorities who fear revolution

    Answer: c   Type: M   Page(s): 540   Key 1: F

23. Minority influence is strongest when

    a) the minority is consistent
    b) the majority had formerly been consistent
    c) the task is easy
    d) the majority must respond in public

    Answer: a   Type: M   Page(s): 541   Key 1: F

24. Fred had always assumed that the world was round, since that's the majority view of his culture. Then Fred heard his neighbor and a few acquaintances state that the world was flat. According to research on minority influence, this will

    a) motivate Fred to publicly state that the world is flat
    b) motivate Fred to ostracize his neighbor and acquaintances
    c) broaden Fred's thinking
    d) narrow Fred's thinking

    Answer: c   Type: M   Page(s): 541   Key 1: A

25. Minority influence has

    a) an immediate effect on acceptance
    b) a latent effect on acceptance
    c) an immediate effect on compliance
    d) a latent effect on compliance

    Answer: b   Type: M   Page(s): 541   Key 1: F

26. Gloria came to be influenced over time, but didn't want to admit it. It is most likely that Gloria was responding to

    a) informational influence from the majority
    b) informational influence from a minority
    c) normative influence from the majority
    d) normative influence from a minority

    Answer: b   Type: M   Page(s): 541   Key 1: A

27. Minority influence is biggest when

    a) the influence is measured immediately
    b) the influence is measured directly
    c) it's a big minority
    d) it's a small minority

    Answer: d   Type: M   Page(s): 542   Key 1: F

28. Divergent, creative thinking results from

    a) informational influence by the majority
    b) normative influence by the majority
    c) informational influence by the minority
    d) normative influence by the minority

    Answer: c   Type: M   Page(s): 542   Key 1: F

29. Hap had always assumed that his 50 fraternity buddies were right in hating Professor Smedley, but then two of Smedley's students told Hap that Smedley was really a great guy. According to work on minority influence, Hap will

    a) not want to lose face with his fraternity brothers
    b) fear rejection by these two students
    c) become less tolerant in his thinking
    d) all of these statements are true

    Answer: a   Type: M   Page(s): 542   Key 1: A

30. Research suggests that in order to have maximal influence, a minority must

    a) be consistent in stating its position
    b) be unwilling to compromise
    c) appear open-minded
    d) do all of these things

    Answer: d   Type: M   Page(s): 544   Key 1: F

31. Your textbook discusses six types of interpersonal power. Which of the following is NOT one of them?

    a) informational power
    b) legitimate power
    c) referent power
    d) peer power

    Answer: d   Type: M   Page(s): 545   Key 1: F

32. Which type of power involves emphasizing a common identity?

    a) collective power
    b) referent power
    c) informational power
    d) legitimate power

    Answer: b   Type: M   Page(s): 545   Key 1: F

33. Irene wanted to have informational power over the women who worked with her. To get this power, Irene must

    a) disclose a lot about herself to the women
    b) threaten to blackmail the women with information she's learned about them
    c) persuade the women that she knows best
    d) have more knowledge that the women

    Answer: c   Type: M   Page(s): 546   Key 1: A

34. Everyone knew that Kathy was the leader of her sorority. Because of the norms of the sorority, they all felt obligated to do what she said. Kathy had

    a) intrinsic power
    b) extrinsic power
    c) legitimate power
    d) illegitimate power

    Answer: c   Type: M   Page(s): 547   Key 1: A

35. Larry had coercive power over his employees. In order to get this power, Larry would have had to

    a) punish his employees
    b) tell his employees that if they didn't do what he said, he would punish them
    c) tell his employees that they had no choice but to do what he said
    d) do none of these

    Answer: d   Type: M   Page(s): 547   Key 1: A

36. Mary and Nancy were managers in a large business firm. Mary managed 10 people. Nancy managed Mary and 99 other people. According to research,

    a) Nancy will use reward power more than Mary
    b) Mary will use reward power more than Nancy
    c) Nancy will use expert power more than Mary
    d) Mary will use expert power more than Nancy

    Answer: a   Type: M   Page(s): 547   Key 1: A

37. Your text discusses three theories of leadership. Which of the following is NOT one of them?

    a) the "great person" perspective
    b) the situational perspective
    c) the reciprocal perspective
    d) the contingency theory

    Answer: c   Type: M   Page(s): 548   Key 1: F

38. The _____ perspective on leadership emphasizes the traits of leaders.

    a) attributional
    b) Zeitgeist
    c) "great person"
    d) situational

    Answer: c   Type: M   Page(s): 548   Key 1: F

39. Otto was chosen to be captain of the basketball team because he was in the right place at the right time. This would have been predicted by the _____ perspective on leadership.

    a) spatiotemporal
    b) situational
    c) contingency
    d) "great person"

    Answer: b   Type: M   Page(s): 549   Key 1: A

40. Patricia was participating in a discussion group. Research shows that Patricia is most likely to be seen as leader of the group if she

    a) says nothing
    b) makes only a few remarks, but those remarks are highly perceptive
    c) talks neither more nor less than the average member of the group
    d) talks more than anyone else

    Answer: d   Type: M   Page(s): 549   Key 1: A

41. According to the contingency theory of leadership,

    a) the group member who acts as leader depends on what the group needs to accomplish
    b) whether or not the group needs a leader depends on what the group needs to accomplish
    c) a leader's power is contingent on the leader's intelligence
    d) a leader's power is contingent on the leader's personality

    Answer: a   Type: M   Page(s): 550   Key 1: F

42. The Least Preferred Co-Worker (LPC) scale is most often used in work on

    a) intergroup conflict
    b) intragroup conflict
    c) social loafing
    d) leadership

    Answer: d   Type: M   Page(s): 550   Key 1: F

43. The contingency theory of leadership emphasizes the differences between two types of leaders:

    a) masculine and feminine
    b) task-oriented and relationship-oriented
    c) thinking and feeling
    d) authoritarian and laissez-faire

    Answer: b   Type: M   Page(s): 550   Key 1: F

44. According to the contingency theory of leadership, when will the best leader be someone who is relationship-oriented?

    a) under conditions that are highly favorable to leadership
    b) under conditions that are highly unfavorable to leadership
    c) under conditions that are moderately favorable to leadership
    d) never

    Answer: c   Type: M   Page(s): 550   Key 1: F

45. Quinn, a highly task-oriented individual, was chosen to be Dean at a women's college. Research indicates that Quinn will feel the most stress if she

    a) has a lot of power to reward and punish subordinates
    b) has moderate power to reward and punish subordinates
    c) has little power to reward and punish subordinates
    d) has clear guidelines about how to do her job

    Answer: b   Type: M   Page(s): 551   Key 1: A

46. As research shows, training on an impersonal task benefits

    a) both task-oriented and relationship-oriented leaders a lot
    b) neither task-oriented nor relationship-oriented leaders
    c) task-oriented leaders more than relationship-oriented leaders
    d) relationship-oriented leaders more than task-oriented leaders

    Answer: d   Type: M   Page(s): 552   Key 1: F

47. Studies of mixed-sex groups show that men are

    a) always more likely than women to be chosen as leaders
    b) always less likely than women to be chosen as leaders
    c) chosen as leaders by groups that have a "masculine" task
    d) chosen as leaders by psychotherapy groups

    Answer: c   Type: M   Page(s): 553   Key 1: F

48. Roger and Teresa, two workers at a small manufacturing firm, were about to get a new boss. According to research on sex differences, which of the two would prefer to have a male, rather than a female boss?

    a) both Roger and Teresa
    b) neither Roger nor Teresa
    c) Roger, but not Teresa
    d) Teresa, but not Roger

    Answer: a   Type: M   Page(s): 553   Key 1: A

49. As leaders, women almost have to be "twice as good as a men"

    a) if the group needs a relationship-oriented leader
    b) if the group needs a task-oriented leader
    c) under all circumstances
    d) when the previous leader was a woman

    Answer: b   Type: M   Page(s): 554   Key 1: F

50. When a woman is chosen to lead a group, the members of the group expect her to

    a) provide information
    b) provide interpersonal support
    c) act like a man
    d) look like a man

    Answer: b   Type: M   Page(s): 554   Key 1: F

51. Experimental research indicates that when a woman takes over solo leadership of a group, the members of the group will

    a) rate her as more effective than a man who takes over
    b) rate her as highly feminine
    c) smile
    d) frown

    Answer: d   Type: M   Page(s): 555   Key 1: F

52. Who were the subjects in the Stanford prison study?

    a) highly stable women
    b) highly unstable women
    c) highly stable men
    d) highly unstable men

    Answer: c   Type: M   Page(s): 557   Key 1: F

53. In the Stanford prison study, some subjects served as guards; others served as prisoners. Who served in which role?

    a) Subjects who had stable personalities served as guards; subjects with unstable personalities served as prisoners.
    b) Subjects who were naturally aggressive served as guards; subjects who were naturally unaggressive served as prisoners.
    c) Males served as guards; females served as prisoners.
    d) None of these statements are true.

    Answer: d   Type: M   Page(s): 557   Key 1: F

54. Sam and Dave were participating in the Stanford prison experiment. Sam was serving as a guard, while Dave was serving as a prisoner. If these two subjects are typical,

    a) Sam will abuse his power, and Dave will obey
    b) Sam will abuse his power, and Dave will rebel
    c) Sam will treat Dave humanely, and Dave will taunt Sam
    d) Sam and Dave will treat one another humanely

    Answer: a   Type: M   Page(s): 558   Key 1: A

55. Why did people act so deplorably in the Stanford Prison study?

    a) because the experimenter ordered them to do so
    b) because of the situation and an arbitrary label
    c) because of their personalities and unusual backgrounds
    d) because of the intense environmental stress they were under

    Answer: b   Type: M   Page(s): 559   Key 1: F

56. The 1967-1974 Greek military regime was successful in training torturers. Who did they select as trainees?

    a) murderers
    b) mental patients
    c) ordinary well-adjusted men
    d) none of the above

    Answer: c   Type: M   Page(s): 559   Key 1: F

57. Subjects in Milgram's obedience studies were

    a) Yale undergraduates
    b) Yale professors
    c) men from a variety of backgrounds
    d) women from a variety of backgrounds

    Answer: c   Type: M   Page(s): 560   Key 1: F

58. Joe participated in the famous Milgram obedience studies at Yale University. At the beginning of the experiment, Joe was told that the study concerned

    a) the effect of reward on learning
    b) the effect of punishment on learning
    c) obedience to evil authority
    d) obedience to benevolent authority

    Answer: b   Type: M   Page(s): 560   Key 1: A

59. In Milgram's studies of obedience, subjects were ordered to

    a) act brutally toward mock prisoners
    b) act brutally toward school children
    c) eat a live worm
    d) give electric shock to a man

    Answer: d   Type: M   Page(s): 561   Key 1: F

60. Milgram asked people to predict how many subjects would obey an experimenter in giving 450-volt shocks to an innocent man. They said that

    a) about 3% would obey
    b) about 33% would obey
    c) about 65% would obey
    d) about 95% would obey

    Answer: a   Type: M   Page(s): 562   Key 1: F

61. In a famous study, Milgram ordered subjects to give 450-volt shocks to an innocent man. What percentage of subjects obeyed Milgram all the way to the end?

    a) about 5%
    b) about 15%
    c) about 65%
    d) about 95%

    Answer: c   Type: M   Page(s): 562   Key 1: F

62. Zach has just finished participating in Milgram's famous study of obedience. In a post-experimental debriefing, Zach will now hear

    a) that he has really shocked an innocent man
    b) that the man whom he shocked was a masochist
    c) that he has not really shocked anyone
    d) nothing -- subjects were not debriefed in this study

    Answer: c   Type: M   Page(s): 562   Key 1: A

63. In a series of follow-up studies to his famous experiment, Milgram studied a number of factors that might influence obedience to authority. Which of the following was NOT one of them?

    a) whether the subject was a psychopath
    b) whether the victim was physically close to the subject
    c) whether the experimenter was physically close to the subject
    d) the number of experimenters

    Answer: a   Type: M   Page(s): 562   Key 1: F

64. In a follow-up study to Milgram's work on obedience, children in Jordan were ordered to administer shock to a same-sex peer. Results showed that

   a) virtually none of the children obeyed
   b) most of the children obeyed
   c) more subjects obeyed an adult experimenter than a child experimenter
   d) more subjects obeyed a child experimenter than an adult experimenter

   Answer: b   Type: M   Page(s): 563   Key 1: F

65. A follow-up to Milgram's study of obedience showed that people in the Netherlands

   a) refuse to ruin an applicant's chances of getting a job
   b) obey when told to ruin an applicant's chances of getting a job
   c) want to ruin an applicant's chances of getting a job
   d) no such follow-up work was ever done

   Answer: b   Type: M   Page(s): 563   Key 1: F

66. Your textbook describes a number of studies that were conducted to follow up Milgram's famous study of obedience. Which of the following is NOT one of them?

   a) a study in Jordan of children being ordered to give electric shock
   b) a study in the Netherlands of people ruining an applicant's chances of getting a job
   c) a study in Japan of college students being ordered to take their own lives
   d) a study in the U.S. of nurses being ordered to give a drug overdose

   Answer: c   Type: M   Page(s): 564   Key 1: F

67. A number of studies have been done on obedience to evil authority. These show that

   a) in general people don't obey evil authority
   b) people obeyed evil authority in Milgram's study, but not in the more recent studies
   c) Americans are more willing to obey evil authority than Germans
   d) in general people are willing to obey evil authority

   Answer: d   Type: M   Page(s): 564   Key 1: F

68. Your textbook discusses a number of factors that increase people's willingness to obey orders to harm innocent people. Which of the following is NOT one of them?

   a) if the people perceive that they are not personally responsible
   b) if the people in fact have no choice
   c) if the person giving the orders has legitimate authority
   d) if the commitment to obeying the orders is gradual

   Answer: b   Type: M   Page(s): 565   Key 1: F

69. Albert wants to use the foot-in-the-door effect to get Alice to loan him $50. To do so, Albert should

    a) tell Alice that Betty is loaning him $500
    b) tell Alice that Betty is loaning him $5
    c) first ask Alice to loan him $500
    d) first ask Alice to loan him $5

    Answer: d   Type: M   Page(s): 565   Key 1: A

70. In a follow-up to Milgram's study, fewer people obeyed orders to give a man electric shock if

    a) they were made to feel personally responsible
    b) the study was conducted in a seedy office building, rather than a University
    c) a confederate disobeyed the experimenter
    d) all of these reduced obedience

    Answer: d   Type: M   Page(s): 566   Key 1: F

ESSAY

71. How do majorities and minorities influence one another? In what ways are these forms of influence similar? In what ways do they differ? In answering this question, be sure to summarize social psychological concepts and research.

    Answer:
    Students should answer this question by drawing on the material on pages 532-544 of the text. As noted there, majorities can exert two types of influence: normative influence (on minorities who want to avoid rejection) and informational influence (on minorities who want to be right). Minorities exert informational influence only. There are different responses to these forms of influence, as noted on page 533. The best answer to this question would elaborate on these points, noting the distinction between public compliance and private acceptance.
    Type: E   Page(s): 533   Key 1: F

72. You are head of an organization that favors increasing welfare payments to single parents. In the current political climate, this is a minority view. Based on research, what can you do to maximize the impact of your minority on the majority of people? What sort of impact can you expect to have? Be specific.

    Answer:
    Students can answer this question by drawing on the material on pages 539-544 of the text. As noted there, minorities are most effective if they are consistent and small. Although minorities are unlikely in the short run to get majorities to comply publicly with their positions, in the long run they may obtain converts and encourage open-minded thinking.
    Type: E   Page(s): 539   Key 1: A

73. There are six types of interpersonal power. Define each of the six types and give an example of each. In what sort of situation is each type of power used? In your opinion, what is the most useful type of power? What is the least useful? Why?

    Answer:
    Students can answer this question by summarizing the material in Table 14.2 (p. 546). Listed there are descriptions of expert power, referent power, informational power, legitimate power, reward power, and coercive power. Students should define and give examples of each of these six. As noted on page 547, higher-level managers are more likely than lower-level managers to use reward power, coercive power, and legitimate power.

    Type: E   Page(s): 546   Key 1: F

74. Discuss the contingency theory of leadership. What is the theory? Does it seem to be valid? Be specific.

    Answer:
    Students can answer this question by summarizing the material on pages 549-552 of the text. The contingency theory of leadership says that different types of leaders are most effective in different situations. Task-oriented leaders are most effective in situations that are either highly favorable or highly unfavorable to the exercise of leadership; relationship-oriented leaders are most effective in situations that are moderately favorable. Research has supported the theory, and suggested that training helps relationship-oriented leaders but not task-oriented leaders.

    Type: E   Page(s): 549   Key 1: F

75. You're afraid that if present trends continue, the U.S. may someday be taken over by an evil authority figure. If so, what is the likelihood that U.S. citizens would obey their leader's evil commands? What factors would increase American citizens' tendency to obey evil authority? What factors would reduce their tendency to obey? Base your answer on social psychological research, and summarize at least two relevant studies.

    Answer:
    To answer this question, students will need to draw on the material on pages 556-566 of the text. The research summarized there suggests that Americans would indeed be likely to obey an evil authority figure's commands. Their tendency to obey would be increased by the authority having legitimate power, by their making a gradual commitment to obedience, to their feeling no personal responsibility, and by there being few people who disobey (p. 566). These conclusions are evident from the results of a number of studies, including the Stanford prison study (p. 557) and Milgram's study of obedience (p. 560). Two such studies should be described.

    Type: E   Page(s): 556   Key 1: F

Chapter 15

Groups

MULTIPLE CHOICE

1. Jack was on trial for murdering Jill. Prior to jury deliberation, the typical member of Jack's jury thought that he should get 25 years in prison for his crime. After deliberating, they thought he should get only 15 years in prison. From research, we can guess that all of Jack's jurors are

   a) men
   b) women
   c) authoritarians
   d) non-authoritarians

   Answer: d   Type: M   Page(s): 570   Key 1: A

2. You are the prosecuting attorney in a murder case. All of the jurors in the case have authoritarian personalities. If your goal is to maximize the sentence the defendant receives, you should urge jurors to

   a) set aside their own personalities when deciding on a sentence
   b) ask some non-authoritarians for input into the sentence
   c) deliberate before deciding on a sentence
   d) decide on a sentence without deliberating

   Answer: c   Type: M   Page(s): 570   Key 1: A

3. Which of the following would a social psychologist consider a "group"?

   a) the 12 people who are taking Dr. Smith's anthropology seminar this semester
   b) all of the people who have ever taken a course in anthropology
   c) redheads
   d) Social psychologists would regard all of these as groups.

   Answer: a   Type: M   Page(s): 571   Key 1: A

4. According to a social psychological definition, _____ are "social aggregates that involve mutual awareness and potential mutual interaction."

   a) collectives
   b) groups
   c) interpersonal categories
   d) crowds

   Answer: b   Type: M   Page(s): 571   Key 1: F

231

Groups

5. All of the following are types of groups EXCEPT

   a) standing crews
   b) embedded systems
   c) crowds
   d) expeditions

   Answer: c   Type: M   Page(s): 571   Key 1: F

6. Which type of group engages in broad activities for a limited time?

   a) an expedition
   b) a crew
   c) an embedded system
   d) a task force

   Answer: a   Type: M   Page(s): 572   Key 1: F

7. Bobbie your roommate notes: "I see Tom Cruise every summer. His vacation home is right next to my family's." Bobbie is

   a) making an upward social comparison
   b) making a downward social comparison
   c) making a horizontal social comparison
   d) basking in reflected glory

   Answer: d   Type: M   Page(s): 572   Key 1: A

8. Basking in reflected glory refers to

   a) taking credit for your current accomplishments
   b) publicizing your accomplishments of the distant past
   c) emphasizing your association with someone who's successful
   d) emphasizing your differences from someone who's unsuccessful

   Answer: c   Type: M   Page(s): 572   Key 1: F

9. Research indicates that on Mondays after a school sports team wins students will

   a) do unusually well on exams
   b) do unusually poorly on exams
   c) wear clothes that display the school name
   d) wear the latest fashions

   Answer: c   Type: M   Page(s): 573   Key 1: F

10. Carl, a student at Skew U., was talking on the phone to his brother David the night after Skew had won a big game. David asked how Skew had fared in the game. We would most expect Carl to say "WE won" if

    a) Carl had just aced an important exam
    b) Carl had just flunked an important exam
    c) Carl had just learned about David's acing an important exam
    d) Carl had just learned about David's flunking an important exam

    Answer: b   Type: M   Page(s): 574   Key 1: A

11. People are most likely to bask in reflected glory when

    a) their individual self-esteem has just been threatened
    b) their individual self-esteem has just been lowered
    c) they're around people who have low self-esteem
    d) they're around people who have high self-esteem

    Answer: b   Type: M   Page(s): 574   Key 1: F

12. Herman, a diehard Notre Dame football fan, had just watched Notre Dame lose a big game 54-0. According to research, watching this game should lower Herman's

    a) tendency to be aggressive
    b) tendency to be altruistic
    c) need to be unique
    d) expectation that Judy (an attractive woman) will accept Herman's invitation to go out on a date

    Answer: d   Type: M   Page(s): 574   Key 1: A

13. Collective self-esteem is

    a) the mutual esteem that group members have for one another
    b) the self-esteem that derives from a positive group identity
    c) primarily experienced by people with low individual self-esteem
    d) more important to psychological health than individual self-esteem

    Answer: b   Type: M   Page(s): 575   Key 1: F

14. Collective self-esteem has four aspects: worthy membership, public respect, identity, and

    a) mutual respect
    b) empathy
    c) private pride
    d) collective values

    Answer: c   Type: M   Page(s): 575   Key 1: F

Groups

15. Worthy membership, public respect, identity, and public pride are four aspects of

    a) collective self-esteem
    b) public self-consciousness
    c) ethnocentrism
    d) the group mind

    Answer: a   Type: M   Page(s): 575   Key 1: F

16. Joanne's softball team did poorly in batting against a new pitching machine. Joanne is most likely to think that the machine is no good if

    a) she is high in collective self-esteem
    b) she is low in collective self-esteem
    c) she is high in public self-consciousness
    d) she is low in public self-consciousness

    Answer: a   Type: M   Page(s): 576   Key 1: A

17. A minimal group is

    a) a group consisting of one person
    b) a group consisting of two people
    c) a group consisting of the minimum number of people who could possibly perform the task assigned to the group
    d) a group formed on the basis of a trivial distinction

    Answer: d   Type: M   Page(s): 577   Key 1: F

18. Research shows that people show favoritism

    a) only to groups of people they have met face-to-face
    b) only to groups of people who are in competition with another group
    c) even to minimal groups of people (but not groups of animals)
    d) even to minimal groups that have animals as their members

    Answer: c   Type: M   Page(s): 577   Key 1: F

19. As part of a psychology experiment, Zelda learned that she tended to perceive figures as wholes, rather than breaking the figures into parts. Then Zelda had the opportunity to divide up $10 that the experimenter had given her between two people she had never met: Vanna (who also perceived figures as wholes) and Wanda (who broke figures into parts). Research shows that Zelda will most likely

    a) demand that the experimenter give her more information about Vanna and Wanda
    b) give $5 to Vanna and $5 to Wanda
    c) give more money to Vanna than to Wanda
    d) give more money to Wanda than to Vanna

    Answer: c   Type: M   Page(s): 577   Key 1: A

20. As research shows, in-group favoritism

    a) raises self-esteem
    b) lowers self-esteem
    c) polarizes one's preexisting opinion of oneself
    d) moderates one's preexisting opinion of oneself

    Answer: a   Type: M   Page(s): 578   Key 1: F

21. Mary, Nancy, Ophelia, and Patty were a four-person relay team. Who is most likely to express favoritism to the team?

    a) Mary, a long-term member of the team who was speaking in private
    b) Nancy, a long-term member of the team who was speaking in public
    c) Ophelia, a new member of the team who was speaking in private
    d) Patty, a new member of the team who was speaking in public

    Answer: d   Type: M   Page(s): 578   Key 1: A

22. George, a student at State U., is drawing an inference about the undergraduates at Private U., State's arch-rival. Research suggests that George will

    a) show an unusually large correspondence bias
    b) show an unusually large false consensus effect
    c) give Private U. undergraduates the benefit of the doubt
    d) infer the worst about Private U. undergraduates

    Answer: d   Type: M   Page(s): 579   Key 1: A

23. In a study of hiring decisions, researchers gave female subjects the opportunity to use either a simplistic or a complex form of reasoning and to choose to hire either a female or a male employee. Results showed that overall the female subjects tended to

    a) use simplistic reasoning
    b) use complex reasoning
    c) use the form of reasoning that would result in hiring a female
    d) use the form of reasoning that would result in hiring a male

    Answer: c   Type: M   Page(s): 579   Key 1: F

24. In the service of making their own group look better than an outgroup, people

    a) rely on simplistic inferential strategies
    b) rely on complicated inferential strategies
    c) rely on invalid inferential strategies
    d) use a variety of inferential strategies

    Answer: d   Type: M   Page(s): 580   Key 1: F

25. Sunil, a Hindu, is being asked why Adnan, a Muslim, saved Sunil's life. Research on group differences indicates in explaining Adnan's behavior Sunil will

    a) make an internal attribution
    b) make an external attribution
    c) use the simulation heuristic
    d) use the availability heuristic

    Answer: b   Type: M   Page(s): 580   Key 1: A

26. A highly abstract description of a person's behavior implies

    a) an attribution to the person
    b) an attribution to the entity
    c) an attribution to the circumstances
    d) an attribution to the describer

    Answer: a   Type: M   Page(s): 580   Key 1: A

27. Matthew (a Southern Baptist) saw Mark (a Northeastern Jew) throw an empty beer can out his car window. Research indicates that Matthew will describe Mark's action

    a) with verbs that use the active voice
    b) with verbs that use the passive voice
    c) abstractly
    d) concretely

    Answer: c   Type: M   Page(s): 580   Key 1: A

28. People give highly concrete descriptions of behaviors performed by a member of

    a) their own group, whatever the group member does
    b) an outgroup, whatever the group member does
    c) their own group, if the group member does something good
    d) their own group, if the group member does something bad

    Answer: c   Type: M   Page(s): 580   Key 1: F

29. In strategic games like the prisoner's dilemma,

    a) individuals are more cooperative than groups
    b) groups are more cooperative than individuals
    c) individuals fear one another more than groups fear one another
    d) individuals are greedier than groups

    Answer: a   Type: M   Page(s): 582   Key 1: F

30. In strategic games, groups are more competitive than individuals. According to research, why?

    a) Cooperative group members tend to be free riders.
    b) The presence of other group members enhances dominant responses.
    c) Groups are more likely to bask in reflected glory.
    d) Groups are more motivated by fear and greed.

    Answer: d   Type: M   Page(s): 582   Key 1: F

31. Groups perform worse than individuals on

    a) disjunctive tasks
    b) conjunctive tasks
    c) additive tasks
    d) subtractive tasks

    Answer: b   Type: M   Page(s): 584   Key 1: F

32. Questions were posed to undergraduate teams in the State U. quiz bowl. Each member of each team wrote down an answer to the question, and if any member of a team got the right answer, the team got 100 points. Otherwise, the team got no points. This quiz bowl is a(n)

    a) additive task
    b) subtractive task
    c) conjunctive task
    d) disjunctive task

    Answer: c   Type: M   Page(s): 584   Key 1: A

33. Tad, Ted, Tim, and Tom were the four members of a swimming team. They participated in an event in which all four swam 200 yards simultaneously and the time for the team was the time it took the slowest member of the team to finish the 200 yards. This is

    a) a conjunctive task
    b) a disjunctive task
    c) a subtractive task
    d) an additive task

    Answer: a   Type: M   Page(s): 584   Key 1: A

34. The sororities at State U. competed each year in a GPA contest. The contest was run as an additive task. This means that the winning sorority would be the one that had

    a) the largest number of students with a perfect GPA
    b) the smallest number of students with a GPA=0.0
    c) the highest average GPA
    d) the least spread in their GPAs -- from the best GPA in the sorority to worst

    Answer: c   Type: M   Page(s): 584   Key 1: A

35. Which of the following is NOT one of the guidelines followed in brainstorming?

    a) Build on the ideas that others have given.
    b) Make your ideas as logical as they can possibly be.
    c) Come up with as many ideas as possible.
    d) Never criticize others' ideas.

    Answer: b   Type: M   Page(s): 585   Key 1: F

36. Alice, Betty, Carla, and Dawn brainstormed together for an hour. During that same hour, Eva, Fran, Gloria, and Hazel worked alone in separate rooms coming up with ideas on the same topic. Together, Eva, Fran, Gloria, and Hazel came up with 200 different ideas. Based on research, it's most likely that as a group Alice, Betty, Carla, and Dawn came up with

    a) 100 ideas
    b) 200 ideas
    c) 400 ideas
    d) 800 ideas

    Answer: a   Type: M   Page(s): 585   Key 1: A

37. Your textbook mentions three phenomena that may explain why brainstorming is counterproductive. Which of following is NOT one of these phenomena?

    a) group polarization
    b) evaluation apprehension
    c) production blocking
    d) social loafing

    Answer: a   Type: M   Page(s): 586   Key 1: F

38. Production blocking occurs when

    a) people try to take credit for one another's contributions
    b) people intentionally sabotage one another's work
    c) people would rather socialize than work
    d) people have to wait their turns

    Answer: d   Type: M   Page(s): 586   Key 1: F

39. A nominal group is

    a) named for one of its members
    b) organized around a charismatic leader
    c) the same thing as a minimal group
    d) not a group, as social psychologists define groups

    Answer: d   Type: M   Page(s): 586   Key 1: F

40. Research suggests that evaluation apprehension

    a) does not occur in brainstorming groups
    b) is bigger in nominal groups than real groups
    c) is bigger in large groups than small groups
    d) is bigger in female groups than male groups

    Answer: c   Type: M   Page(s): 588   Key 1: F

41. Evaluation apprehension is most likely to influence

    a) the correspondence bias
    b) brainstorming
    c) basking in reflected glory
    d) social comparison

    Answer: b   Type: M   Page(s): 588   Key 1: F

42. Social loafing occurs when

    a) people are especially motivated to be sociable
    b) people have been working on a task for an unusually long time
    c) people believe that their contributions to a group won't be identified
    d) people believe that their group is going to fail no matter what they do

    Answer: c   Type: M   Page(s): 588   Key 1: F

43. In brainstorming, real groups generate as many ideas as nominal groups if

    a) an experimenter gives the real group a high performance standard
    b) an experimenter gives the nominal group a high performance standard
    c) an experimenter gives the real group a list of ideas
    d) the real group is left to its own devices

    Answer: a   Type: M   Page(s): 589   Key 1: F

44. Research shows that there is an illusion of effectiveness in

    a) group polarization
    b) group moderation
    c) group brainstorming
    d) use of the anchoring-and-adjustment heuristic

    Answer: c   Type: M   Page(s): 589   Key 1: F

Groups

45. Walt is CEO of a large business firm. Walt most likely believes that brainstorming

    a) brainstorming is effective
    b) brainstorming is ineffective
    c) brainstorming leads to risky decisions
    d) brainstorming leads to conservative decisions

    Answer: a   Type: M   Page(s): 590   Key 1: A

46. Jack and Jerry brainstormed together on a problem, writing down their ideas. Meanwhile, Luther worked on the same problem alone, writing down his ideas independently. Later, a psychologist transcribed all of these ideas, and showed the list to Jack. Research shows that Jack is most likely to claim that

    a) the ideas that Jerry wrote down were ideas that Jack wrote down
    b) the ideas that Jerry wrote down were ideas that Jack was having anyway
    c) the ideas that Luther wrote down were ideas that Jack wrote down
    d) the ideas that Luther wrote down were ideas that Jack was having anyway

    Answer: b   Type: M   Page(s): 590   Key 1: A

47. Group polarization occurs in

    a) performance of additive tasks
    b) performance of conjunctive tasks
    c) performance of disjunctive tasks
    d) decision-making

    Answer: d   Type: M   Page(s): 591   Key 1: F

48. Group polarization refers to the fact that

    a) groups can rarely make unanimous decisions
    b) groups can easily make unanimous decisions
    c) groups make extreme decisions
    d) group members compromise with one another

    Answer: c   Type: M   Page(s): 591   Key 1: F

49. By virtue of group polarization, groups make

    a) better decisions than individuals
    b) worse decisions than individuals
    c) the same decision as the average group member
    d) extreme decisions

    Answer: d   Type: M   Page(s): 592   Key 1: F

Copyright © 1997 by Harcourt Brace & Company. All rights reserved.

50. Your textbook discusses three factors that contribute to group polarization. Which of the following is NOT one of them?

    a) informational influence
    b) normative influence
    c) attributional influence
    d) social identity

    Answer: c   Type: M   Page(s): 593   Key 1: F

51. Normative influence occurs when people want to

    a) draw self-esteem from a group
    b) stand out from a crowd
    c) be likable
    d) be right

    Answer: c   Type: M   Page(s): 593   Key 1: F

52. When a group is trying to reach a decision, _____
    causes the members of the group to pay attention to persuasive arguments.

    a) normative influence
    b) informational influence
    c) social facilitation
    d) social contagion

    Answer: b   Type: M   Page(s): 593   Key 1: F

53. Roger, Sam, and Ted, three professional burglars, had each individually decided on houses that they might rob as a team. Then the three got together and discussed each house. Research indicates that after this discussion, Roger, Sam, and Ted will be

    a) more concrete in their descriptions of the robberies
    b) more abstract in their descriptions of the robberies
    c) more willing to take risks
    d) more cautious

    Answer: d   Type: M   Page(s): 594   Key 1: A

54. By virtue of _____, people go along with what other members of their group want to do.

    a) normative influence
    b) informational influence
    c) cognitive balance
    d) psychological reactance

    Answer: a   Type: M   Page(s): 594   Key 1: F

Groups

55. Normative influence causes group polarization by virtue of

   a) possible selves
   b) social comparison
   c) cognitive dissonance
   d) persuasive arguments

   Answer: b   Type: M   Page(s): 595   Key 1: F

56. _____ occurs when each individual in a group falsely assumes that other group members know more than he or she does.

   a) False consensus
   b) False uniqueness
   c) The correspondence bias
   d) Pluralistic ignorance

   Answer: d   Type: M   Page(s): 595   Key 1: F

57. Ursula was serving on a jury. The actual consensus opinion of the other 11 members of the jury was that the defendant should receive a moderately severe sentence -- 15 years in jail. Research suggests that Ursula will perceive that her fellow jury members' consensus opinion is for a sentence of

   a) 15 years in jail (that is, the actual consensus)
   b) 10 years in jail (less extreme than the actual consensus)
   c) 20 years in jail (more extreme than the actual consensus)
   d) no research has been done on individuals' perceptions of group consensus

   Answer: c   Type: M   Page(s): 597   Key 1: A

58. At a highly publicized rape trial, the judge told the jury that they had to reach a unanimous decision -- no matter what. Research shows that this will

   a) increase informational influence
   b) reduce informational influence
   c) increase normative influence
   d) reduce normative influence

   Answer: c   Type: M   Page(s): 598   Key 1: A

59. In civil trials, juries can award the plaintiff compensatory damages for medical bills and lost wages. They can also award the plaintiff exemplary damages -- to punish negligence. Jury decisions over compensatory damages are most likely to be determined by

    a) normative influence
    b) informational influence
    c) social identity
    d) groupthink

    Answer: b   Type: M   Page(s): 598   Key 1: F

60. Group polarization is LEAST likely when

    a) the group must make a unanimous decision
    b) there is a correct solution to the task
    c) the members of the group are friends
    d) the group is competing against other groups

    Answer: b   Type: M   Page(s): 599   Key 1: F

61. Social psychologists attribute bad decisions, like the decision to coverup the Watergate break-in, to a process called

    a) social loafing
    b) social impairment
    c) the group mind
    d) groupthink

    Answer: d   Type: M   Page(s): 601   Key 1: F

62. Groupthink occurs when group members

    a) seek consensus
    b) try to compete with one another
    c) ignore one another's opinions
    d) are not interested in the task at hand

    Answer: a   Type: M   Page(s): 601   Key 1: F

63. A highly cohesive group consists of

    a) individuals who are similar to one another
    b) individuals who like one another
    c) individuals who draw collective self-esteem from the group
    d) all of these

    Answer: d   Type: M   Page(s): 601   Key 1: F

64. Your textbook discusses three factors that contribute to groupthink. Which of the following is NOT one of them?

    a) a threat to group identity
    b) free riding
    c) cohesiveness
    d) restrictive decision procedures

    Answer: b Type: M Page(s): 602   Key 1: F

65. Groupthink is most likely to occur when the group leader

    a) allows the other members of the group to meet in the leader's absence
    b) is directive
    c) appoints one member of the group to play devil's advocate
    d) is too willing to seek public input into the decision-making process

    Answer: b Type: M Page(s): 602   Key 1: F

66. An "illusion of invulnerability" is most important in producing

    a) groupthink
    b) productivity losses in brainstorming groups
    c) informational influence
    d) social anxiety

    Answer: a Type: M Page(s): 603   Key 1: F

67. The President of the United States assigned a foreign policy problem to two independent groups of advisers. The State Department group consisted of 14 highly similar Ivy Leaguers who knew and respected one another. The Pentagon ad-hoc group consisted of 14 very different individuals who had not known one another prior to formation of the group. According to research, which group will offer the President better advice?

    a) the State Department group, if the problem has a correct solution
    b) the Pentagon group, if the problem has a correct solution
    c) the State Department group, if both groups feel threatened
    d) the Pentagon group, if both groups feel threatened

    Answer: d Type: M Page(s): 604   Key 1: A

68. Who is least vulnerable to groupthink?

    a) Kathy, who is high in need for cognition
    b) Laverne, who is low in need for cognition
    c) Marianne, who has a dominant personality
    d) Nell, who has a submissive personality

    Answer: c Type: M Page(s): 604   Key 1: A

69. The members of a group are most likely to share information with one another when they

   a) assume that the problem at hand has a correct solution
   b) assume that the problem at hand has no correct solution
   c) must reach a unanimous decision
   d) don't have to reach a unanimous decision

   Answer: a   Type: M   Page(s): 605   Key 1: F

70. Psychological entrapment occurs when

   a) opposites attract
   b) people throw good money after bad
   c) people can't escape from a discrepancy between their real self and ideal self
   d) people commit themselves to a charismatic leader

   Answer: b   Type: M   Page(s): 606   Key 1: F

ESSAY

71. What are the consequences of an individual's social identity? What impact does social identity have on an individual's thoughts, feelings, and actions? In answering these questions, be sure to describe relevant research.

   Answer:
   In answering this open-ended question, students could draw on the material from pages 572-583 of the text. They might discuss the individual's tendency to bask in reflected glory (p. 572), to have collective self-esteem (p. 575), to show in-group favoritism (p. 576), and to compete against outgroups (p. 582). In elaborating on these aspects of social identity, students should describe some of the relevant research.

   Type: E   Page(s): 572   Key 1: F

72. Sometimes people show favoritism to members of their own group. What are the minimal circumstances under which this in-group favoritism is evident? Under what circumstances is in-group favoritism strongest? Why do people show favoritism to members of their own group? In what ways is in-group favoritism shown? In answering these questions, be sure to describe relevant research.

   Answer:
   In answering these questions, students should summarize the material presented on pages 576-582 of the text. As noted there, ingroup favoritism is evident even in "minimal groups." In-group favoritism may be strongest for people who are new to the group, especially if it can be shown in public. People derive self-esteem from showing in-group favoritism; and show this favoritism by allocating rewards to in-group members, by outgroup derogation, and by giving in-group members the benefit of the doubt when making inferences. The best answer to this question would summarize some of the research studies on which these conclusions are based.

   Type: E   Page(s): 576   Key 1: F

73. Is brainstorming in groups the best way to come up with ideas? Why or why not? What factors influence the productivity of brainstorming groups? Be specific.

Answer:
Students could answer this question by summarizing the material on pages 584-590 of the text. As noted there, individuals are more productive than brainstorming groups. Groups may be non-productive because of production blocking, evaluation apprehension, and social loafing. Students should explain the impact of each of these factors.

Type: E   Page(s): 586   Key 1: F

74. How do decisions made by groups differ from decisions made by individuals? Why do they differ? Under what circumstances do group decisions and individual decisions differ the most? Answer these questions by summarizing research and concepts related to group polarization.

Answer:
Material for answering this question appears on pages 590-599 of the text. As noted there, group decisions tend to be more extreme than individual decisions. They are more extreme because of the impact of informational influence, normative influence, and social identity. This group polarization is most evident if the group must make a unanimous decision on a task that does not have a single correct solution. The best answer to this question would describe research that supports these conclusions.

Type: E   Page(s): 593   Key 1: F

75. Having just read a social psychology textbook, the President of the United States has hired you to develop better decision-making procedures for the Federal government. In particular, the President wants you to develop procedures that will help government officials avoid groupthink. Tell the President how the government can avoid groupthink, being as specific as possible.

Answer:
To answer this question, students should draw on the material on pages 599-606 of the text. As suggested on page 602, groupthink could be avoided if the government used groups that weren't highly cohesive, if the groups didn't feel threatened, and if restrictions weren't placed on groups' decision-making procedures. The best answer to this question would describe research and elaborate on these suggestions.

Type: E   Page(s): 602   Key 1: A